'Quite astonishing war adventures . . . written with the personal modesty which characterises most brave men'   Robert Kee, *Observer*

'Many brave men come from this part of the world [New Zealand] . . . few can write like Thomas . . . a story that loses none of its excellence for being modestly told, without heroics of any sort'
Lt Gen Sir Brian Horrocks, *Sunday Times*

'His book is a record of great personal courage and resourcefulness and an adventure story of the highest order'
Edinburgh Evening News

'His book, modest and engaging, is interesting not only as a genuine document of escape, but as a . . . vividly written description of Greek landscape'   *TLS*

'Astonishing – Absorbing – Amusing adventure story. A stunning book'   Sir Terry McLean

'I was riveted by [the] book from beginning to end'
Sir Noël Coward, *Middle East Diary*

In 1939 'Sandy' Thomas was a bank clerk in New Zealand; the next year he came to England with the 23rd New Zealand Battalion. He has had a most distinguished record as a soldier; in July 1945 Lt General Sir Bernard C. Freyberg, VC (later Lord Freyberg), who commanded the Allied Forces in Crete, wrote: '. . . I have watched him develop from a very young Second Lieutenant through all ranks, until in the last year of the war he became one of the most dashing and seasoned Commanding Officers of infantry in the 2 NZ Division.' He became Major General W.B. 'Sandy' Thomas, CB, DSO, MC and Bar, ED, Silver Star (USA) Army Commander, Far East Land Forces.

DARE TO BE FREE

One of the greatest true stories of World War II

W.B. 'SANDY' THOMAS

CASSELL

Cassell Military Paperbacks

An imprint of Orion Books Ltd,
Orion House, 5 Upper St Martins Lane,
London WC2H 9EA

An Hachette UK company

First published in 1951
by Allan Wingate (Publishers) Limited
First published in paperback in 1954
by Pan Books Limited, London
Published in hardback in 2001
by Dryden Press, New Zealand

This Cassell Military Paperbacks edition 2005

British Library Cataloguing-in-Publication Data.
A catalogue record for this book is available
from the British Library.

Printed and bound in Great Britain by
CPI Mackays, Chatham ME5 8TD

www.orionbooks.co.uk

To

Gay, Ce & Jo
and to
Tyson

Contents

List of Illustrations

Preface

To tens of thousands of men in the New Zealand Division, W. B. 'Sandy' Thomas, D.S.O., M.C. and Bar, Silver Star (USA), was a fabulous character, a legend.

He was brought up on a farm in Riwaka at the top of the South Island of New Zealand, attending school in rural Motueka, not far from Nelson. Thomas's great grandfather had been a colonel in the Indian Army, and Thomas applied for the Royal Military College at Duntroon in Australia. He was declined entry because he had taken agricultural science instead of chemistry at high school. Consequently, this young man started work as a clerk in the Bank of New Zealand but, ironically, the future would find him lecturing at Duntroon.

Thomas gained his commission in the Territorials before the war. In 1940 he sailed with the great convoy of troopships destined for the Middle East, but urgently diverted to the United Kingdom to counter the threat of German invasion after Dunkirk. From England he went to Egypt, Greece, and then to Crete. Thomas was left badly wounded and a prisoner on Crete, where this adventure begins. The story of his escape is still as gripping as when first published in 1951 and this edition is largely unchanged, but includes a postscript relating the astonishing coincidence of what occurred when he eventually crossed the Turkish border to Syria. The *Official History of New Zealand in the Second World War 1939-45, 23rd Battalion* records for 11 May '… the happy occasion when Lieutenant Sandy Thomas, who had been left wounded on Crete, arrived across the Turkish border at Captain Dick Connolly's Post.'

German paratroopers, Crete – May 1941

Chapter One

Crete 1941

'Cripes!' said Sergeant Templeton, stumbling over his mess-tin as he stepped back for a better view, 'cripes, they can't be real! They're only dummies!'

The parachutists certainly seemed unreal, difficult to comprehend as anything at all dangerous. Seen against the deep blue of the early morning Cretan sky, through a frame of grey-green olive branches, they looked like marionettes, like little jerking dolls whose billowy frocks of green, yellow, red and white had somehow blown up and become entangled in the wires that controlled them. Standing next to Sergeant Templeton I struggled to grasp the meaning behind this colourful fantasy, to realise that those beautiful kicking dolls meant the repetition of all the horrors we had known so recently in Greece.

The invasion of Crete had begun. 'They're parachutists, Sergeant,' I shouted, suddenly waking up and realising that something was expected of me, 'get the men ready for action immediately! Those Huns will fall about five hundred yards from here, but the next lot might come right on to us. Look at those planes!'

Circling slowly above us were eight or nine flights of transport aircraft, ugly Junkers 52, with their black crosses showing clearly as they turned. In a few minutes the sky had filled with fighters, with gliders, and these flights of fat troop-carriers, each consisting of nine aircraft packed in close formation.

We had stood to as usual that morning some two hours before daylight, cursing as we stirred from the meagre shelter of the olive trees and wishing that we had some of the blankets and overcoats which had been left behind in Greece. There had been the normal bombardment, perhaps a little more frenzied than other mornings, of the Maleme Aerodrome less

German aircraft at Maleme Aerodrome   ATL DA-02059

than a mile along the coast road from us. We had received our share of the overs, as well as a rigorous machine-gunning from some low-flying Stukas, but after a fortnight on Crete we had grown to expect such treatment. When the roar of the fighters had died away a little we had stood down from our posts to rummage about for some breakfast, assuming that the remaining drone of engines came from reconnaissance planes which were always over our heads, unchallenged and confident.

The first inkling that the day was to be very different happened just before the appearance of the transport planes, when a glider swished over the olive trees on its way to the aerodrome.

The noise now built up to a tremendous crescendo. Bombs crumped and roared in the distance, rifles crackled from the olive trees as the troops came into action. Machine-guns chattered as they plucked at the swinging forms in the sky, men yelled and wounded parachutists, still in their air, screamed with fear and pain. The few remaining Bofors guns joined in with their steady sharp quarks, while from nearby a three-inch mortar whoofed as it lobbed its bombs high into the air. Above it all, a deep bass rising and falling in intensity but ever present, was the drone of aero engines, punctuated by whistling bombs and diving fighters. It was a real bedlam.

My platoon organised themselves into their sections quietly and efficiently, startled perhaps, but ready for anything. I looked them over quickly, proud that they retained a soldierly appearance in spite of their experiences and losses in Greece. They were a grand crowd, I thought, as I waved them to take cover in the slit trenches until our orders arrived; they had been wonderful company for the past year. It was, in fact, just over a year since I, a very raw Second Lieutenant of twenty years, had welcomed them all into the mobilisation camp at Burnham, New Zealand. They were all in civilian clothes then, and a rough assortment they looked. Most of them were from my district and were either miners, bushmen or farm hands. There were also those who, like me, had been country bank clerks, or shop assistants. We spent four terribly busy but happy months training in New Zealand and then sailed for England where we completed our training.

It was tragic that after so much enthusiastic drill and study of war we should have been sent via Egypt to such a hopeless debacle as Greece, where these men fought valiantly, but against such frightful odds that withdrawal and evacuation had been inevitable.

Major Thomason, my veteran Company Commander, came winding through the olive trees with his distinctive limping gait, calling to me as he approached. He grinned at me, unruffled by the confusion all around, and said, 'Well, young Thomas, here's the war for you, brought

2nd Lt W. B. 'Sandy' Thomas

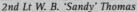

15

right to your doorstep. Now pay attention. Those Huns we saw falling are part of a whole battalion group which has fallen on the 22nd Battalion positions. The Colonel thinks that some of them were dropped wide of their objective. At the moment they're getting organised between our own 23rd Battalion positions and the main 22nd area on the high ground by the airfield. They could build up quite a threat there and prevent the execution of our counter-attack role.' He paused and looked straight into my eyes, commanding and aggressive. 'Move out with your platoon and clean 'em up.'

I worked my mouth for a few moments, speechless, and a little out of my depth. Then I realised that this was the real thing, this was how I had always read orders were given in battle. I sprang into action and, briefly shouting our task to the platoon, set off with the sections spread at some twenty yards' interval. We passed through the forward troops, all alert in their slit trenches, and then made through the grove towards the area where we had seen the parachutists fall.

Outside our battalion perimeter things seemed unnaturally still at first, the medley of battle noises seemed to be shut out of the valley as we hastened down the terraced slope. I presumed the enemy were still at some distance and pressed forward at the head of the platoon, my mind gloriously clear and alert. Only the fighting man can experience that clarity when danger expunges all irrelevant worries and crystallises the brain for that deadliest of pastimes, the stalking of fellow man.

I approached the bottom of the valley and soon stood immediately below the first of the waist-high ascending terraces on the far side. I was in the very act of clambering up, indeed I had my hand on the stone ledge and one foot raised, when something, quite unaccountable, stopped me; some chill of premonition arrested me and made me duck. I had heard nothing, and I was not expecting any sign of the enemy until we reached the crest of the next small ridge. There was no reason, even had I considered it very carefully, why I should not have continued my forward rush. But something more urgent than reason said 'stop a while' and I heeded it.

Looking behind me, I was concerned to find that my men were a good fifty yards back, advancing with a certain amount of caution. I signalled them to hurry forward, impatient at the delay.

I had several grenades in my pockets and they were heavy and uncomfortable. I took the one from the left pocket of the battledress trousers and, more to get rid of it than to counter my dread of climbing the terrace, I withdrew the pin and lobbed it forward. 'Three, four, five, six,' I counted under my breath as I crouched in readiness, and the instant it burst, on the seventh second, I leapt up the stonework of the terrace.

Before I could get my balance I saw something dark-green, a German steel helmet almost hidden by a thick olive trunk, and a revolver raised from the ground next to it pointing right at me. I pulled the trigger of my rifle, the parachutist's shoulder jumped, and with a sudden thrill I realised that I had fired instinctively from the hip and killed him, had involuntarily killed my first German.

There was no time for any exultation or repugnance; in the next split second I discovered at my very feet, grovelling on his back, a second soldier, fair-headed, his face a sickly green. He had a revolver waving shakily in his right hand. I jerked the muzzle of the rifle down to his head, reloading en route, and screamed at him to drop it. He continued to wave it aimlessly. I could see from the saliva oozing down either side of his mouth, and from the gibbering sounds he was making, that there was no fight in him. I stepped over his body and kicked the revolver from his grasp.

I glanced around me quickly. Amongst the olive trees immediately in front there was no further movement, behind me the platoon, cautioned by my firing, were only just approaching the terrace.

What did one do with a prisoner? No one had ever told me and I had never thought of capturing one. I could not take him with us, he would immeasurably complicate the cleaning up of the pocket I vaguely imagined some distance away, and surely it would be wrong to waste a soldier to take him back to Headquarters? If I took twenty prisoners and sent them all back I would soon have no force left. Obviously I had either to tie him up, or somehow dispose of him until we could collect him on our return.

Callous as it seemed, I decided to put the first prisoner I had ever taken to sleep, to give him a little pat on the head sufficient to keep him quiet until we could pick him up on the way back to the lines. His steel helmet was off and lying some feet away, so I bent down and suggestively patted his head in explanation of what I had to do. The frantic gibbering increased but, after all, I had a job to do; why should I let one skulking German keep me from it?

17

Then I did a very foolish thing: I turned my rifle upside down. I clasped the warm muzzle to administer a light tap. Just as I raised the rifle two or three feet above his head, there was a burst of machine-carbine fire, and a host of olive leaves and twigs dropped down on my head and shoulders from the branch above me. Glancing up in quick apprehension I saw a giant of a German rushing at me through the olive trees. His tommy-gun was pointed straight at me.

For a split second my mind shot off to a foolish thought that this fellow did not know that all tommy-guns fire high in bursts. Then the urgent danger of the position registered like panic. My first reaction was to complete the downward motion of my rifle butt. Even as I did this I realised that my panic had made me strike far, far too hard. The butt entered the side of the fair head as though it was plywood.

I dropped to the ground behind him, and grabbed the discarded revolver. I pointed it at the charging figure and pulled the trigger. Nothing happened. It was jammed.

The big German stopped about three paces from me. As I cringed closer to the still twitching corpse he raised him tommy-gun to his shoulder. Slowly, deliberately, and coldly, he took aim. I saw his right eye screw up as he focused the sights. The barrel steadied.

I was frozen stock-still. I could not move. Then in a flash it was all over.

Simultaneously, I saw his shoulder jar as he pulled the trigger, and a red splodge appear on his forehead. Something plucked at the corpse by my face. I saw the German topple to the ground, his face covered in blood.

Corporal Rae Thompson, his rifle smoking, was looking at me with inquiry from over the edge of the terrace.

'Near thing, sir,' he grinned, clambering up to have a look at his bag. 'Don't think you should move so far ahead of us, sir, if you don't mind my saying so!'

'Believe me, Corporal,' I rejoined in as normal a voice as I could muster, 'your advice is not necessary. In future I will command from well in the rear!'

We advanced warily, carefully examining each bunch of foliage where there were parachutes of any colour. We found that the yellow parachutes nearly all denoted canisters of supplies, and destroyed as best we could the guns and ammunition we found in them. Before long every man in the platoon was wearing a Luger revolver and a pair of Zeiss binoculars, and our morale ran extremely high.

The patrol continued thus for the rest of that day, the 20th of May 1941, and when we found that the area designated by the Colonel was clear of the enemy we made to return to the battalion perimeter. As proof of our success we carried the identity discs of twenty-nine Germans killed, and three prisoners, as well as an assortment of weapons and stores which would be of great value to replace the equipment lost in Greece. Sadly, my platoon also had lost two fine men killed.

Shouting to herald our approach, we entered the battalion perimeter to find that our exploits were small stuff compared to the excitement the companies had experienced since we left. A whole parachute battalion had landed late in the morning right on to the battalion strong-points, and there had been a simple slaughter, for the parachutists were almost helpless until they landed and got out of their equipment. The whole area was an unforgettable sight, with parachutes of all colours draped from practically every tree. Some of them still had their soldiers held in harness, swinging to and fro from the branches. The Colonel, the Quartermaster, the Adjutant and the Sanitary Corporal all claimed their man, and there was a glow of confidence on all sides. Even though we had left our carriers and most of our mortars in Greece, thought the battalion, we could still make Jerry sit up and take it. The men were ready for anything.

We waited all that day, and all the next night for the expected orders to execute our planned role of the counter-attack on the aerodrome at Maleme. We knew the 22nd Battalion was in grave peril there and that the main weight of the attack had come in against them.

But, even when two companies, sent up for reinforcements, returned to report the position confused, no order was forthcoming. It was not until early the next morning, when the men of the 22nd Battalion began to stream into our lines, that I realised the order never would be given. Yet, without any doubt, the initiative up to that time was ours for the asking. From that moment the tide of battle began to swing in favour of the side with enterprise, and as that side was building up each hour and had such aerial supremacy as was never to be seen again, I began to see that the Battle of Crete might go against us. I felt very bitter.

The position up to the withdrawal was never acutely dangerous compared with the battles we were to experience, and win, in later years. At the early stage of the war, however, there was a disinclination to study the difficulties and the fears of the enemy, and a tendency to build up a false picture from the vivid accounts of men in their first action. The worst reports came from those stark-eyed men who would arrive at Headquarters as 'the sole survivor of X Company', or as a self-appointed runner to say that the enemy was advancing in 'thousands' on his Company front when, in fact, the position all round was sound and secure.

The Germans had thought the olive grove wherein our whole battalion was contained was clear of any English troops, and had dropped their reserve regiment right on to us. This had demonstrated the value of concealment and camouflage which had been the Colonel's particular fetish. He had insisted that no one showed between the trees, that no smoke rose, that not even a bit of orange peel was to be seen when there was a German aeroplane within sound of the area. There was no doubt that this foresight paid astounding dividends; the few parachutists we took alive expressed their astonishment at our presence. They told us that they had expected to land unmolested, form up and advance as a unit to the aerodrome. They even dropped the Quartermaster and the unit clerks, so sure were they that there would be no fighting initially.

Even after the lack of initiative had thrown away this tremendous advantage, there was much to be gained from deception. The enemy air force was not certain of the position of our sector; he was aware that he had dropped a regiment there and was therefore chary of attacking it. Furthermore he hovered above, ready to reinforce it. When we discovered on the corpses large red swastikas and silk strips we laid out some in speculation, to be rewarded with showers of canisters. Mortars, rifles, ammunition and food all floated down into our midst, and we made good use of them.

On the morning of the third day of fighting, the counter-attack by the Maori Battalion and the 20th Battalion, delayed by hours for various reasons, at last got under way. Such a delay in any battle makes a bad start; on Crete it was catastrophic. Instead of taking advantage of the darkness of the early hours the troops were forced to debouch in open formation in broad daylight in the face of almost complete aerial supremacy. They fought magnificently. But by this time all the scattered little bands of parachutists had been centralised, had been reinforced with units and heavy weapons brought by transport plane or dropped on multi-parachutes.

The Germans might have still lost a night attack by these warriors, when they were in the dark they so hated, and without their hundreds of planes on call. But this deliberate daylight advance, however much it frightened them and however near it came to success was, after all, their chance of effecting a quick decision on the island. The Germans fought back with confidence.

From back in the 23rd Battalion positions we watched the initial success of the advancing troops together with the light tanks under Lieutenant Roy Farran. We had high hopes at first that the day would be ours, but presently a stream of wounded Maoris began to come in, and with them the stories of the determined opposition. Before the day was well advanced there were indications that our attack had failed.

That evening, the third night of the battle, the pressure all round was obviously more intense. Calls came from all companies that they were under attack. My small force, dwindling with casualties, was used now on one side and then the other as the Germans felt for a weakness, until about midnight things seemed to quieten down.

At one in the morning the Colonel called a conference at Battalion Headquarters. As Major Thomason was now the unit second in command, I attended as O.C. of the company. The conference was, I found to my horror, to receive orders for the complete withdrawal of all British Forces from the Maleme area. It appeared that our battalion alone remained intact on this front and that we were to withdraw to Platanius and form a line there. C Company under my command was to fight as rearguard of the force; we were to hold the present positions until the other rifle companies could extricate themselves from their forward positions and pass to the rear.

About four in the morning they began to file through us in the dark, quietly and sadly. There was no enemy interference.

Corporal Rae Thompson, a dour, intrepid Section Leader, was standing by me, his rifle gripped tensely in his hands as he glared into the dark. 'Why the hell are we withdrawing, sir,' he whispered urgently, 'why can't we attack by night and knock the bastards into the sea?'

'I don't know, Rae,' I replied wearily, 'maybe to give the Navy a chance to shell the area and the 'drome from the sea.' However unconvincing, this was one of the current rumours. 'In any case we'll probably get all the scrapping you want when the Hun wakes up to the fact that the companies are on the move!'

Corporal Thompson grunted and moved off to check his men. I knew they would ask him the same questions. They all felt the same. They had seen so many of the enemy dead that their morale was quite unshaken by the terrific air attacks by day. Man for man they considered that they could lick the German despite his superior weapons and equipment. Their fathers had made a name in the first war for ruthless and invariably successful night attacks, and these ex-farmers, ex-miners, ex-bank clerks who had come so far to do the job, felt sullenly critical of the powers that were withdrawing them.

The battalion was retreating over the low hills at the rear of our positions and I knew it would be daylight by the time I could assume them safely away. Before dawn, therefore, I sought out Colonel Leckie who was preparing to follow the companies, and asked permission to choose my own withdrawal route in view of the danger of my men being caught on exposed hills by the aircraft that would come with the sun.

I preferred the plains, well cropped and dotted with olive groves, which ran along the northern side of the island parallel with the sea. The Colonel was at first dubious, as there had been enemy reported in strength in various places on the plains, and it had not been possible to bring vehicles up that way for some hours. However, I explained that I knew the area well and that I felt the enemy would have withdrawn those scattered flank positions during the night. The Colonel agreed that I should leave at eight o'clock in the morning, and then choose my own route back according to the circumstances. If necessary, I was to fight through to rejoin the battalion.

At a few minutes before eight, with the fire from the direction of the aerodrome steadily increasing, the platoons assembled in the hollow of Company Headquarters. When the sergeants had checked everyone present we wound quietly back through the olive trees, stepping over the swollen bodies that lay on the path. Behind us, as we passed the small church on the battalion's seaward flank, we could hear the sound of intensified battle, and the area we had left became full of bursting mortar shells. We had timed it nicely.

We crossed the Platanius River and made across the fields through some holding troops to the village, perched up on a steep and commanding cliff. I contacted the battalion and was told to hold a line from the sea on to the village. In actual fact I found that there was already a platoon on the flat below the ridge; it was the third platoon of the company commanded by Rex King which had left earlier than we had by some error. In conjunction with three other subalterns, all commanding companies—Jim Ensor, Ted Thomson and Bridge Gray—we tied up the defence of the village. Below us, in the direction of the airfield, we could see long columns of enemy troops reaching out towards us. The exasperation of seeing such targets with neither the aircraft nor the guns to engage them was tremendous, and occupied all our thoughts until the full weight of the attack hit us.

A hovering Heinkel picked up our positions. Soon we had flight after flight of Stukas jettisoning their bombs in quick succession into the village, followed by even more deadly mortar fire from the approaching troops.

We took heavy casualties. They were all so serious that one felt helpless to deal with them. There were head gashes, loss of limbs, and painful stomach wounds. We bound them up as best we could, but there was no means of getting them down to the doctor while the blitz was on. We made stretchers from ladders and from the timber of the pulpits of the church which had served as our headquarters and medical aid post. When we ran out of bandages we were forced to use the white robes found in the church.

There were eighteen wounded in the church when the building was registered by the enemy; mortar after mortar crashed on to the roof, so that the reverberations were almost unbearable, and the wounded were showered with falling masonry. Some of them whimpered quietly as a dog might, but none lost their control.

I went outside, flinching at the screaming splinters which spattered against the walls from all sides. The planes seemed to be engaging targets farther back at that stage, so I presumed the German infantry must be closing in for the attack. Let them come, I thought; once we were at close grips the odds would be more even.

To see my own men wounded and dead was bad enough. We were, after all, soldiers and expected to face these things. But to find the streets littered with mangled women and children was almost too much.

As I walked down the village I was suddenly astounded to see an old lady, bent almost double over her stick, hobbling quietly up the street, tranquil and apparently quite oblivious of all the danger. I had no sooner hurried her, protesting, into a building when a young woman came running, breathless and sobbing, down the street. She stopped by every crumpled form until she was almost up to me. Then with a cry of indescribable anguish, she darted almost to my feet and fell on to a fair-headed child. It was lying face down and inert on the road. I approached her awkwardly. She sat up with the mangled head cradled in her lap, but she would not move until I carried the tiny body as gently as I could into a nearby wineshop.

I had a look all along the front, from the right where we could see the troops on the narrow strip to the sea, to the very left where the highest ground made good positions for the fast-approaching attack. I passed several dead parachutists who must have landed away from the main force. That they had fallen to the villagers was gruesomely obvious. These Cretan women were already widowed from the fighting in Albania, and they made short and ghastly work of any Germans who fell into their hands.

Evening fell and with it came the attack. For perhaps an hour every rifle and bren-gun that we had blazed forth as the men retaliated for the punishment we had taken during the day. On the left the line wavered and then stabilised. In front two sections, depleted by casualties, came back a little and then fought forward again. By ten o'clock the enemy had withdrawn some distance to lick his wounds. The night became strangely quiet. From outside the church all I could hear was the quiet groans of the wounded and the crying of the children within the houses.

Chapter Two

The Battle of Galatas

We withdrew under orders soon after midnight, carrying our wounded on improvised stretchers down the steep cliff-face and along a difficult clay creek bed to the road. Then we marched until nearly dawn. I was impressed by the continued discipline of the men. Mile after mile we trudged. Everyone was tired. All were vaguely resentful, although none of us could have put a finger on the reason. Those who could bear the strain better carried the rifles and bren-guns of those who were fatigued. Len Diamond, a rough and lovable West Coast miner, with a difficult stammer, raised a smile whenever things seemed a bit strained.

We rested throughout the next day and night, just stretched out fully dressed under the olive trees near Canea. The enemy pressure was obviously increasing, and there was always the danger of being bombed. Indeed, a reconnaissance Heinkel hovered over our area most of the day. It was alarming now to see how this affected some of the men. They would cringe close to the ground and huddle around the trunk of an olive tree, and their eyes, opened unnaturally wide, showed the beginning of panic.

Feeling fresher after a full night's sleep I reorganised the company. Late in the morning the Colonel informed me that Captain Mark Harvey was to take over the company, and when he arrived at midday I went round the platoons with him. At first I felt a little disappointed at losing my new command, but remembering that Mark was a grand fellow with years

25

of experience and that I was after all only a very young Second Lieutenant, I was happy to rejoin my platoon.

News from the front had been scarce, but the sounds of ground fighting steadily nearer gave some credence to the fantastic rumours. So we were not surprised when at about five o'clock orders arrived for an urgent move forward to stabilise the situation on the coastal strip near Galatas. The battalion moved up in single file, the sections moving apprehensively from cover to cover. All ranks were dreading the slaughter which would happen if that persistent reconnaissance overhead was to discover so large a movement of troops.

Before we had reached the turn off to Galatas it became obvious that some serious collapse was threatened. Wild-eyed men, unarmed, came running frantically back through the trees, shouting with terror.

'Back, back,' they screamed, 'they're coming through in thousands. Back for your lives. It's every man for himself.'

At first this spectacle frightened me. Then I was worried about the effect it might have on our men. But now that they were on the move forward, our boys were quick to shout their contempt.

The sounds of battle grew nearer. Odd bullets, almost spent but still lethal, zipped twigs from olives. We were all very shaken at having to pass the Colonel lying wounded on the roadside. Although he was obviously in great pain he managed to call a cheerful greeting to each subaltern as we passed, wishing us luck. The men bucked up as we remembered that our old Company Commander, Major Thomason, would now assume command. We all had the highest regard for the Major. He had taught us all we knew and given us a terrific confidence in his shrewdness as a tactician.

By the time we had reached the foot of the hill below Galatas it was clear that the situation was desperate. As we deployed on the right of the road I saw a perspiring and dishevelled runner talking urgently to Captain Harvey. There was a change of plan. Galatas was reported in enemy hands and we were to counter-attack. We reformed and wound up the rough road.

Galatas came into sight, a small village on a commanding hill. Behind it flare after flare climbed into the dusk, and an incessant crackle of small-arms fire rose above the roar of the planes. An occasional mortar shell burst in our path ahead, the sudden flash showing a brilliant orange in the gathering gloom.

As the shadows deepened so our spirits rose. Darkness blinded the vicious Stuka and evened up the odds.

A lone Dornier, zooming low over the village and no doubt in answer to the flares, swung ominously towards us. From its belly and rear red and green tracer streamed down on the road.

We took shelter in the ditch. It was from here that I first saw a slight figure, pipe in mouth, standing unconcernedly on the road in contempt of danger. When the plane had passed I saw him in conference with Mark and Rex King. Later I heard that this was Lieutenant Colonel H. K. Kippenberger, Commanding Officer of the 20th New Zealand Battalion, who was acting as Brigadier of a composite group.

The enemy fire was still of great volume when Captain Harvey called a quick conference to give us the situation.

The enemy was fully organised and concentrated for a break through to Suda Bay. He had captured Galatas in the early afternoon and was even now forming up for a fresh advance. If he should have further success that night, the whole Division would be placed in an extremely dangerous position.

Galatas was the key to the whole situation. As far as our own troops were concerned, on the right from Galatas to the sea the 18th Battalion had been badly mauled and further resistance from them could not be expected until they had been given a chance to rest and reform. A and B Companies of our battalion were deploying on the right to close the breach and to make a firm base from which to attack. On the left of Galatas and, indeed, even forward of it, a small and hard-pressed force of Service Corps was holding out gallantly under Lieutenant Harold Rowe. In spite of being heavily engaged by determined infiltration patrols, the Divisional Cavalry and the 20th Battalion held firm, on the rear left.

All this Captain Harvey revealed in a matter of minutes. He said that Kippenberger believed the fate of the whole division depended on the recapture of Galatas.

'... and we've got the job of doing it,' he finished.

'Hell,' said Rex, throwing a startled glance at the objective, 'surely not on our own!' Kippenberger had told him of two unsuccessful attempts earlier in the afternoon.

'Oh, no,' Mark replied. 'Kipp has things well jacked up. D Company will be attacking on the left of the road and we have two tanks in support, but the whole show is stiff with Huns. It's going to be a bloody show, but we've just got to succeed.'

'Sandy, you will be on the right, Rex on the left. Now for Pete's sake get cracking!'

I rejoined my platoon. I gave the situation to the N.C.O.s and those standing near in as few words as possible. We moved forward to a mud terrace, lined up and poised for attack. Less than two hundred yards ahead the first few buildings of Galatas seemed quiet enough, but from deeper in the village the guttural shouting of the enemy could be heard. I looked along the line.

On the right Corporal Rae Thompson was talking quietly to his men—on the left Lance Corporal Irwin was stuffing extra ammunition in Len Diamond's pocket, and Bellamy was fondling his tommy-gun. Everyone looked tense and grim and I wondered if they were feeling as afraid as I, whether their throats were as dry, their stomachs feeling now frozen, now fluid. I hoped, as I sensed the glances thrown in my direction, that I appeared as cool as they. It occurred to me suddenly that this was going to be the biggest moment of my life, that now even more than during the last few hectic days the men looked at me to see them through. Something was expected of me. I looked up to the twinkling stars and prayed fervently for guidance.

We had been waiting for the tanks and now they appeared, rumbling slowly up the track, two old Mark VIs, built between the wars and to all intents and purposes useless as tanks—even armour-piercing bullets fired from an ordinary rifle could penetrate their sides. Kippenberger, who had been moving quietly amongst the waiting troops, walked over to the leading tank and spoke to the fair-headed officer.

Meanwhile the activity within the village was increasing. Guttural orders and spasmodic shooting rang clear now that the last of the planes had left. But there was yet no direct fire on to us, and somehow I found this strangely ominous, for surely any alert sentry must have seen us form up.

Suddenly the tanks revved their motors into a roar, and passed through our ranks. The fair-headed Commander who was leading waved to us as he passed,

This was our signal to attack. Someone blew a whistle. Orders barked along the line. I found myself shouting to my men, and we were away, two hundred men in line, advancing steadily and grimly.

As the tanks disappeared into the first buildings of the village in a cloud of dust and smoke, the whole line broke spontaneously into the most blood-curdling shouts and battle-cries. The effect was terrific. One felt one's blood rising swiftly above fear and uncertainty until only an inexplicable exhilaration, quite beyond description, remained.

We moved as one man into the outskirts. From the village a pandemonium of multi-coloured flares burst in frenzy, and in answer the German mortars came quickly into action. But we were by now almost at grips and the ugly black and orange 'K-K-rrumps' sounded safely behind us.

By the time we entered the narrow streets, before the first German was sighted, every man was firing his weapon to the front or in the air, and every man, one could feel it, was flushed with confidence. Nothing could stop us. We were attacking not as our fathers had done with artillery pounding ahead, but as their fathers had with cold steel and savage battle-cry.

Then something happened. One of our tanks came flying down the road towards us in hot retreat, slowing only when it saw our close ranks. The men gaped—dismayed—and the shouting sobered. From the turret a frenzied head and shoulders appeared, a frantic face with eyes popping in the madness of panic. He screamed at us.

'Let me through—get out of the road'—then as the panic rose in him— 'for cripes' sakes run for it—the place is stiff with the bastards.'

There was a murmur from the quietened ranks. I realised with sudden dread that this was the emergency, the crisis, I must face.

'Turn round,' I said, surprised at the harshness of my voice, 'this is no time for turning back—turn round and we'll come in with you.'

'Not ... likely. They've got the other tank, killed my officer—killed him I say—get out of the way or I'll run you down.' Suddenly as I stood in the tracks of the tank I saw a white face looking through a square aperture in the armour—the driver. I thrust my pistol to within inches of his forehead and shouted, 'Turn round and advance or, by heavens, I'll shoot!'

It was strange that, for all the fever of excitement, the anxiety, the fear and danger of that night, my most unforgettable memory was the startled reproach in the driver's eyes.

'I'm game, sir,' came a Cockney voice. 'There's no need for that. I'll do anything I'm ordered—it's the bastard above who needs the pistol.'

And immediately the tank began to turn. It smashed its way about by crumbling the stone wall of one of the houses which formed the narrow street, and roared its engines, preparing to move again into the attack. As it moved off the maniac in the turret leapt from the tank and ran stumbling back through our ranks. His screams and curses were an immediate danger to the success of our attack. When one man breaks, he affects the man who is wavering, and in no time a strong company can become a rabble.

I raised my revolver, hesitating. My duty as an officer was quite clear. But I couldn't bring myself to do it.

A shot rang out and the screams ceased. A private soldier with a smoking rifle looked grimly around his friends. No one said anything. We just all moved on again, quieter now, but I think the better for that.

The road widened a little, and straightened. From ahead a Spandau spat and the bullets cracked over our heads. Sharp flashes spoke from the shadows under the walls and there were answering ejaculations of pain amongst us.

We surged forward. Three forms rose from the shelter of some corpses on the left and we fell on them. They stood their ground and bayonet clanged against bayonet. One collapsed clutching Templeton's bayonet on his throat. One died from a burst from Diamond's tommy-gun. I thought perhaps the third fell to my revolver.

But the defender's fire was vicious. From the road, from window and from low roof-tops, rifles and Spandaus spat brilliant tracer in all directions. Most of it was frenzied and inaccurate, but the effect was terrifying. We sheltered temporarily behind the first tank—the one which had turned back. It was now lying knocked out in the centre of the road, at a point where it broadened into a small square.

Within the tank all was still. Occasionally shots would ricochet off its turret. I groped round the side and reached through to the driver's seat. How horrible a dead face feels, and how surely in an instant one can know it for a dead one. I returned to the men. They were reloading their weapons. Across the square a Spandau flashed, sending staccato bursts over our heads to zip and twang off the houses in the rear. We could hear unmistakable guttural orders. Diamond and Bellamy were firing answering bursts from under the tank. Somebody was dressing a form in the gutter and saying, 'She's OK, Dig—we'll soon get you out—just lie back and relax.'

I realised that my force was rapidly dwindling. Action, quick action, was essential. I decided to charge. The boys rose as one man. We jostled each other for the lead and, firing from the hip, we advanced step by step across the square.

At once we realised the enemy's consternation. Screams and shouts showed desperate panic in front of us.

I suddenly knew, with that particular clear insight which occurs only in battle, that we had caught them ill-prepared and in the act of forming up. Had our charge been delayed even minutes the position could easily have been reversed.

By now we were stepping over groaning forms, and those which rose against us fell to our bayonets. Bayonets with their eighteen inches of steel entered throats and chests with the same horrible sound, the same hesitant ease, as when we had used them on the straw-packed dummies in Burnham.

The enemy seemed in full flight. From doors, windows and roofs they swarmed wildly, falling over one another to clear our relentless line. There was little aimed fire against us now.

The earlier exhilaration returned, victory seemed assured.

But where the streets narrowed, seven or eight men suddenly charged down towards us. Short bayonets glinted as they fired into our midst. A group of diehards. Someone shouted, 'Look out—that bastard on the roof,' and I fired, together with several others, at a helmeted form in the act of dropping a grenade. As I turned to face the attackers, something in the back of my mind recorded the tinkle and rattle of the grenade as it fell immediately behind me.

The enemy were ten paces away, in line. There were only four now, and before I could aim at the biggest he stumbled and fell. They were right on us. A bayonet glinted not three yards from my pointed pistol. As I pulled the trigger, even as that helmetless figure plunged down towards my groin, I saw a mop of fair curly hair, a young face with teeth bared in a savage shout. My pistol jarred in my hand. On the instant that I noted the shudder that shook his frame, something like a sledge-hammer hit me on the thigh, lifted me up and back. It is hard to describe, but I knew that even as I tumbled I felt numbed, cold and sick. Before I crashed to the ground the grenade behind me exploded. From the nape of my neck, all over my back and buttocks, down to my calves, I was peppered with stabs of pain.

For a few seconds everything was black. I had fallen hard and I had great difficulty in regaining my breath. The shrieks, curses and groans, the cracking of the bullets overhead, all welled and receded in my ears as I struggled for self-control.

My mind cleared slowly. One of my men, Schroder, of platoon headquarters, was groaning quietly on my right and trying to get to his feet. Above the babble of voices and groans I could hear a very English voice calling, 'Good show, New Zealand, jolly good show, come on New Zealand....' finishing in an exclamation of pain. It was the young tank officer, Roy Farran.

Roy Farran's tank, Galatas   ATL DA-12645

Bellamy, Knowles and Diamond bent over me, and I thought it was Logie who said urgently, 'Are you OK, sir, are you OK?'

I pulled my hand from under my chest and rolled over. My back hurt, but I somehow knew that that wasn't serious. My stomach felt like a lump of lead, but from there down I was quite numb. No pain at all. Just an awareness that something was terribly wrong. I felt gingerly downwards. My groin seemed untouched. My right thigh as far as I could feel was intact. But as I shifted my hand over on to my left thigh it sank deep into a warm, mangled mess. At first it might have been someone else's leg—no pain at all—but one of my fingers groping deeper touched something

32

hard. My whole body jarred, the blackness welled up again and I felt weakly sick.

Logie cut away some of my trouser leg and ripped it open. Diamond did something with a field dressing. I lay back and left it to them.

'Hell,' said Diamond, stammering as usual, 'these are no good—needs about a dozen to fill that up.'

Ahead things seemed much quieter now. There were still desultory cracks both in front and behind us, but it seemed safe to assume that the field was ours.

'You'll have to go on, chaps,' I said weakly, 'consolidate on the outskirts of the village and then send a runner to find Captain Harvey.' I didn't know at that stage that Captain Harvey and Rex King, as well as five of our senior N.C.O.s were also wounded. The men demurred a bit. There was no officer or N.C.O. to lead them and they were worried about me and the other wounded.

Then Len Diamond, the rough, lovable platoon wit, stood up and, starting gamely down the dark road, stammered, 'C-c-c-come on you b-b-b-blokes, let's get s-stuck into the bastards and be done with it.'

Then they filed past me, saying touchingly comfortable words such as 'Bad luck, sir,' 'Look you up in hospital,' 'Sure you'll be OK, sir?' and so on.

Logie finished playing with my leg and stood up. 'I'll come back as soon as things settle down,' he promised, 'and we'll get you out of this hole.'

The sound of their feet had hardly faded when the door of one of the houses burst open and five Germans poured into the streets, obviously bent on escape. I groped and found my revolver. I wondered whether it might be wiser to lie low and sham death.

They swung in our direction. I fired point-blank into the leader's stomach as he passed. He staggered on a few paces screaming. The second one was almost on me. I pulled the trigger, but nothing happened, and I knew that I had used the last of my ammunition. But there was really no danger. These men were driven by blind panic. They charged on. The last one trod full on my chest and almost fell. They clambered over a low stone wall and disappeared.

Silence once again descended on the square. Only quiet groans and whimpers could be heard. I felt colder than ever in my life, yet the night had been mild before. I kept stopping myself from talking aloud.

Then the Germans started mortaring the village. The pitiful whimpers, both German and British, freshened with fear. Schroder, with one leg

ATL DA-12652

*The Germans re-enter Galatas. A few hours earlier, I lay
wounded in this gutter between my dead comrades.*

flopping uselessly, dragged himself over to me and by pushing and
shoving got me into what small shelter the gutter against a stone wall
afforded. He inspected my wounds and fumbled around my groin and
thigh. I realised dimly that he was applying a tourniquet.

When he had finished he worked slowly with immense pain and effort
out into the midst of those yellow flashes, amid the deadly whistling
shrapnel, until he had most of the wounded in comparative safety.

Once a young Greek girl, not more than twelve or thirteen years old,
brought out a glass of hot sweet milk which to our parched mouths was
real nectar. She brought rugs and carpets and covered us where we lay.

Soon after midnight, Logie, Bellamy, Knowles and Diamond came back
and reported that things seemed quiet. They had obtained permission to
get the wounded out. There were, of course, no stretchers available. The
difficulty was solved by pulling doors off the bomb-shattered houses.

At dawn, I was carried into a rough, stone-walled courtyard already
filled with stretcher cases. The building which framed it formed an
Advance Dressing Station which was hopelessly crammed. The medical
orderlies were doing sterling work, but they couldn't cope with the
numbers.

They made an attempt at feeding us soon after we arrived. They gave me a slice of bully beef. I was by now wholly taken up by selfish thoughts. The sight of the meat repelled me; all I wanted to do was to be quiet and worry over the fact that it was sixteen hours since I had been wounded and I had seen no doctor. It occurred to me that with loss of blood and shock it was imperative that I should eat something. But my most determined effort would not let a mouthful down my throat, and only brought on painful vomiting, so I desisted.

Roofing the stretchers and part of the courtyard was a lean-to built with heavy beams and roofed with tiles. It had obviously housed the farmer's pigs and cows. The stench was almost unbearable, attracting thousands of flies which buzzed greedily around until our blood-stained garments were almost covered by their horrible blackness. Above, in the eaves, pigeons billed and cooed. We would have been less annoyed if they had confined their activities to that.

At last my turn came for attention. A young, fresh-faced doctor introduced himself as Lieutenant Ballantyne and asked me how long it was since my wound was last dressed. He was most concerned when I told him that it had not yet been dressed at all. As he took my temperature and felt my pulse it occurred to me that in spite of his forced cheerfulness he was nearly all in, probably had not slept for days. He seemed to be the only doctor there, and upwards of eighty people were on his hands, requiring urgent surgical attention.

I was carried out of the courtyard by four orderlies, and had a brief glimpse of the countryside.

We were on a low hill. A mile away across the valley I saw a large red flag, with a swastika, clearly laid out on the hillside for aerial identification. I had thought the enemy were miles off. I pointed it out to the orderlies, but they were quite unconcerned, pointing to the large red cross on the rude flagpole over the building and saying confidently that the Hun would not dare to fire on that. I was not so sure.

They took me through a narrow doorway into the 'operating theatre'. Here Ballantyne was busily arranging gruesome-looking knives and syringes. The operating table on which I was placed consisted of two planks bridging two small barrels. I was given morphia and at least four other injections, including anti-tetanus serum. The morphia made me drowsy and I was only dimly aware of something plucking and tugging at my leg until some instrument touched my bone and nausea engulfed me. When the doctor had finished with my leg he dabbed, tugged and dressed the small grenade wounds on my back and buttocks.

He said quietly, 'Your leg is in a bad way. How did it happen?'

I told him briefly.

'That's no ordinary bullet wound—I'm afraid the Hun is using explosive bullets. I have seen quite a few of them,' he commented.

Mention of the enemy reminded me how near us they were.

'Do you know they are almost on us?' I asked him.

'Are they?' he replied, almost without interest. 'I've been too busy to worry about them. Do you think they'll play fair?'

I didn't answer. I didn't think they would, but somehow it didn't seem to matter much.

'We'll soon know, anyhow,' said Ballantyne, stretching elastoplast over some of the smaller grenade holes. 'The sooner the better; I'd like to get some urgent cases down to the hospital. It's out of the question until the fighting stops.'

I pondered over this for a few moments. 'Would I be one of the "urgent" cases?' I demanded finally.

'Well, yes, you would. I can't do much to your leg here.'

'Do you mean I'll lose my leg?'

'Not necessarily,' he replied casually. 'Now I'll give you a little more morphia. Try and relax and get some sleep.'

Chapter Three

I become a prisoner

Within the courtyard there was a growing tension, an excited apprehension, as both wounded and orderlies realised that a climax was fast approaching. The aerial activity increased into an angry roar, above which rifle shots rang clear and close at hand. Mortar shells burst more frequently on the hillside.

I was well fuddled and heavy from morphia, but I looked slowly around the faces I could see from my stretcher. Perhaps I looked for assurance, to see if some strong character could give comfort from his confidence that all would be well. But, with the single exception of an old-looking gunner who was still unconscious, there was the same trapped, furtive look on every face. No one spoke, but eyes shifted their gaze imploringly from person to person seeking the same assurance.

Some time later a Stuka circled lazily around the Advance Dressing Station, not much higher than the large red cross flag fluttering prominently in the breeze. The bomb bays were open and we could clearly see the rows of small black anti-personnel bombs in the racks. It swung away and climbed, and as it turned I knew we were for it. The bombs came away, fell diagonally down towards us and we covered our heads and pressed down into our stretchers. One hit the building opposite where I lay, the remainder fell in a bracket on the other side of the high stone wall.

This seemed to be a pre-arranged signal with the ground troops. Mortars began to fall horribly close all round and bullets spattered into the buildings. In the courtyard some cursed and some prayed. Inside the house someone started to scream. The wall of the courtyard shook and crumbled in places. The pigeons took wing in fright. A few of the tiles became dislodged and fell amongst the stretchers below. Immediately above me a wooden beam at least a foot thick showed signs of slipping from the stone niche in which it was embedded. I watched it apprehensively.

The bombardment continued for perhaps a quarter of an hour and ceased as abruptly as it had started. We all tensed.

Then through the door of the courtyard burst one, two, three, four figures, waving tommy-guns and revolvers aggressively, and shouting unintelligible orders. Ballantyne approached them quietly and fearlessly. We were prisoners.

Presently the four were joined by twenty more. Lying back on my door I studied them. They seemed just youths, some fair, some dark, but all were arrogant and flushed with victory. Here and there were the Spandau or machine-gun men, who wore long belts of shining ammunition draped round their shoulders like mountain brigands. Almost immediately three of them clambered up from the lean-to on the opposite side of the square and nailed a large black swastika with a red background on to the flagpole in place of the red cross. As if in answer a Stuka swooped low and banked around the building. The co-operation between the German air and land forces was almost perfect. Now the three soldiers waved from the roof cheerfully and the pilot leaned out of his opened cockpit to wave back.

Meanwhile those below moved amongst the orderlies and wounded demanding military information. For the most part the men were excellent—gave their number, name and rank, and refused to speak further.

A rather fine-looking boy knelt over my stretcher and addressed me in quite flawless English.

'Your name and rank, please.'

'Thomas, Second Lieutenant.'

'Your regiment and division,' very smoothly.

'I am not required to give you that information.'

The German smiled, not the smile of a Nazi nor an enemy, but a spontaneous amused flash of attractive even teeth. His eyes were twinkling still as he tried all the usual gags for getting information.

'You are not forced to give this information—agreed,' he replied, 'but should you do so I could arrange through Red Cross to have your people advised of your safety'—and so on.

I made no reply.

By now the numbness in my left thigh was creeping into my groin and stomach. I don't recall the numbness as painful; rather it was sickening, and I had the impression that my leg was now four times its normal size. I must have either fainted or dozed off. When next I opened my eyes it was well into the evening and Doctor Ballantyne was kneeling over my stretcher with his hand on my forehead. But who was this other elegant person? I raised my head to get a better view.

'This is Doctor _____' said Ballantyne, pushing a thermometer into my mouth, 'he has agreed to your transfer to the hospital and has promised to try and have you evacuated to Greece tomorrow.' The German doctor bowed stiffly. He was quite an elderly man, with grey hair and moustache. As he turned to leave I noticed that he wore a small ceremonial sword.

Presently four orderlies moved me on to a stretcher. I was horrified at the amount of clotted blood which was left on my door and for the first time a sudden dread clutched me—was my condition dangerous?—was it possible that I might die? And as the orderlies picked me up and took me from the courtyard I groped anxiously around my thigh and stomach and wondered whether the creeping numbness might be gangrene.

They carried me shoulder high down the hillside, over terraces and through fields of grapes. The sun was just dipping below the horizon; both the sea and the clouds nearby were a glorious pink. The air seemed sweet and pure after the courtyard. I wanted desperately to live.

We arrived at the hospital. It had been bombed and machine-gunned and looked very battered. They left me on the floor of a large room with fifty or sixty other stretcher cases. On my right was a badly wounded German who was panting and holding his breath alternately like a dog with distemper. But on my left was fair hair worn too long and a cheerful English smile. We introduced ourselves. It was Roy Farran of the Third Hussars, the officer in command of the tanks we had used in Galatas. He had been wounded when his tank was almost destroyed and had been lying in the square during our pitched battle. My men had carried him out. We made friends immediately and refought the battle.

Eventually I dropped off to sleep.

In the morning I realised that the horrible stench that I had thought to be some corpse outside was coming from my leg. Someone had thrown a blanket over me during the night, and as I lifted it my gorge rose. I was terrified.

When young Fred Moodie, the doctor, came down I was beside myself with panic. He, however, seemed unimpressed and with the typical casualness of his profession prophesied that I would smell a great deal worse before the day was done. He brought me a cup of hot cocoa to cheer me, but I could not hold it down.

There was something rather hopeless and final in the thought of flying north in a German aeroplane. I pondered on it for a few moments, feeling very sorry for myself. However, there was not much time for reflection. Presently a German orderly arrived with four stalwart stretcher-bearers and I was carried out and placed with other wounded on the back of an open truck. It was no comfort to realise that this vehicle was one of the very few sound machines on the island and that it had been captured intact from the R.A.F. The driver was wearing over the top of his uniform the jacket of a British officer's mess kit with a Captain's badges of rank. He was obviously well pleased with his loot.

When we reached the aerodrome the wounded were unloaded by some of our own men who had been prisoners at the airstrip for over two days. I was greatly heartened to be discovered after a few minutes by Captain Ron Stewart and Captain Bob Griffiths, our Battalion Medical Officer and Padre respectively. They had elected to remain behind with the wounded of the first engagement, and we had left them in the path of the German advance. They told me of their experiences, of how the Germans had treated them well when they found their own wounded well tended in the combined Regimental Aid Post. They had been permitted to establish a rough hospital in a group of houses near the aerodrome where, largely unmolested by their captors, they were collecting both our own and German wounded.

I was carried down on to the main airstrip. There seemed to be several hundreds of other stretchers lying in long rows on the edge of the runway.

We lay in the sun for nearly five hours. It was very hot and the stench of my leg and blood-soaked blanket was almost unbearable. The men nearby complained that this stench made them feel sick and the orderlies moved them away from me. I felt lonely and miserable.

Later, one of the orderlies took pity on me and came over for a chat, although I was conscious that he kept his face well averted and sat to the windward. He described to me the scene on the aerodrome, how there were over one hundred planes crashed all round the edge of the airstrip, and how some of them near the beach still had their full crews and passengers seated stiffly in the positions they had been in when hit by our machine-guns. Planes were coming in and taking off continually, quite unmolested. Troops were debarking from the incoming troop-carriers in well-organised sections and moving straightway off down the road which led to the front. The empty planes taxied to the end of the runway and loaded up with wounded, being airborne again in a matter of minutes. Most of the manual work, such as unloading stores and clearing wreckage, was being done by our own men under armed guard. There were also a few hundred scruffy and reluctant Italians who had been freed from their prison camp by their ally only to be put to work, also under armed guard.

There was an exciting incident before we left. One of the bigger planes, a great yellow-nosed Dornier, came in to land, but apparently misjudged his distance. It came almost the full length of the runway and then tried frantically to gain momentum to take off again. It could not make it and crashed in a sheet of flame in the olive trees. There was a subdued but definite cheer from the lines of waiting stretchers.

German Junkers 52

Merv Simm

41

A giant Junkers 52, a troop-carrying plane, drew out to the edge of the runway not far from where I was lying. I was carried over to it by four English medical orderlies.

Nothing further happened for half an hour or so, and I recovered sufficiently to study the interior of the plane. It seemed immense. The main compartment, empty but for me, was twenty feet in length, about twelve feet wide and six feet from floor to ceiling. The walls were of a type of light corrugated metal and I noted with a certain morbid satisfaction that several groups of small punctures indicated that our ground fire had been effective.

Rising on my elbow I saw that the floor-boards, too, carried clear evidence of blood in places corresponding to the holes, so there was no doubt that the bullets had found a target. On the walls, farther up, were an assortment of machine carbines with neat rows of additional magazines and belts of cartridges.

If I cocked my head forward on my chest I could look right up the main compartment, through a small door. There I could see the two pilots chatting, as they waited at their controls. They looked amazingly casual and complacent, as though all the carnage and destruction was no concern of theirs. They were just doing their normal day's work. They revved the twin motors alternately every few minutes, making the whole plane vibrate.

Presently there was more movement outside the plane and, one by one, three stretchers were loaded aboard. As soon as the orderlies had dropped back to the ground two German soldiers clambered in and closed the doors behind them. The twin motors of the transport plane revved in unison and we moved, slowly at first and then with heavy lumbering speed, down the runway. In a few seconds we were airborne and climbing slowly into the sky.

Chapter Four

Life in a POW hospital

We touched down on an airfield some miles from Corinth in the Peloponnese, and drew down a long airstrip lined seemingly by hundreds of planes. The door was opened by four stalwarts in *Wehrmacht* uniform, and in no time we were carried to a waiting ambulance. It was very hot.

Everything seemed to be well organised. A medical orderly quickly examined the particulars on our casualty cards, and in a few minutes we were speeding along a tar sealed road and over the makeshift bridge the Germans had thrown over the Corinth Canal. Soon we entered the town.

It must have been about seven in the evening when we arrived. We were taken into the foyer of a hotel used as a hospital. An orderly came out, looked at us, gave all a dose of morphia and disappeared.

Corinth Canal, Greece WBT collection

43

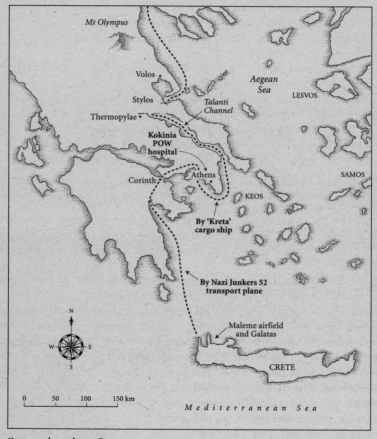

Crete and southern Greece

About an hour later a German sister paused and gazed at us for a few moments, then repeated this performance, in spite of my protests, for it seemed to me that people had been injecting morphia into me all day, and I had no wish to pass away with an overdose. I remember faintly that we were moved to some other place in an ambulance and then carried along a street, crowded with interested Greeks, into another hotel. A German orderly approached me with a syringe, but I managed to persuade him that I had no need of it. It was then nearly midnight.

'You are an officer, yes?'

I nodded, and he said, 'Your wounds smell bad. I will arrange to have them attended to. Can you walk?'

When I replied in the negative he disappeared for a few minutes and returned with an elderly and portly officer whom I took to be a doctor. He addressed me in French which I understood well enough to describe my wounds and the treatment I had already had. He pulled his grey moustache for a few minutes thoughtfully and then called to some orderlies. I was taken in the ambulance to yet another emergency hospital, and about two in the morning I was placed on the operating table.

The doctor was now garbed in a white coat and as he pulled on rubber gloves he smiled at me. All around the table stood white-coated orderlies— about eight of them. They undressed me and made me comfortable in such a friendly and sympathetic way that I found it difficult to realise they were Germans.

The doctor started on my leg, calling short orders which were promptly answered by one or other of the orderlies handing him some syringe or instrument. He was not hurting me; indeed at that time my leg was quite numb from my groin to my foot. But I raised my hand a little apprehensively, and the doctor stopped his cutting. He spoke to one of the orderlies. An ether pad was put over my face and by gesticulation and example I was persuaded to count aloud as it took effect. I came round once during the operation, all sorts of mad noises and voices crashing in my ears, and became aware of these strange faces bending over me and beyond them the ceiling which had a weird Eastern pattern. I was violent and they gave me another whiff, for when I woke up, vomiting from the ether, I was lying in the corridor. My blood-stained blanket was over me, but its stench was now overpowered with ether.

Presently the portly doctor came out, saw me, and after a few words in French, had me taken up flight after flight of stairs to a really delightful room on the top floor. There he visited me, and told me quietly that I would be given transfusions and that when my blood count was normal my leg would be amputated. He ran his finger across my thigh to indicate where it would be lopped off.

Through the window I could see blue ocean, with here and there the sails of Greek fishing-boats. Down below in the street I could hear a military band playing stirring march tunes, and later what I took to be a battalion of soldiers marched past singing. The bed was soft and comfortable. Strangely enough, I was not at all worried about my leg. Perhaps it was a reaction from the shock, or more likely the ample injections of morphia they gave me, but I was held by a strange lassitude which lasted for several days. I glanced idly at the instructions for transfusions and amputation, written boldly in German and repeated in different handwriting in English on my card. It did not seem to concern me at all.

Early in the afternoon, I was told that all the wounded prisoners were to be concentrated at a hospital in Athens and I was taken away with others in an ambulance. It was a long, hot journey. At various turns I could see beaches and open sea out of the back of the ambulance. It was late in the evening when at last the ambulance slowed up and a sentry allowed us to enter a barbed-wire enclosure. A bell rang loudly and eight or nine orderlies gathered round the back of the ambulance. They questioned us in cheery English and I realised with delight that they were Australians, great strapping fellows well browned by the Grecian sun.

I had arrived at the 5th Australian General Hospital which had been captured some six months before. The building, which had been built by the Greeks for a borstal, consisted of four blocks, each four storeys high. I was carried into the lobby, and from there to a ward which was to be my home for many months.

POW Hospital, Kokinia, Greece

ATL DA-12318

46

The journey from Corinth had left me exhausted and I did not take much notice of my fellow wounded. The orderlies fussed around, made me comfortable and produced the inevitable syringes.

Then the doctors arrived, and over my bed they discussed the instructions on my card. I listened dully with my eyes closed until I realised that they were arguing over the German decision to amputate. I tried to imagine what life would be like without a leg, but I was dozy again and strangely enough it didn't seem to matter very much. I felt confident that I was in good hands. The doctor smiled at me as he fitted a large syringe into the crook of my arm.

It seemed days later when I woke up and looked around. I was immediately conscious that I felt better, I racked my brains to remember how I had arrived in that comfortable bed, and suddenly realisation chilled me. I had been to the operating theatre—had I lost my leg?

I could feel nothing at all. I pushed my hand down slowly; now there was no apathy, just an awful dread. Then I felt a great wad of bandages and cotton wool and, below that, still numb and foreign feeling, but unmistakably there, was the continuation of my leg. Thankfulness surged through my body and my eyes smarted as I tried to express it in prayer. It was an unforgettable moment.

Presently the doctor arrived. He took off my bandages, and I raised my head to have a look. A terrific red gash ran from my groin across the top of my thigh and down the side of my leg, the wound roughly the shape of a four-pointed star. In size it was seventeen inches long and ten inches wide. Its edges puckered out untidily like frills and in the centre, criss-crossed with dabs of flesh, a portion of bone was visible.

The doctor explained that everything now depended on my lying very quiet and avoiding any sort of movement to excite bleeding. My grenade wounds in the back were smarting and troubled me far more than the leg, but he assured me none was serious although some still retained their shrapnel which, he mentioned casually, would not do any harm. I pestered him to give an estimate of how long it would take to heal, but all he would say was that it would not be healed in six months. His diagnosis was more or less accurate. Actually, it was fifteen months after I had been wounded that the two edges united for the first time.

And so the days began to pass. Some of them were interminably long, and having a watch made them seem longer. After being woken for the dawn dressing whole days would seem to drag slowly past until a glance at my wrist would show but an hour's difference. And the longest hours were those when three or four of us would discipline ourselves not to touch our morning bread for a certain period. Someone would always give in, and then we would either pounce on it and devour it in seconds or continue our restraint to the extent of slicing it with a razor blade into thin wafers and applying these one by one to the tongue at timed intervals. Yes, as appetites came back, food became everything in life, the only real topic of conversation, the only means of satisfactory barter. And hated with jealous intensity was the man in the ward who received more than his fair share, or wangled a second helping.

Some ten days after my arrival, the grey-haired German doctor who had cleaned up my wounds in Corinth visited the hospital on a tour of inspection. He walked into our ward with an entourage of lesser doctors and medical orderlies, beaming benevolently at everyone. He did not examine every patient; in fact, he only looked at about six; but when he arrived opposite my bed his face lit up in recognition.

'Ach, the New Zealand boy!' he exclaimed in French, 'my patient from Corinth. And how do you find yourself?'

I replied as cheerfully as I could and, encouraged, he demanded to have my wounds shown to him. He was quite astonished to find I still had my leg, and sent one of the doctors off for my records. I could make out that he was explaining in some detail to the younger doctors why he had ordered an amputation.

The results of this visit were twofold. First my thigh wound was photographed (to the envy of the ward), and a long list of younger doctors came to inspect the progress of it from day to day. The second result was more important and exceptional. I was put on extra rations as an interesting case, and the grey-haired doctor himself commenced to visit me periodically, often bringing grapes and sweets. Of course, I was bound to share the extra food with my comrades, but even the portion I retained made a vast difference to the diet. Soon I realised I could do without further dope and that I was getting well. I no longer needed transfusions, my bodily vigour was re-established and the chance of a relapse very remote.

With this change in health came the first clear realisation of my plight. Any attempt I had made before this period to sort out my thoughts had always ended in dull despair, but now it seemed quite straightforward. I was in the hands of the enemy, a prisoner of war. I must get back. I must escape.

My leg gaped sarcastically at me as I watched each day for signs of healing, but my mind was full of plans and ideas. Some were wild and impossible, just pleasant and exciting daydreams, but others had their practical side. In any case, I had found a line of thought to keep my mind healthily occupied as I lay in bed, and the hours did not seem so terribly long. I started to save the German marks which they paid me as an officer each week, and for a period I collected a store of dry bread crusts. I managed to keep up my monetary savings, but the store of bread crusts did not last long. One night after I had been storing for nearly six weeks I woke up and just could not get back to sleep. After tossing restlessly for an hour or so I started sucking one of the crusts. By dawn there was none left.

The general attitude among the prisoners towards escape was apathetic. There had been practically no training for the emergency of capture, and the majority of prisoners gave way to the strange selfish lassitude which was a feature of all prison camps. The days, the weeks, the months dragged slowly by. The edges of my main wound became less ragged and week by week began to round off and work towards the centre.

May, June, July and early August were marked off on the large calendar at the end of the ward. I still lay on the same bed, always on my back, waiting impatiently for some real signs of recovery.

In the second week of August I made my first move towards getting fit enough to escape. On a hot, uncomfortable afternoon when all the orderlies were away sunbathing on the roof I gathered all my will-power and worked my good leg out of bed and on to the floor. Then, over a period of an hour or so, I slowly worked myself out of bed and on to my feet. I felt dizzy and sick and soon collapsed, and in consequence had a bad night. Apart from the wound itself, which still had several inches to close over, my legs and arms, indeed my whole body, was wasted and feeble.

Nevertheless, it was a start. The next day I repeated the performance, the day after I managed to step by clutching the side of my bed. At the end of the week I managed to move shakily from bed to bed down the whole ward, stopping to chat and rest all the way. Soon after I could make the latrines if I took it in easy stages, and I was able to confound the orderlies in the days that followed by refusing the much-hated bed-pans and bottles.

Each day I exercised my arms and my good leg, and enjoyed the feeling of the youth in me responding well to the challenge. At the end of the second week, carefully guided and assisted by two of the walking patients, I made my way down the two flights of stairs into the open court-yard below.

That was a very happy day. I took off all my bandages and let the sun stream down on the raw flesh, while I revelled in the fresh air which was so sweet and pure after the ward atmosphere of dirty wounds and plaster cases. All the men of the 23rd Battalion who were captured with me came round to make their congratulations. Some of them were on crutches, some with sticks, others had their chests covered in plaster and their arms held at queer, uncomfortable angles in wire frames called 'Airplane splints'.

We used to meet most afternoons after that, either in the courtyard or up on the flat top of the roof of my block. I liked this latter place best, as there was such a glorious view.

To the south, not more than three miles away, lay the harbour of Piraeus, with the white sails of the fishing vessels, and beyond the harbour entrance there was the royal blue of the Aegean. To the east, skirted neatly by whitewashed suburbs and crowned by the Acropolis, lay lovely Athens. We were told that with field-glasses one could see plainly the German and Italian flags flying from opposite ends of the Parthenon but, personally, I was glad I had lost my own binoculars.

It was strange, during these afternoon meetings of ours, how seldom we discussed escape. It was not a subject which lent itself to easy conversation in a large group. We soon found that there were always conflicting views on the question, and that to bring it up in moments of quiet enjoyment was to ask for discord.

The escapes which occurred during the period, including Roy Farran's, while gratifying to many, were most unsettling to me. They made me impatient with my wounds and miserable with anxiety that by the time I was fit to go additional precautions would make escape impossible.

One morning I went up on the roof of the hospital. The sun was just rising beyond Athens, and the air was crisp and delightful. I sat for a few minutes thinking of the long period I would have to wait until my leg closed over; then I took off all the bandages, gauze and padding to have yet another look at it. I flexed my leg back and forth and watched the muscles working smoothly under the raw, clean flesh. If I was careful, if I had luck, if I could be reasonably certain of medical supplies, I would have a chance of success, even with the present state of my leg. It was worth the risk.

I decided not to wait any longer.

Chapter Five

The first attempt

Pte Stan Schroder, DCM

Private Stan Schroder had been an original member of my platoon when we formed the battalion from civilians in 1939. He had never been particularly outstanding during the training period. His rough, genial appearance rather went against his chances of standing out as a soldier. In battle, however, it had been another matter, and he had demonstrated a surprising ability and a high degree of casual bravery. His worth on Crete was recognised later with the award of the Distinguished Conduct Medal.

Schroder had been one of my most frequent visitors when I had been bed-ridden, and on more than one occasion had asked me to include him in any escape plan I might make when we were fit. In captivity he was quite unchanged, rough as ever, his hair long and untidy, and his clothes draped untidily about him. Yet for all his unkempt demeanour this soldier retained in prison camp something far more precious than personal appearance: he never at any time lost his sense of duty.

So, when I had done up my wound, and had made up my mind that the leg and thigh would carry me satisfactorily, I sought out Schroder.

I found him sitting in a large group of Australians playing 'two-up' on a hospital blanket. The game did not appear to have its usual pep and excitement, and Schroder had only a few cigarettes in front of him, so I guessed he would not mind an interruption. I beckoned to him.

He rose from the group slowly and stiffly.

'Morning, sir,' he smiled in his normal easy manner. 'Did you want me for anything?'

'That rather depends on you, Stan,' I replied. 'Do you feel like a change of surroundings or are you content with the life here?'

His dour face lit instantly.

'Are you on to something, sir?' he demanded, glancing around to see if there was anyone within earshot. 'Because if you are I'm with you all the way. I've only been waiting to get a bit more flesh on my knee myself, and if I never saw this place again it would be too soon for me!'

We made our way together to the top of the main block. There was no one on the roof, so we sat down on the balustrade and looked out over the guards on to the blue Aegean.

The first thing to do was to clear our minds of all the optimistic flights of fancy we had both been harbouring—wild schemes such as the theft of a lovely yacht lying down in Piraeus anchorage. We soon realised that the whole of our concentration was necessary to get over the first hurdle, the actual escape from the hospital compound. Once free there were all sorts of alternatives, all of which would depend very much on the luck we might have in finding the right sort of friendly Greek. The plan uppermost in my mind for that phase was a long march north and east of Athens to the coast of Porto Rafti, from where I had embarked in April for Crete. Once there I was confident that we could make our way by boat across the Aegean to Turkey in easy stages.

'Can you sail a boat, sir?'

'No, not really. I've done a bit at Kaiteriteri, you know, but no ocean-going stuff. But those Aegean islands must be little more than thirty miles or so apart. They need never be out of sight and we could row there, hopping from one island to the other.'

'Don't need legs for rowing. It would suit me, sir. But that doesn't get us out of this bird-cage. What's the form on that?'

We were back again to the main snag. We talked on most of that day, and again later in the evening, whispering in a dark ward corridor. But we would always wander away from the main point to some wonderful plan starting from our successful escape, and then once again we would wake up to the fact that we were evading the main issue. The only decision we came to was that a further ten days or fortnight was necessary to allow us to make a careful study of the sentries and their habits, to collect the necessary tools and equipment for the escape and to save enough food for the journey. The delay would also benefit our wounds.

We continued to collect a store of food with the help of a friend of Schroder who worked in the cookhouse. I got a pair of pliers which we could use as wire-cutters from a Greek electrician who visited the hospital. We got a compass from a wounded New Zealand officer, exchanging it for a German camera which Stan had taken from a dead paratrooper, and successfully concealed it in his stretcher on capture. This meant that we were almost complete in the equipment we thought essential for a successful escape. We could now crystallise our plan.

A careful study of the changing of the German Guard had revealed a weakness which was, perhaps, typical of the Teuton mind.

The four blocks of four-storeyed buildings of which the hospital was composed were very close together, so that the area to be guarded by the Germans was not by any means excessive. Roughly the outer wire perimeter consisted of a rectangle some three hundred yards by two hundred yards. In addition to the outer wire, which was double dannert, well-laced and interlaced, the guard placed some reliance on the twelve-foot wall which linked the blocks, limiting exit to two doors.

There was no vegetation at all in the enclosed area, nor indeed any outside for some thousands of yards. Thus a sentry on the gate and one each at opposite corners of the compound was a completely adequate guard by day.

By night the guard of three was doubled, providing an additional sentry on the two remaining corners and one sentry to prowl around the whole enclosure. Again, this was a completely adequate guard for night duty; the ground was both light and open, so that movement in the dark could be easily picked up. Furthermore, there was an order restricting all prisoners within the actual walls of the Borstal after dusk.

Now the important thing was this. The time laid down during the summer for 'dusk' and for doubling of the guard was eight o'clock and, because it was so ordered, the German Guard adhered strictly to that time.

53

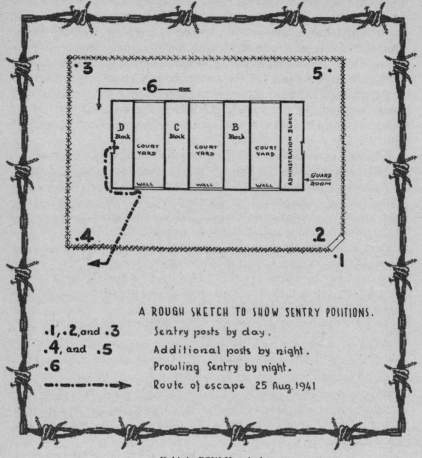

A ROUGH SKETCH TO SHOW SENTRY POSITIONS.

.1, .2, and .3   Sentry posts by day.

.4, and .5   Additional posts by night.

.6   Prowling Sentry by night.

·–·–·–·–>   Route of escape 25 Aug. 1941

Kokinia POW Hospital

But, with the drawing in of the autumn evenings, it was almost pitch dark at fifteen minutes to eight.

We planned to make use of this brief period when the long distance between the two day sentries offered a reasonable chance of not being seen. We chose a stretch of wire with a few flaws, between the sentry at the gate and the one at the northern corner, taking into account that the

54

sentry at the gate for most afternoon shifts was an elderly man with spectacles. We hoped he would be particularly short-sighted in the dusk.

We had chosen a date well in advance, between the seventh and the tenth of September. Our main reason for this choice, apart from the collection of necessities, was the fact that a new moon was in the sky during the afternoons. By the dates we had chosen it would rise sufficiently late to allow us maximum darkness for the actual break and some good light for our first night's march after we were clear of the compound. Our excitement and impatience rose with each hour that passed.

Although by then we fully appreciated that the biggest hurdle was the initial escape, we did not entirely neglect the second stage, the long march to Porto Rafti. We studied the maps we found in various books in the hospital library, and plotted out our route and how far we would travel each night. We copied an outline of Greece on to a piece of linen and sketched in the roads, and all the small islands which stretched over the Aegean to Turkey. For the possibility of recapture we spent an amusing hour carefully ridging a route on the map in the opposite direction to the one we intended to take, writing 'see Mr "X" at Police H.Q.' or similar remarks against certain villages. This map was to cause more concern and also more amusement later.

We were continuing with our preparations when one day a blow fell. In the evening Schroder came to see me.

'I've got some bad news, sir,' he said, very quietly.

'What is it, Stan?'

'The hospital Sergeant Major warned me today that I was to get ready to move to Germany with the next draft.' He paused and looked away from me, out of the window. 'The draft is to leave here on Monday,' he finished.

This was a serious blow. Everything was nicely planned for ten days away, and it would be a pity to hurry our preparations. Besides, there was the moon to consider.

I thought it over for a few moments. 'Have you tried to get your name taken off the roll?' I demanded.

'Yes, I spent the whole afternoon jawing with the Sergeant Major, and even saw the doctor of my ward. But they say the German doctor has made up the list and they have no say in it at all.'

'That's serious, Stan.'

'Yes.'

There was a pause for a minute or so. There was only one course open as far as I could see, but at first I was a little worried. We continued, dropping our voices automatically to a low whisper.

'How big was that damned moon tonight?' I asked him.

'About quarter, or a little less, I should say. Went down about nine o'clock just before I came up here.'

'Was it very light?'

'It was rather, but not too light. I couldn't see the sentry by the gate from the far end of "D" Block.'

'What about giving it a go tomorrow night then?'

'I'm on if you are. Only don't think you have to make it now, sir. If you left it until the moon was right and took someone else you would have a better chance.'

'And what about you?'

'Oh, I would make it somewhere else. On the train on the way up perhaps.'

'No, we'll go together tomorrow night. I'm sick of waiting anyway. We'll have to pray for a nice fat cloud to fix that moon, that's all.'

'What if there's no cloud? This Greek summer doesn't seem to produce any at all.'

'We'll go in any case. At fifteen minutes to eight tomorrow evening we'll get out on to the path by the main building opposite the spot we fixed. At about ten minutes to we'll set off. By eight o'clock we'll be free men.'

A few more details remained to be sorted out. We debated, still in whispers, in the now sleeping ward until we were clear on all that had to be done on the morrow. Then Stan rose to go. He stood awkwardly at the end of my bed for a few minutes, and then, mumbling something with emotion quite foreign to his normal self, he seized my hand, shook it, and stumped off out of the ward.

After he had gone the night orderly came through on his rounds. I feigned sleep, but my mind surged with excitement. Optimism carried me through ecstatic moments as I pictured various scenes which would follow our success. I saw my arrival back with my battalion, the congratulations of the Brigadier. I saw myself walking quietly along the path through the garden at home, to surprise my mother as she picked the morning roses. Sleep was quite out of the question.

The morning of Sunday, 25th August 1941, broke clear and bright. There was not a cloud to be seen.

To the orderlies bustling to and fro with thermometers, meals and bed-pans, it was just another day of hard, thankless work. To the patients it was the start of many more weary, heartbreaking hours of partial hunger and complete boredom. But to me, up early and carefully shaving, it was the dawn of a new life. A half-ration of breakfast did nothing to affect my exuberance. I could even survey the ugly bug-spotted walls of the ward with that peculiar affection one sometimes experiences for unlovely things to which one has become accustomed. After all, I would not be seeing them again.

After lunch we checked over our stores. Food, money, compass and dressings for our wounds, and the map I had traced on to a piece of linen. Schroder had prepared for haversacks two old pillowslips, by the simple means of dipping them in *ersatz* coffee. We stowed everything away and spent the afternoon saying farewell to those of our friends who were 'in the know'. We listened as patiently as we could to all the good advice they gave us. It seemed that if we followed their directions the whole thing was simple, a foregone conclusion. They finished by optimistically writing down addresses and messages for people at home.

But by late afternoon most of my optimism and exuberance was gone. Stan seemed as cheerful as his normally glum face would allow him to be, but I felt a rising dread, a sort of numb sickness such as one used to feel while awaiting the headmaster's caning at school. The sentry on the gate looked so grim and brutal, his square helmet fitting down below his ears, his hands forever fondling his rifle as though he were praying for such a chance as we were to give him. And the wire seemed so much more formidable now. I wondered just how sharp our wire-cutters were.

I joined Stan in the passageway below and we waited, trying desperately to appear unconcerned and cool. Orderlies, both Australian and German, seemed to look at us suspiciously as they passed.

We moved along to the big double door at the back of the block. It was quite dark outside, not pitch black by any means; one could see the dark form of the rear sentry over in his corner. We hurried around the corner of the building and sat down at the spot we had chosen to wait for the extra darkness an additional five minutes might bring. Down by the gate we could faintly see the only sentry who would worry us. He was kicking his feet against the side of a small bridge which formed the entrance to the camp. We could not be sure that it was the one with spectacles.

Over the Aegean the new moon smiled wanly down and we cursed her silently.

A few patients, taking a last walk round the block before the doors were closed, observed us as they passed, and continued on their way whispering excitedly. I felt desperately afraid and had to clench my mouth to stop my teeth chattering. I realised that had I been on my own I would have funked it. It would have been so easy to go back to the ward with some plausible story of bad luck.

Then, suddenly, I wanted to get it all over. That wonderful clarity which comes in moments of emergency took possession of my mind. I jumped to my feet. Schroder followed more slowly.

We debated in whispers which way the sentry was facing. It was impossible to be certain.

Then Stan said, '... and anyway, it's a fifty-fifty chance.'

That settled it. We set off across the open towards the wire. It was like stepping out on to a road directly in front of a speeding car. We moved too quickly, yet we knew that fast movement would attract attention.

We threw ourselves down by the first fence. I started cutting. The pliers worked like a charm. I cut three strands.

Suddenly there was a harsh shout from the bridge. It was followed by the unmistakable working of a rifle bolt, as a round was forced into the breech.

'Hurry,' said Stan, pressing against me from behind. 'Hurry, we've been seen!'

Seconds passed, and all I was aware of was a rising commotion down by the sentry post. I cut four more strands. Then there was a crack and a flash together. A bullet hit one of the iron uprights about two yards away and ricocheted into the sky. We ducked momentarily, then carried on. Stan bent back the strands as I cut them.

We were into the middle barricade when the second shot twanged over our heads. After that a succession of spurts in the clay and stones within feet of us sped us through.

Of course, we should have stopped and called out. Once discovered, it was madness to continue. But the pliers were working so well, and the last apron of wire was taut. It cut as easily as butter.

I broke through and started to run. Then I heard Stan call out, so I went back. I was afraid that he might have been wounded. There were three rifles firing at us by that time and one of them was only about thirty yards away. But Stan was not hurt, he was stuck with his bulky clothing in the gap I had made. I helped him through. We picked up our pillowslip-haversacks, swung them over our shoulders, and sped off into the night.

The whole German Guard was streaming out of their quarters, shouting and cursing. Several of them were firing wildly in our general direction. The sentry on the bridge screamed information of our whereabouts and they all started in pursuit like a pack of hounds. We could hear them coming.

But we had the start of the two hundred yards from the main building, down through the only gate, and then back to where we had breached the wire. With luck, with a great deal of luck, we could still make it.

The hospital, by that time, was fully aroused. From every window, and from a tremendous crowd on the roof of each block, came cheers and well-meant suggestions. Then someone organised them into chanting to hide the sound of our running footsteps.

We pushed on, hoping that the darkness might throw off our pursuers. We heard them reach our haversacks, which we had dropped when we heard one of our friends shout that their light colour showed up in the dark. They seemed a good two hundred yards away. Then they fired a volley of bullets into a clump of stunted trees well to our left. We began to take heart, although our wounds were pulling us up almost to a walk. I felt rotten, covered in sweat and battling for breath. But I still thought we might make it.

Then something loomed up out of the darkness in front of us. In uniform. A Greek civil policeman.

We veered away from him, but he closed in and drew a revolver. He called out. He was one of the Gestapo-type police brought by the Germans from their Greek community in Berlin. But he was obviously a little uncertain. He waved his revolver at us and kept on shouting, but somehow seemed reluctant to do any more. I thought he looked scared stiff.

Stan made short work of him. He closed in with a right and a left and sent him sprawling on to the ground. We sped on.

The Greek policeman let us get away some twenty yards and then started to blow a whistle. He began to follow us. We could hear the Germans changing direction and swinging over towards him. Gradually they closed in on us. They caught up with the Greek policeman and the shrill whistling ceased. They started planting shots nearer and nearer.

I bumped into Stan as I stumbled forward. My lungs were bursting, and my legs flopping around almost out of control.

'No go, Stan,' I panted. He gasped something in reply.

We sat down and waited for them to come up. We were terribly exhausted, too much so to be really afraid. But I was conscious above everything of my disappointment.

The Germans were furious. I thought for one moment as they pushed their short rifles into our chests that they were going to kill us there and then. But after bruising us somewhat, and kicking us with their hobnail boots, they dragged us to our feet and packed in around us. Evidently they lost all leave for long periods after each escape, and they wanted to work off their wrath on us.

We set off back to the hospital. I received my worst bruise from the sentry at the gate. He was beside himself with fury. He rushed at me with his rifle, reversed, in both hands like a club. I raised my hands in defence, but could not hope to avoid a grievous injury with my hands alone. The Guard Sergeant, however, shouted an order, and thrust his own rifle forward to deflect the blow. Even so, the reduced force was sufficient to knock me to the ground and to inflict a bruise that was painful for many months.

We were shepherded roughly through the main doors, where all the fit prisoners were being forced back from their gaping by the German orderlies. A few called out, 'Bad luck,' but the big majority just gaped at us as though we were strange animals. It was very embarrassing.

The guard pushed us into the orderly room and gathered around us. A soldier busied himself with the telephone. Then they searched us. The only satisfying moments of that night came from their consternation and disbelief as our stores were laid out. It was amusing, too, to see their excitement over the rudely traced map—I had taken the precaution of marking a route through Corinth to the Peloponnese, many hundreds of miles from Porto Rafti, and now they believed they were on the track of some secret organisation whose headquarters they took to be the villages I had marked at random. I felt sure we would hear more about the map.

During the search my heart was in my mouth. I knew we would lose nearly everything, but it would be a great blow to lose the compass and our money. The latter I had secreted between the dressings of my wound. It was reasonably safe. The compass hung between my legs from a cord around my waist. So when I was ordered to undress I took off my coat, shirt and civilian trousers, but left on a pair of drill shorts which concealed the prize. When I was first ordered to remove these I pretended not to understand. They insisted, so I feigned acute embarrassment. Stan, standing naked, grinned sheepishly as he realised what I was up to, so I was very surprised when the Sergeant relented and satisfied himself with turning my empty pockets inside out. The compass was saved.

From the start I liked the look of the Sergeant. He was a heavily built, quietly spoken lawyer from Vienna. His face would have been quite pleasant had it not been dreadfully marked with ugly duelling scars which the graduates of many German universities took a pride in acquiring. I decided that any leniency we might receive would come from him, and treated him accordingly.

A car skidded to a halt outside and the guard froze to attention as a smartly uniformed officer strode arrogantly into the room. If I had liked the Sergeant, I felt immediately apprehensive of the officer. If ever a face was evil, his was. Thin, almost pinched, he had eyes which darted from person to person and smouldered with animosity. Lieutenant Walther Bruning, of the Gestapo, was clearly the nastiest of types. I was to hate him intensely in the weeks that followed. He now addressed the Sergeant aggressively, obviously slating him down. The Sergeant stood stiffly to attention throughout, but he held his head proudly, and there was no mistaking his disdain. It was my first indication of the general loathing some German soldiers had for the S.S. or Gestapo.

The Lieutenant turned to us, and asked something in German. The interpreter was brought forward, and we went through the same questioning the Sergeant had already put us through. But it was much more unpleasant. I felt my temper replacing my apprehension as he kept hurling obviously foul epithets.

Then he started on Stan. When his name was given as 'Schroder' the officer worked himself into a terrific rage and slapped Stan's face four or five times with his open hand. Stan took it stoically, just glared at him, saying nothing. The interpreter translated dispassionately that the officer believed Stan to be a German and therefore a traitor to the Reich. As such he was to be shot. I was studying the face of the Sergeant when this was said and could have sworn that he winked at me; certainly his eyelid flickered. Anyway, neither of us felt particularly worried at that moment.

We were ordered to dress, and then taken down into the basement of the old borstal and thrown into separate cells. There was a leaking sewer pipe running along the roof of mine and the floor was covered in an inch or so of foul water.

The iron door was locked and the guard clattered away.

A few minutes passed and the Sergeant returned with a chair for me to sit on.

The hours dragged slowly by. I paddled up and down the cell, wondering what they could do with us. I imagined courts martial, prison and, as I became more cold and miserable, I even thought apprehensively of firing squads. It wasn't a very happy night.

In the morning we were taken by car to the Headquarters at Kofisia, a suburb of Athens, and interviewed by a very dignified and slightly pompous old Captain. He took us separately, but the main object of the interrogation was obviously the marked route and ringed towns on my pillowslip map. I like to think that we both managed, by refusing to give any explanation, to leave the impression that some very secret organisation flourished in those innocent villages. No doubt a considerable number of intelligence men, who might otherwise have been used to better purpose, were directed to clear up the mystery.

When he had finished the normal questioning, and had abandoned the idea of getting any sense from me in connection with the marked map, the Captain paused. He assumed an even more pompous attitude, drew his head back and looked down his nose. I realised that he was about to announce my punishment.

He spoke at length of the many punishments he was empowered to inflict, spending some minutes on firing squads in relation to Polish offenders he had dealt with in Warsaw. Then he talked of labour camps and how very few were ever able to complete their sentence. Bread and water for months on end with very little bread completely broke a man, particularly if it was served throughout in a dark solitary cell infested by rats. He finished his gruesome tirade and glared at me.

'Mr Thomas,' he said, 'when you were wounded, the men you were trying to kill brought you from Crete to hospital.'

'That is correct, sir,' I answered. All the horrors of his power prompted the 'sir' quite easily. In any case, he was my senior.

'You have had good treatment; no power but the German Reich would have given prisoners such good treatment.'

This was a bit much. I was almost scared enough to agree, but managed to reply, 'You have treated us in accordance with the Geneva Convention, yes.'

'We do not recognise the Geneva Convention, Mr Thomas. The Third Reich is not bound by any outside laws. Our treatment is prompted by the national decency of the German people.'

I remained silent.

'But the point in question is this.' He thumped the table. 'You show your ingratitude by escaping. You return our kindness by being a nuisance, by bringing reprimands and disgrace on the very officers and N.C.O.s who have been caring for you. What do you expect to gain? What prompts this unruly behaviour? Why do you want to escape?'

He was just approaching a show of temper. It occurred to me that, unless I said something soothing, anything could happen.

I realised that his manner, apart from his native pomposity, had been strictly correct and military throughout the interview. I wondered if it would help if I climbed on to my own dignity.

'Sir,' I said, as coldly as I could, 'I have only done my duty as an officer. I am honour bound to do my utmost to escape, as you well know. Surely in attempting to rejoin my own forces I am only doing what you would expect of a member of the German Officer Corps in similar circumstances?'

I tried to say it coldly and pompously, yet to me it sounded very ingenuous. But the effect was beyond anything I had expected. It was as though I had suddenly presented a toffee-apple to a sullen child.

The Captain lifted his portly frame out of his chair and came around his desk towards me, all smiles. He was almost purring as he fumbled at my side for my hand.

'Of course, of course, Mr Thomas,' he beamed at me, 'we officers have our honour and our duty. We have our code. You are quite right, quite right.'

It was more than embarrassing: it was a little sickening. I realised I had touched an Achilles heel and decided instantly, that ingenuous or no, I would exploit it to the full in future.

The outcome of it all was fifteen days' solitary confinement on bread and water. It could have been much worse.

We were taken back to the hospital and put into the cells below, next to the German Guard. This time, however, both cells were clean and dry.

The Guard Sergeant had beds sent down from the hospital and even made no objection when I persuaded the Australian orderlies to bring both sheets and blankets. The Sergeant himself went to the hospital library and brought a variety of books for us to read. I started my term of cell-life quite happily.

Schroder, I found, was harder hit by our failure. His disappointment was keen; he was quiet and a little sullen. He stirred himself to appear cheerful whenever we could get together for a few minutes, but I noticed that he took nothing to read for the long hours in his cell.

I was younger than Schroder. I found that the thrill of the experiences of the previous few days greatly alleviated my own chagrin at the failure. I had always been a day-dreamer longing for adventure, and I had suddenly found myself in the middle of a grand adventure, far more exciting than any of my youthful dreams. The idea of being in an iron-barred cell with no conscience at all was somehow pleasing. I chuckled at the thought that some day in the future I could tell the story in detail to my people at home. I was more determined than ever to get away, and somehow more confident.

Life in the cells had its lighter side. I enjoyed every hour of the fifteen days. We were far better off on so-called 'bread-and-water' diet than anywhere else.

The day began with Lieutenant Bruning's rounds, about seven in the morning. He was always furious to find us still in bed and would scream his anger at us. The idea then was to turn the head to the wall, pull the blankets around the ears, and enjoy his rising passion until he called for the sentry. Then one stood up and did whatever he wanted. I am sure the Sergeant got quite a kick out of these daily scenes. He never interfered nor gave us orders to be up before the Lieutenant arrived.

While we dressed, our bread and water would be brought in by one of the guard. Four ounces of black German bread and a flagon of water to each of us. Sometimes we ate a little in our separate cells; I rather liked it.

But as soon as we heard the arrival of the guard's breakfast, heralded by the clattering of plates, we would rattle our doors loudly, and demand to be let out. Always we claimed we wanted to go to the latrines urgently, the same excuse every single morning for the fifteen days. They would comply.

In no time we would be seated at one of the two long tables in their guard-room. And we would have a good breakfast, a very good meal. The first morning we tried this had been most amusing. We returned from the ablutions and, without actually planning it in advance, went to the nearest table and sat down.

The German soldiers sat back in amazement. I reached over, took a plate from a pile and loaded it with some meat rolls from a large tin dish in the centre of the table. I passed a plate to Stan and he followed suit.

It was a glorious feeling; I was almost exploding with mirth. Then I nearly went too far. I touched the arm of the German soldier on my right and pointed to the bread. He jerked his arm away, shocked into action. He swore, then looked towards the Sergeant at the head of the table. He was not too sure of himself.

The Sergeant had been as aghast as the rest of the guard. But now when something was expected of him he had to make a decision. He took the easier course. He shrugged his shoulders expressively, and then looked down at his plate and went on with his breakfast. The soldier next to me passed the bread with a rather sheepish half-smile, and from that moment we had no difficulty. We only had to nudge and point and we got everything we wanted. The guard were all quite cheerful about it; indeed, I thought they enjoyed the irregularity of it all.

And so we had three good meals a day, with a welcome cup of coffee in the morning and afternoon. In addition, as a bonus, we had our four ounces of black bread.

I found interest and enjoyment in studying the guard. They were much the same individually, and as a team, as a normal-war-time New Zealand guard of soldiers. They had their clown, who was up to all sorts of childish tricks, the simpleton who was the butt of all jokes, the bad-lad who was doing extra guard duties, and the over-conscientious soldier who was going all out to curry favour with the Sergeant. They all seemed to get on well together and went about their duties conscientiously.

I found them interesting to talk to. They were mostly from Vienna, two were from Czechoslovakia, and they all spoke freely of their homes. One rather simple lad who often embarrassed me with his constant saluting told me of his young wife and family near Bremen and how his father had been a prisoner of war in England in the last war. His father had directed him, 'Always treat an Englishman well; remember he is a gentleman and plays fair,' which was surely unusual advice to give a German son off to the wars.

I was able to hide the compass and our money on the first of my daily visits to the hospital to have my leg dressed. The civilian clothes were a little more difficult. They were in an empty locker in the guard-room, and it was only by a masterpiece of play acting and deception that we secured them. Stan as usual took the uncomfortable role. He reported that he had found a louse in his clothing and as we had expected he was immediately rushed off to be disinfected. From there it was an easy matter to mention casually the possibility of the civilian clothes being verminous, and to suggest I should take them along to the disinfecter. The simple guard from Bremen was detailed to accompany me, but as he spoke no English he was not to know that I had asked the Australian in charge of disinfestation to hold the clothes for our later use.

Chapter Six

The coffin plan

When we were released from the cells and sent back to our wards in the hospital, I found that life there had assumed an entirely different aspect. Existence as a prisoner was no longer hum-drum, small annoyances and quarrels no longer a worry.

Everything had become a stupendous adventure, a sort of real-life game with definite rules and penalties. The goal at the end was freedom. But one had to dare to be free.

The piquancy of having duty on one's side in law-breaking was exhilarating. The mind seemed never free from some thrilling or amusing idea which would help towards the goal. To steal the German pay-roll and use the funds to hire a boat for Egypt, to lock the guard in their guard-rooms with the great iron doors which led into their quarters, to purloin a German uniform from the hospital store and walk out at night unmolested, to go out concealed in a large bundle of hospital laundry with the connivance of the Greek contractor, or buried under the rubbish of the rubbish cart—all these were almost feasible. To explore their possibilities kept the mind healthy.

Schroder's departure from Athens, which happened soon after our attempt, threw me in with a group of officers who were all bent on escape. Their enthusiasm made life very pleasant indeed. The leader, or rather the older member of the group, was a Captain Shannon.

We had a great number of ideas, some of which were put to the test with varying degrees of failure. The first really sound idea, however, was one which would fire the imagination of any lover of adventure.

It arose from an inspiration of 'Skipper' Shannon after he and I had been to a funeral. A young Maori officer, Lieutenant _____ who had been grievously wounded in a bayonet charge on Crete, died peacefully, having struggled valiantly to live for five long months. We had all thought highly of _____, and admired his cheerful pluck during the period at the end when he knew there was no hope. Consequently twelve officers applied for permission to attend his funeral. It was granted on sworn parole.

The funeral took place only a few hours after the certification of death, a necessary custom in the heat of Athens. We draped the secretly held Union Jack over the rude coffin, knowing that the Germans would not object. Then we carried him down from his ward and out to the main entrance.

An army truck was waiting there with a guard of a Corporal and three men, all armed. We stowed the coffin aboard carefully and clambered on. The truck drew out of the gates and down a series of secondary roads until we approached a small suburb of Athens.

When the truck drew up we found ourselves at the gates to a walled cemetery. The walls were ten feet high and of stone and mud.

I could never subscribe to the popular opinion that all Germans were bad. On the contrary, I often found men in their army whom I could respect. On this occasion the guard did not come into the cemetery at all, but contented themselves with leaving the truck at the gate and placing a sentry at the four outer corners. Thus the whole of the ceremony inside was British.

We carried _____ up a lane of cypress trees until we were met by two Greek priests who, without speaking, guided us to where a shallow grave had been prepared. The priests joined us in sympathy as one of our own padres committed _____ to rest. We saluted at attention for two minutes and then left him. It was a simple and touching ceremony.

Before we left the cemetery the two priests invited us into a small annex to the chapel and offered us *ouzo*. In the absence of the Germans they were very friendly and full of confident stories of the arrival of the Allies in the near future. Just before we left we realised that we had not brought the Union Jack, and were somewhat surprised when the priests offered to return it with the coffin. They explained that, for the sake of economy, bodies were removed from the army coffins before the grave was filled in. All the many dead from the hospital had used the same coffin.

We returned to the gate, in no great hurry, and the Corporal of the Guard recalled his sentries. In half an hour we were back at the hospital.

That night Shannon came up to my ward, acting in an excited and mysterious manner. I was convinced that he had hit on something. We went up on to the roof, by then deserted, and Shannon revealed his plan.

'Sandy,' he said, 'I've discovered the perfect escape route! It's absolutely foolproof; it's a certainty if there ever was one!'

This from Skipper was startling. He was usually so conservative—even pessimistic. I pressed him to go on. But he could be a tantalising person, and he took his time.

'There's no possible way it could go wrong,' he declared emphatically, nodding his head at each word.

'What is it, Skipper—are you going to let me in on it?' I demanded.

'Of course. Do you know, Sandy, if this comes off it will make headlines; it will make a best seller of any "escape" book.'

I noticed the 'if', but my impatience got the better of me. I pummelled him on his ample waistline until he surrendered. Even so, he went about his explanation at his leisure.

'That's just the trouble with you youngsters,' he grimaced, 'you get brainstorms about impossible schemes and when they all fail you bully us old-stagers into giving you the perfect solution—do you mean to say you didn't get any ideas today?'

'Well, if one was prepared to break a sworn parole....'

'No need for that,' Skipper broke in, '*think*, man. Use your grey matter.'

Finally he gave up teasing. He had enjoyed his fun. He said very quietly, 'There was one of us in the party today who did not give a parole.'

'Who?—the Padre?—yes, he did,' I said, a little at a loss.

'No, not the Padre.' He paused. 'What about W_____ in his coffin. Did he give a parole? Eh?'

He stood back and let the full significance of this take effect. I saw it all in a flash.

'Of course not!' I cried. 'And had he been alive he would be free in Athens now. And the Germans would never know that he was around— never look for him!'

I stopped to give Skipper an excited hug. 'Old man, dear old Methuselah, you have hit on an idea in a million. We can die off one by one, or somehow take the place of patients who die, and the rest will be easy. If things go anything like today we will only have to get out of that shallow hole and drink *ouzo* with the priests until the guard takes all the mourners back.'

'Yes. It's not bad, is it?' Skipper beamed his pleasure. 'The coffin could be loosely lidded with a few airholes for comfort. A chap could stow all his escape kit in easily. It is a really de-luxe way of going.'

'I expect every case of death is the same. What I mean is, do they let our doctors make out the certificates?'

'Well, I've known of three officers dying here, and in each case the Germans left it entirely to our own doctors.'

'That seems OK. But what about putting the corpse into the coffin? Is that a British fatigue or a German?'

'You can be sure that any dirty work such as that is left to our own orderlies. No, if the doctors will play, the scheme is foolproof.'

'Now what about details at the cemetery? Suppose some dumb-cluck of a grave digger buried one of us just to be a bit different?'

'That's not so difficult. We would have to take Padre _____ along with us: he speaks good Greek. He could get hold of the two priests and they would fix it. The only dirt that need go on the coffin would be the stuff they throw during the "ashes to ashes, and dust to dust" part of the ceremony.'

In the morning we approached the doctors. They were vastly tickled with the originality of the plot, but were rather hard to pin down for co-operation. We had to appreciate, they pointed out, that failure would bring a large measure of blame on to the doctor concerned. The Germans were particularly harsh in punishment of any abuse of the privileges accorded to protected people.

However, a young New Zealand doctor, Ron Stewart, was willing.

We drew lots to decide who should have first turn, and I won.

In half an hour I was in bed and it was generally known around the ward, and later around the hospital, that I had a temperature of a hundred and four.

For a whole week the chart over my bed showed alarming temperatures, and people started talking in low whispers about my condition. Some of the medical orderlies who were not in the know became really worried, and helped to create the atmosphere we wanted. The Padre became a constant visitor.

At three o'clock in the morning of Friday, 14th September 1941, I died peacefully in my bed from pneumonia. Friday was a good day to die, because on that day Lieutenant Bruning left early for Athens and did not get back until night—so it gave a man a decent twelve hours to be buried in.

As dawn crept into the ward a group of mournful figures could be seen standing around my bed. Their voices were respectfully lowered and probably only I from under my shroud could tell that their sympathetic whispering consisted mostly of derogatory remarks about me. As it grew lighter I could see that I would have trouble to prevent the sheet over my head from rippling up and down as I breathed.

Ron had come up at three. I heard him now saying that the German Sergeant had been very sympathetic and was arranging for a later afternoon funeral. That sounded very satisfactory. Skipper Shannon was heard saying in sepulchral tones that he thought it would be difficult to get a Greek coffin long enough for me, and in the event of it being too short, did Captain Stewart think he could take off the feet or perhaps the head? Ron thought that would be easy enough. After a pause he sent off one of the orderlies to bring a Padre. I cursed them all. It was difficult enough not to giggle as it was.

An hour dragged slowly past. Breakfast arrived and, hungry as I was, I had the infuriating experience of hearing the orderly say with an unmistakably sniff and almost a break in his voice, 'Here you are, Goodwin'—sniff—'you better have poor Mr Thomas's breakfast this morning. He'—sniff—'won't be wanting it.'

I was snoozing complacently about ten o'clock when I heard the orderly whispering urgently as he scrubbed the top of a dresser near my bed. I could not make out all he said, but his message came through like this ... '... worried ... German doctor ... grey hair ... maybe coincidence, but ...' and then he was interrupted by a shout from the far end of the ward.

I immediately thought of the portly, grey-haired doctor who had dressed my wound in Corinth and later showed a kindly interest in me. What if he should choose today of all days to visit the hospital!

There was a commotion at the end of the ward and, oh horrors, someone was coming towards me speaking German. I froze stiff—I was not acting; it was sheer panic. As they came nearer someone said to someone else in a very German accent, '*Parlez-vous Français?*' and I knew that my worst fears were realised. It was my doctor friend. The party clattered to a halt at the foot of my bed.

Someone said, '*Et si jeune, il n'a pas vingt-deux ans.*'

Someone moved quietly down to the head of my bed and stood there a moment. I could hear him breathing. Then, very gently, the sheet was raised from above my head, drawn reverently back and down my face. I could stand that. Then though I had my eyes closed I felt a hand coming near my face. It was too much. I gave a snort and a giggle and looked up into the startled blue eyes of the German doctor.

There was a moment of utter consternation. What was going to happen now? But the German doctor stepped back a pace in fright, and then broke into peal after peal of uncontrollable laughter. He sat down on the next bed, held his ample waist with both hands, and just shook and shook as though he was unable to stop. Of course, we all joined in. Soon the whole ward was rocking with merriment. I think the last to join in was the German Sergeant, who gaped at his senior uncertainly before blending his guffaws with the rest.

The Germans took no action whatsoever. I doubt whether Lieutenant Bruning was ever told. But, of course, the coffin plan was hit on the head. We swallowed our disappointment and looked around again.

Chapter Seven

Wings beat against bars

Pursuing a policy of preparedness which I had started early in October, I was lounging late one morning around the front of the hospital. In my pockets were bandages and lotions for the wound, in a small haversack under my shirt were dried crusts enough for three frugal meals, while secreted in the dressings round my wounded thigh were the marks and drachmae I had saved and borrowed.

For several days I had been watching the various vehicles which called at the hospital, weighing up the chances of clinging to the axle underneath this car, or getting in the back of that lorry. It seemed possible, now the guard was reduced and more or less slack, that one day an opportunity would be presented to be driven out in style.

On this particular morning over six cars and trucks had visited the hospital, but the opportunities had been ruined by three of the guard. They were off duty and spending the morning smoking and reading in the sun near the hospital entrance where the vehicles were parked.

I had just decided that there was nothing doing and was thinking of going in to lunch when the situation changed. A smart car sounding a loud klaxon wound towards the prison entrance. The three loafers looked up, and then dashed headlong into the guard-room—no doubt they knew an officer was arriving and it would go ill for them to be caught, as they where unshaven and without their tunics. The car slowed up as it passed through the entrance and the sentry presented arms smartly. It skidded to a halt, and a very smart Major sprang out of the driver's seat and disappeared into the building. Here was my opportunity.

The ration truck, which had been parked all morning, was due to pull out any minute, to take the Greek driver home for lunch. It was parked right under the nose of the sentry, and to clamber into the back of it without his knowledge was normally impossible. But if one only had four certain seconds when the sentry was fully occupied it would be fairly easy, and the five- or six-inch side- and tail-boards should screen a prone form as the truck passed out of the enclosure. The sentry's smart salute revealed possibilities: he had put his whole heart into it from the moment the car appeared until the officer had left his car.

I decided that a golden opportunity would present itself, providing the Major left before the ration truck.

I lounged over to the truck and lazily inspected the make of tyre and chassis and radiator. The sentry watched me idly for a few moments, and then resumed his alertness for the return of the officer. Long minutes passed and I was fast running out of things to inspect when I heard the sentry's heels click loudly, as only a Nazi's heels could.

The Major was starting his car. He backed it away from the truck to turn it, changed gear and moved slowly forward towards the sentry. He passed only five paces from where I stood.

It was now or never. I put a foot on the hub of one wheel, pulled myself over the side-board, and sprawled as flat as I could on the floor.

So far so good. There was no action at all from the sentry; I could hear the officer's car fading away in the distance. The only worry was some excited comment from a group of patients on the roof where they could look directly down on to me. I twisted my head and glared furiously at them. They saw my point and shifted their gaze to a more innocent and lazy study of the general landscape. I noticed with apprehension, however, that their numbers were fast growing as more and more gathered to see what was happening.

I could not tell what effect they were having on the sentry and the suspense was agonising.

It seemed hours, but I think it was actually only ten minutes before the Greek driver came whistling out of the ration store and clambered into the truck. Out of the corner of my eye I saw a ripple of excitement move along the gallery of the roof. The truck backfired and stuttered into life, backed some twenty yards to turn, then moved slowly towards the entrance. It was a very tense moment.

The Greek said something to the sentry and it raised a laugh. We passed over the culvert-bridge and the gears clashed as the driver prepared to speed up.

I thought for a few wonderful moments that I had made it. If intention and will-power had anything to do with it, I was as flat as a pancake on the floor, but people have told me that certain parts of my anatomy are very large even for my height. Anyway, the sentry just caught a glimpse of the seat of my trousers as we bumped down the road. I heard his frantic shout and realised immediately that the cat was out of the bag. I still hoped against hope that the driver would not hear the shouting over the clatter of the engine, and that we would go far enough for me to choose a lonely spot and throw myself off. But it was not to be. A bullet cracked high over the truck, followed quickly by another. The truck stopped with a jerk which threw me into a heap by the cab; the Greek driver leapt screaming into the gutter and the game was up.

This time I felt far more disappointed than afraid. As the whole guard came streaming through the gate I clambered down and walked slowly towards them. There was only a small amount of anger; the Sergeant prevented any brutality. As I was taken through the gates once again I found the gaze of hundreds of curious spectators very galling, however sympathetic they may have been.

They took me down into the basement and locked me in my old cell. I think they were quite pleased to have me back. The rather simple lad from Bremen asked me if I had lunched and, on my negative, fussed around and fried me up some eggs and potato. That evening I resumed my practice of eating with them, and the Sergeant, after furtively bolting both doors into the guard-room, produced a bottle of cognac. We all became quite convivial. The best joke of the evening was a demonstration by a heavily built German of my lying prone and thinking that a certain part of my anatomy was slim enough not to show over a five-inch tail-board. The whole attempt to them was as funny as a bit of string.

But, however friendly they were, I realised that any one of them on any future occasion would not think twice about putting a bullet into me. They were amiable because they were on top.

Lieutenant Bruning wasn't amiable at all. He came fuming into the guard-room during breakfast next morning, his face working with rage. The guard all sprang to their feet and I rose as slowly as I could. It was obviously no time for bravado: he might easily have used his pistol in the state he was in. He began to rave and curse, shaking his puny white fist under my nose. However, when at last he had spent himself, and his anger had changed to exasperation at my stolid uncomprehending stare, he gave some order to the Sergeant and strutted out. We sat down to our breakfast again, everyone a little embarrassed until I caught the Sergeant's eye and he grinned. Then everyone broke into laughter. Lieutenant Bruning was no favourite with the guard.

The gist of Lieutenant Bruning's orders to the Sergeant became apparent later in the morning. Soon after breakfast I asked for permission to go up to my ward and have my wound dressed. Permission was granted readily and without escort, but I was asked to be as quick as possible. I made my way up to see the medical officer.

I had not been there for more than half an hour when one of the guard came into the ward and asked me to follow him. I protested that my wound had not yet been dressed, but he ordered me out peremptorily. I followed him down to the main entrance.

Outside a staff car was waiting, and into this I was hurried. The soldier sat on one side and the Sergeant clambered in and, with an apologetic sort of grin, sat down on the other side. Another visit to the pompous Captain at the Army Headquarters at Kofisia was indicated.

I relaxed. There was nothing to be scared about, and the chance of another drive into Athens was welcome. With any luck I would get a decent stretch on bread and water, and it occurred me that if the Sergeant was going to make a habit of producing cognac in the guard-room life there would have its bright moments.

We wound through the crowded streets of Athens. The famine and misery the city was to undergo later was not yet apparent. Great stalls in the streets displayed luscious bunches of grapes, and as the headquarters at Kofisia was at least twenty minutes the other side of Athens, the Sergeant agreed to stop at my suggestion and sent the soldier over to buy two or three bunches. I enjoyed his blank astonishment when I produced and offered a thousand drachma note to pay for them—he had searched me fairly thoroughly the day before and not found a sou.

We arrived at Army Headquarters and clambered out. I noticed with satisfaction that the soldier who had been so officious in hurrying me from the ward, now had several dark splodges on the back and seat of his uniform from the grapes I had surreptitiously placed for just that purpose. It seemed childish, but then a prisoner had to have his little bit of fun sometimes. The Sergeant noticed them immediately, and his consternation was so amusing that I had the greatest difficulty in controlling myself. The Sergeant decided to leave him sitting in the car, and we proceeded up the impressive steps without him.

The first thing that struck me as we entered was the terrific industry. Greeks were rushing to and fro with buckets and mops, German N.C.O.s were shouting orders at one another and at the Greeks. Brass door-knobs and oak doors were being strenuously polished. The quiet dignity of the hall which had impressed me on my first visit was completely lacking. I guessed that someone fairly important was due any day.

Even the sentry who on the last occasion had been alert and officious was obviously not on the job. He was giving orders to a very attractive Greek girl, and as we passed him he emphasised a point by playfully pulling her hair.

We passed along a wide corridor, where each door was adorned with horrible German names, and finally arrived at the double doors of the Captain's office. The Sergeant made as though to knock and then desisted and frowned. I could see that something was worrying him and I thought that he was wishing he had brought the other soldier.

Finally he knocked.

Someone called from inside and after some hesitation the Sergeant ushered me in. There were eight or nine people, mostly officers, in the room, all looking with obvious displeasure at our intrusion.

Someone barked a question savagely at the Sergeant who, to my surprise, was in a cold sweat. He stammered out some reply which seemed to be a description of me and why I was there.

The same voice broke into a harsh tirade, finishing in an order. I understood it to be something like, 'Get that English swine to hell out of my office.' It was certainly no welcome. The Sergeant saluted awkwardly and ushered me out into the passageway, but as the voice had started again he himself returned, not without first throwing me a look of agonised appeal.

Up to that moment I had not given the chance of escape a thought. But, as the door closed behind me and the echo of angry questions rang through the building, I saw my opportunity, and set off down the long corridor as fast as I dared.

It was easy. I had no time to get scared or even excited.

At the end of the corridor, just where it opened into the big hall, a Greek woman was working with a mop and bucket. Inspirations just flashed one after another from nowhere that morning. I walked straight up and, ignoring her astonished protest, took both bucket and mop; armed with these, I marched through the hall.

The sentry was still standing by the girl, and from the leer on his face I guessed he had stopped giving orders. In a second I was past him and starting down the wide marble steps on to the street. On the left was parked the car with the disgraced soldier. I swung right and, still with my mop and pail, joined in the throng of midday shoppers. Free!

But before I had travelled a hundred yards a lot of my confidence ebbed. The shirt I was wearing had my single pip on each epaulette and, complete in khaki, I was a glaring target for suspicion. Several soldiers opened their eyes in astonishment as I passed, and I realised that the only reason they didn't stop me was that they thought it impossible for an English officer to walk unescorted down the street so near their headquarters. They did not like to make fools of themselves in a possible mistake. And then I expect the mop and pail were confusing.

But the Greeks can always pick an Englishman. Furtive, excited whispering came from all sides as I jostled in the crowd. Two small boys, in misplaced patriotism, started to follow me, calling 'Engleez, Engleez' in dangerously loud stage whispers. They put up their dirty thumbs in the greeting we had taught them during the short period before the German invasion. It was most uncomfortable.

I was wondering what was the quickest way out of the town when I saw two German military policemen approaching. I could not conjure up sufficient courage to pass them. There was a wine-shop-cum-restaurant advertised on the other side of the street, so I walked quickly across and pushed through its swing doors.

The large and rather dingy saloon was comparatively empty, but just inside the door were two German privates talking earnestly over a large flagon of red wine. They looked up as I passed them and then resumed their conversation. I deposited my pail and mop near the hat-stand and selected a table at the back of the room where I could watch the door. The room was dim enough for me to hope that the Greeks at a nearby table would continue with their voluble argument.

The minute hand of the large clock over the hat-stand seemed unbearably slow. My mind was at a standstill. I tried to concentrate on a plan, but at any thought of movement from my chair, a cold fear froze me numb. And yet I was aware that my opportunities were fading with every minute I wasted. The only possible comfort was that with extraordinary luck I might stay in the saloon all day without detection and slip away when it was dusk.

The Greek proprietor was moving in a worried fashion through the empty tables. Then suddenly his eyes lit up as he found a customer as yet unserved.

He hurried towards me, his face beaming. But not for long. At three paces from the table he stopped short, his smile vanished and he all but dropped his tray. How he knew so quickly that I was English was a mystery which was to repeat itself again and again throughout my stay in Greece.

His agitation was dangerous, whatever his sympathies might be. Across the room the two Germans were watching idly, and the Greeks on my right were staring curiously. I quickly pulled out all my money—some eight thousand drachmae—and held it carelessly in my hand. He hesitated further, fumbling with his tray and throwing beseeching glances at his colleagues. Then he made his decision. He stooped down, pick up some imaginary rubbish from the floor and approached the Greek table as though that had been his intention all along. He took orders from them, conferred in low tones for a few moments and then disappeared behind the screen which evidently concealed the entrance into his combined kitchen and cellar.

The certainty that he was on my side, however frightened and for whatever purpose, was heartening. Had he been other than patriotic he could have called to the two Germans, who had now resumed their conversation.

A few minutes passed and the proprietor reappeared, a tray in either hand. His smile was certainly a little fixed, but apart from that he was acting superbly. He came over to my table and to my astonishment put the larger of the trays down. I had misjudged him, he would not even look at the 1000-drachma note I offered. He gabbled at a terrific speed in Greek, and before I could open my mouth to thank him, he was away serving the next table.

I looked at my tray, and most of my confidence came back. A beautifully fried fish with lemon and abundant chipped potatoes. In addition, a flagon half-filled with red wine. With something to do with my hands it was easy to look casually around. The Germans were still disinterested, and the Greek who was facing me positively beamed when I winked at him. I wondered if they would help me when the Germans left.

I tried some wine. It was fresh and furred the mouth, but still it was pleasant. In a few minutes I could feel the warm glow of it spreading through me, and from then I started to see the funny side of the situation and almost enjoyed myself.

An hour passed uneventfully. I finished my flagon and it was replaced. The Greeks left, smiling encouragement. But the Germans seemed to be making an afternoon of it. They were drinking steadily and I hoped their reason would soon be dulled, for occasionally one of them would stare hard in my direction. In spite of my new confidence I lacked the courage to walk past them to the door.

It was nearly three o'clock before the climax came. Feeling warm and content from the wine, I was musing over the good Sergeant's reaction when I became aware of some commotion outside. Then, with sudden dread, I saw, through the panes of the door, square-helmeted figures jumping from the back of a truck. The door burst open and eight or nine soldiers clattered in, shouting orders and making a terrific din with their heavy boots on the wooden floor. The two Germans were instantly attacked with questions. I knew it was all up. Two accusing fingers and ten rifles were pointing at me as they closed in. I raised my hands above my head and stood up slowly.

Back at the Army Headquarters the Sergeant identified me. He was very frightened and his eyes reproached me bitterly as an interpreter went through the normal questions. I felt sorry for him, but convinced myself that my action had been correct. It was surely my duty not to befriend or consider any German.

A different guard took me back to the hospital and I was once again securely locked in my cell. Lieutenant Bruning took pleasure in warning me that a court martial had been ordered.

Life in the cells in the next few days lacked its former amusing and almost cordial atmosphere. The guard was civil and allowed me to eat with them, but was silently disapproving. The acting Guard Commander explained to me one evening that the Sergeant had been given a week in detention cells for his carelessness. And the German Army detention cells were known and feared.

After a few days I visited the Kofisia Headquarters again—this time for my court martial. After a fair and correct trial I was found guilty. Much to Lieutenant Bruning's chagrin, the punishment was negligible because of my wound. I was ordered to pay the cost of the bucket and mop, and warned to be a model prisoner in future!

Back in hospital, I was put to bed for four days and quite enjoyed the rest. However, when I started moving around again I found things rather difficult. The greatest difficulty, perhaps, was the fact that all the guard now knew me both by sight and name. Though I was always greeted with a salute and smile from them, I was watched closely in whatever I did. After much deliberation, therefore, I decided that Athens had exhausted her opportunities for escape. I persuaded the doctor to pass me as fit, and to recommend that I should be sent north towards Germany.

Chapter Eight

Salonika:
The final escape

The Sergeant, with his usual good nature, held the trucks up until all goodbyes were complete, and then they drew slowly out of the hospital compound and wound down the rather squalid streets to the bomb-blasted port of Piraeus. Here forty-nine of us were shepherded with our belongings into three ranks while the Sergeant obtained a receipt for us from a very young German naval officer. Before he left us the Sergeant came over and shook my hand. He was a German certainly, yet I would have been somehow disappointed if he had not; moreover, it cost him, in his position, more than me to show feeling. The young naval officer rebuked him sharply.

We were marched along the devastated wharves and led on to a small cargo steamer of about 5,000 tons. Here we were guarded on deck by three untidy German soldiers until the ship, the *Kreta*, had cast off and anchored out in the harbour.

The pilot came aboard and at dusk we pulled out through countless wrecks including the famous *Nea Hellas*, the Royal Yacht which had been criminally bombed when full of wounded. We anchored out in the stream for the night.

I was very bitter about that trip north. There was never in history such an opportunity for a spectacular escape. To guard us we had a Corporal and six soldiers, and as a section I had never, on either side of the firing line, seen anything so slack and casual. Three sentries were posted, three rested. The three on duty hung over the rails and allowed parties of prisoners to press around them. On any signal the three could have been overboard in the twinkling of an eye. The other three rested with the Corporal in a galley which had a swinging iron door. To close it would take a casual lounger less than a second. The German officer wore no revolver, although he may have had one on the bridge. The two marines on the bridge were the only worry.

The general idea was obvious. The trip was to take four or five days. If on any evening other than the first the ship could be taken over, Turkey was almost within a night's sailing. The evening was the best to avoid air pursuit, for we could not be certain the wireless operator could be dealt with before he could send a signal.

On the second night out I easily evaded the guard, when at dusk they battened the prisoners in the hold. I slipped down an alleyway into the Greek seamen's quarters. They greeted me warmly and we fell into long and difficult conversation in a variety of languages and gesticulations. They explained carefully that they only worked for the German master to feed Greece and to save their own families from destruction or reprisals. But before I left at dawn they trusted me more and said definitely that, should we mutiny and succeed, they would take us to Turkey or even on the long and dangerous trip to Alexandria. They would not take part in the fight; in fairness to their families they could not. But we were to rely on their passive assistance for the battle and their full co-operation once we gained success. I was more than satisfied.

There were two or three men I knew would co-operate. We leaned over the rails and worked out the details. To be certain of success we would need three men for each guard on duty, two men to lock the remainder in the galley, and finally myself and four others to rush the bridge. That made a total of sixteen.

We approached the other fifty prisoners. But in spite of our persuasion, our pleading and finally our anger, only seven came forward out of the fifty. One officer and one sergeant spoke to nearly everyone against the plan. They said there were explosives on board and that the Nazis would blow up the ship if we looked like succeeding. The German Guard had been decent and given us a 'fair go'—therefore we should do the same in return.

So we had to give up the idea. I was near to tears in my disgust. At a future date I was to be shown an Intelligence file in General Headquarters, Cairo, which contained news of the plans we had to take over the *Kreta*. The information had come back to them via three members of her crew who had managed to escape to Egypt.

We wound through the islands of Keos and Laurium, then north inside of Negroport, up the Talanti Channel. The ship anchored each night at dusk and remained anchored until dawn. The fear of our submarines was apparent. On the third morning the hills of Thermopylae could be clearly seen to port, and we swung east at Stylos to anchor that night at the entrance of the Gulf of Volos.

Soon after midday on 30th October, with snow-capped Olympus on our left, we steamed up the Gulf of Salonika to tie up in that historic port.

Above the harbour the old stone city walls, the towers and the fortresses standing out on the hill gave a medieval atmosphere, but around the dock things were modern enough. There was a small amount of German and Italian shipping about, with here and there a cruiser or a destroyer from Mussolini's fleet. German marines, none of whom seemed more than 18 years old, paraded on the wharves, constantly saluting their smart-looking officers. Everybody seemed busy, but all were very interested in the Englanders as we were off-loaded and shepherded into Red Cross vans. We were driven along the water-front, past the great circular tower of Salonika and in a few minutes were at the gates of the prison camp.

My heart sank at the sight. Here was no hospital wire. This was a real prison camp. High mazes of barbed wire ran at all angles. Throughout the camp were great towers on which sentries could be seen fondling their machine-guns. From behind the wire near the gate a crowd of unkempt and undernourished prisoners gathered to gape forlornly as we were formed into ranks and our luggage checked.

It was almost dark by the time all our personal belongings had been strewn in the gravel and the Guard Officer satisfied that we carried no implements for escape. The great gates opened and we poured in, to be ushered into various buildings.

In a large dormitory I met again quite a few of the officers who had come up from Athens in the hospital ship. We all fell to exchanging experiences, and I felt quite at home amongst them. Two in particular I came to respect immediately. Lieutenant Colonel Le Soeuf, tall, dark and quietly spoken, had been captured with his unit, the 7th Australian Field Ambulance, when they were overrun at Heraklion in Crete; Major Richard

Burnett, a regular officer, had been C.O. of his unit on Crete and had been captured while making a reconnaissance in the dark.

Salonika was a bad camp in every way. In the past many shocking atrocities had been committed by guards who had been former members of the Nazi Youth Movement. Burnett was even then investigating a horrible case. A German sentry had thrown a grenade into a latrine packed with dysentery cases and the carnage had been frightful. The only explanation given on Burnett's protest was that the men were whispering in a suspicious manner. The authorities supported the sentry's action.

In a recent unsuccessful attempt at escape, three men had been shot out of hand and their bodies left for days in the hot sun, while for other escapes soldiers had been bound with barbed wire and whipped as a warning to all. Drunken guards had been known to walk into the compound and cruelly maul unarmed prisoners, while it was said that the officer in charge of the young Nazis would ask daily of his guard how many English swine they had killed and congratulate the murderer effusively.

It was an alarming picture, quite different from the treatment I had experienced in Athens. Listening to it all I regretted very much that I had ever left the hospital.

The camp had been an old Greek Artillery Barracks, but the Germans had allowed it to deteriorate badly, so that now it was in a terrible state of sanitation, with practically no drainage at all. Millions of flies swarmed around the latrines and cookhouses and formed ugly black heaps where refuse was dropped. Scores of mangy cats slunk among the barrack rooms.

The prisoners in the compound were the stragglers of the large army which had already passed through to Germany. There were thirty officers and some two hundred men, one hundred and fifty of whom were maimed in some way.

About fifteen were men who had lately been caught in and around Salonika. These were a grand crowd of fellows, and I made a point of talking to them and gaining much valuable information.

Some had been out and recaptured four or five times; indeed, the greatest joke amongst them was the case of the Australian who was picked up as a matter of course by a German patrol every Friday at a house of ill fame. Others with higher motives for escape had been free for long periods, only to be recaptured either on the very borders of Turkey or at sea moving south to freedom.

One, a tall New Zealand Sergeant with a sense of humour, had seen his chance on a day of pouring rain, when a German officer had visited the camp hospital. The officer had walked into the lobby, and hung up his dripping coat and hat before entering the German guard-room. The Sergeant had donned these quickly and marched out into the rain. The sentries had all, one by one, frozen into a salute. Thereafter, he walked down into the streets of Salonika. It was truly an escape to fire the imagination.

A long-haired lad from Sussex had clung to the bottom of one of the contractor's drays and had been carried out of the camp. A very young Cockney told us of his adventure in going out in a bag of rubbish.

The prisoners were even then working on a mass escape plan, and they had the shrewdness of experienced escapists. It was some days before I was to be allowed into their confidence.

Meanwhile the atmosphere in the officers' mess was unpleasantly strained. There were bickerings over food all round, the quarrels between the Medical Corps and the combatants over such futile things such as seniority and the post of Senior British Officer in Captivity. On one occasion feeling ran so high that one side actually asked a German N.C.O. to consider and settle the dispute.

It was not a pleasant place. Consequently I was pleased when Dick Burnett asked me to share a room accorded him because of his rank.

Burnett was keen on escape. He had been free on more than one occasion in Crete and in spite of his forty years was determined to risk all the hazards to get back to his regiment. For as long as he was to be a prisoner he was firmly resolved to cause as much trouble for his captors as possible.

For the first three or four days, I think, he was weighing me up as a possible partner for the months we might have to spend together before reaching British lines.

Then we began to lay our plans.

The section of the camp we were concerned with was only a small part, a sub-section, of the main Salonika Prison Camp. Most of the other sub-sections were now empty and unguarded, with the exception of the one immediately to the west of ours. This held political prisoners from Greece and Yugoslavia. In there one day we had seen an old lady awaiting execution for aiding British escapers.

The sub-section was an oblong, some three hundred yards by two

Salonika POW Camp

hundred, containing seven large barrack huts, a cookhouse and a large new building. The only exit was the gate at the north-west corner, and apart from the roving sentries within the compound, the Germans relied mainly on the guard posts immediately outside it. At the southern end these consisted of two twenty-foot towers, each with two sentries, a machine-gun and a movable searchlight. At the northern end there were the sentries on the gate, those on a tower by the gate, and two sentries with machine-gun and searchlight on the roof of a small shed used for storing horse fodder. The south and west sides were bounded by other sub-sections, the north by an open space and the Salonika road, and the east side had a wide gravel road which separated the compound from rubbish and salvage and which led along to the stables.

A whole morning spent watching guards, drawing innumerable diagrams and getting annoyed with one another disposed of the front, the west and rear sides as quite impossible. Only the east side was left, and we had little hope that it would produce the answer. In common with the others it had some three hundred yards of wire tangle, ten feet high, ten feet wide, but there was one difference. There were two buildings which broke the obstacle, that is the wire tangle ran in between them, and rambled up and over them. It did not run along the back.

One of these was the cookhouse. It had a thick cement wall for a back and, furthermore, was less than a stone's throw from the southern sentry tower. We mooched around it for half an hour after lunch and rejected it as impracticable.

The second building was a fairly new three-storeyed building. A preliminary examination revealed no possibilities; all the windows facing out were heavily barred with steel and barbed wire, while even if work could free them it would be too dangerous to be lowered to the road below in full view of the searchlights at either end.

But just as we were deciding dejectedly that a tunnel was the only solution, we espied a staircase winding down from the ground floor to hide what must be a back doorway on to the gravel road below. The passage down was blocked by large empty crates. The door was of itself unimportant. There were still the searchlights and machine-guns covering the road outside. But Dick had an idea and we climbed again on to the first floor to discuss it.

The two searchlights which concerned us covered the road very efficiently. The one at the south end from the tower had an unobstructed view, while the one on the roof of the hay shed was only limited by its position from seeing the actual back of the building in question. But, and on this our plan depended, these posts had the additional task of covering the south and north wire respectively: their searchlights were on swivels and they would swing from one task to the other every few seconds. For the most part one or other of the posts would have its light focused on the gravel road, occasionally both would play together along it for minutes on end. But with an understandable human error, often for a few seconds, both crews would switch simultaneously on to their secondary task. This would leave the road in darkness until either of them realised the position and swung his searchlight back. Burnett and I considered that, given luck, this erratic few seconds would give us the chance to make the initial dash across the road and use the scant cover of a shallow culvert before the searchlights swung back.

And so we examined the door. The crates barring the steps down from the first floor were really no obstacle and would afford good cover for

A plan of Salonika Camp

any work we should do. The steps ran down in two short flights on to a very small landing, and the door-frame was set firmly in stone. There were steel and wooden bars across it, both bolted and nailed, and the whole was covered with barbed wire on staples. Formidable certainly but, provided we were not hurried, we thought it could be done.

One remarkable thing about our work on this project was the complete absence of the adventure spirit and the elation of imaginary success. Every step we took in this venture was coldly methodical. We took very few into our confidence.

Amazingly enough, the tools for the work were no trouble at all. I bought a pair of excellent pliers from a Greek electrician working in the barracks; Burnett made some useful crowbars from sections of our beds; and Fred Moodie, a camp doctor, provided a pair of strong plaster cutters. Fred also arranged for me a good supply of the German cod liver oil salve which had proved very soothing and beneficial to my wound.

We started work that night. Immediately after the evening check we made our way to the building with innocent unconcern and talked to various orderlies until curfew, then we slipped behind the crates under the first flight of stairs until all was quiet.

The work was necessarily slow, and not a little nerve-racking. Each nail, each bolt had to be worked out slowly and with great caution; a loud squeak would leave us perspiring and fearful for long minutes. Every now and then the crunch of heavy feet on the gravel outside would hold us up, and on three occasions during the first night two of the guards talked for a long time just outside the door.

By four o'clock we had removed all the wooden bars and two of the six more formidable steel bars. We tacked the bars back loosely into their old positions and generally tidied up the evidence before setting off on the quite hazardous trip back to our barracks. The two sentries detailed to prowl around inside the compound had orders to shoot on sight after curfew, and though the twenty minutes they took on their regular rounds provided ample time for us there were the searchlights to pin us down occasionally and always the chance that the sentries might vary their tactics.

We reached our room without incidence and were sound asleep for the six o'clock room check. Having previously convinced the Germans that it was less trouble not to order us out to stand by our beds each morning (as laid down), we were left to slumber on until almost lunch time.

Our progress on the second night did not compare with the first night. There were too many interruptions—stable-hands coming home late from leave and arguing out on the road, restless sentries and irregular changing of guards. And we were discovered at work by a group of Australian and British medical orderlies and it took us some little time to impress on them the need for absolute secrecy. However, we worked out two more steel bars and managed to loosen a third before an early rooster, crowing beyond the stables, warned us of approaching day.

On the third night we made very good progress indeed; by eleven o'clock the last of the steel bars was disposed of. We had brought a rough chisel and a screwdriver to remove the lock but, to our amazement, we found that it was not, in fact, locked. A few nails had been hammered at random around the edges however, and just after midnight the last was worked out and we were able to move the door.

It opened two or three inches and then stuck. We realised that there was an apron of barbed wire stapled on to the outside. With some difficulty it would be possible to worm a wrist with pliers through the opening. After a short consultation we decided to leave it as it was until the night of the break, knowing that it would only take a few minutes to open it.

We made our way carefully back to our room, secreted our tools under our mattresses and in the stove, and undressed in the dark. It was only about one o'clock and, tired as we were, the prospect of a few extra hours' sleep was very pleasing.

No sooner had we said good night, however, than we were suddenly startled by the tread of heavy feet in the passageway outside. There was a guttural order, our door burst open, and three soldiers rushed in. Torches flashed in our faces, our blankets were pulled off roughly, and the room quickly but not thoroughly searched. Then, as if satisfied, the officer barked an order and the party clattered out and away, leaving two very shaken men behind.

Now that visit was unfortunate. The explanation was quite beyond us, particularly as ours was the only room searched. Perhaps someone had discovered and reported that we had not been sleeping in our beds at night; or perhaps it was merely a check on me as a known 'bad lad'. But the effect was this: Burnett decided not to come. Three nights' work had taxed his nerves badly and now he thought our whole plan was discovered. Even when daylight proved that no attempt was made to re-fix the door, Burnett saw the possibility of a trap—a machine-gun covering the exit to make an example of anyone who attempted to escape. He was still as determined as ever, but with the caution of forty years he weighed the chances as too dangerous, and started straightaway on a new plan to throw ourselves from the train on the way through Yugoslavia.

His pessimism shook me not a little. I spent the morning watching the area near the cookhouse, and after lunch sat down and tried to come to some decision. His arguments were very sound; the plan had been hazardous enough without the new threat. Yet at the back of my mind was a conviction, however unfounded, that the plan was still secret.

Finally I took out a piece of paper and, ruling a line down the centre, wrote in two columns all of the pros and cons I could think of.

That was a poignant half-hour. I knew well that the wrong decision might cost me my life. Yet I felt very strongly that it was a case of 'now or never', that, if I let this opportunity pass, I might never be presented with another.

As the page filled up, Burnett sat quietly watching me. I knew that he was apprehensive but, having stated his arguments once, he made no attempt to dissuade me further.

Before I could make up my mind we were besieged by some five or six of the more hardened card players and I was quite willing to procrastinate an hour for a game of pontoon. Perhaps it was my abstraction, but within half an hour, without effort, I had taken every drachma off the whole school. After a drink of cocoa from my Red Cross parcel they all departed very disgruntled, threatening that they would come back on the morrow to get it back. As soon as they had gone, at Burnett's suggestion, I entered under the pros the fact that I now had 8,000 drachmae for escape purposes.

At six o'clock I made my decision. It was, I am sure, the decision of my life. Our original plan had been to get some greatly needed rest that night, Saturday, and escape on Sunday about nine when the guards not on duty were on leave. But now, as things appeared to be moving rapidly and because my nerves were so tense that I could not sleep, I decided to go on my own that night.

When Burnett saw that I was determined, he gave me everything he had; all his bread, condensed Red Cross food, a civilian coat, and all his savings, including some English money. He cooked me up a wonderful farewell meal and set himself to do a thousand and one little things to help me to get ready.

It was now after curfew. It was therefore necessary to move with great care over to the building. Soon after eight-thirty, I said goodbye to Burnett. He was terribly apprehensive of the risk I was taking and heartily miserable that he was not coming with me. I realised I was going to miss his company very much.

It took me almost an hour to go the two hundred yards from our barracks. The searchlights seemed particularly restless and the roving patrol sat down and talked for nearly half an hour while I lay in what shade a wire-netting fence afforded. When they finally moved off I ran quickly up the steps and through the door into the hall of the medical building. As soon as I latched the door behind me a startled voice greeted me.

'Are you *mad*? Surely you know that it's dangerous to be out after curfew?'

It was an Australian medical orderly. When I told him of my plans he immediately offered his help.

We moved on to the first landing, from where we could look through the barred window down on to the road. Everything seemed quite normal. We watched for half an hour but, with the exception of a team of horses being taken out from the stables, only the usual movement was apparent.

The orderly and a friend appointed themselves to keep watch while I worked. We arranged a code of signals whereby, should they wish to warn me, they would throw something small down the steps leading to the escape door. The 'all clear' would be one or the other whistling from *Rigoletto.*

The door was as we had left it. I removed all the loosely held bars and convinced myself that no one had tampered with them. The door opened noiselessly some three inches and even with great caution it took me only twenty minutes to cut the eight or nine restraining wires on the outside.

As I cut the last one and felt the door suddenly swing easily towards me, the first alarm signal in the form of a leather slipper clattered down the stairs behind me. I closed the door quickly, my heart in my mouth. Outside I could hear heavy feet crunching slowly down the road. As they approached the door I held my breath in apprehension. With the searchlights full on I felt that no one could miss the tell-tale loose ends of wire. But, although I could have sworn there was a slight pause just level with the door, the danger passed and in a few seconds I heard a soft but unmusical attempt to whistle the arranged all clear.

I opened the door a few inches and studied the ground. The road was only some fifteen feet across, but I realised that unless the searchlights settled down I would never get over without being seen. The sentry in the tower on the south end was unusually restless; his light was flickering to and fro every few seconds. I decided, as it was then nine-thirty, to wait until the ten o'clock change of sentries with the hope of getting someone more placid. During the wait I worked out each step across the road, and the point where I should get over the low wall into the rubbish on the other side.

Just before ten the team of horses, which had gone out earlier, returned noisily up the road and, although I did not look, I imagined they were towing some vehicle. When they had passed up towards the German stables I stole a look out. I thought for one moment that the opportunity was ideal, for one of the searchlights was playing on the stable yard, probably to help the unhitching of the horse. I had just made the decision to go and was in the act of opening the door when some object clattered down the stairs behind me. A second later came the sharp order of the Corporal of the Guard as he turned his ten o'clock relief up the road—I shivered as I realised how very nearly I had run right into them.

For fifteen minutes after the old guard had clattered past the door on their way to the guard-room, the searchlights on both ends were seldom still for more than a few seconds, but soon after that the new sentries began to tire of their vigilance. Sitting back on the stairs I could count up to four seconds while no light shone through the keyhole or under the door. So I opened the door cautiously and looked out.

Looking across the road, I realised that although the tower at the south end shone direct on to the exit, it would be the light from the roof of the hay shed which would be most dangerous, as it shone over the rubbish. I started counting the irregular breaks of darkness. Sometimes there would be one or other searchlight shining on the road for over ten minutes, then for an erratic five minutes it would be in darkness every few seconds.

'One—two—three,' I counted, 'one—two—three—four getting better now, one—two—three—four—my word, I could have made it that time, one—two—three—phew, just as well I didn't then ...' and then there would be another period of light. The most unnerving thing about it was the fact that there was no way of knowing how long any particular period of darkness was going to be. I knew that whenever I made the decision it would be final. The success or failure of the whole plan depended on nothing more than luck.

I think perhaps I must have been poised there for half an hour. But it seemed years to me. I alternated between self-reproach for having missed a good chance and a chill of horror when a period of darkness lasted only one second.

And then I went. Not running, but carefully over the road, my stocking-covered shoes making little noise on the gravel. But as I prepared to throw myself over the low wall on the other side of the road, I sensed the return of one of the lights and involuntarily dropped to the ground, realising instantly that I must present an ideal target to either sentry post.

First the light from the hay shed played idly up and down the road, and so brilliant was it that it shone right into the gravel where my face was buried. Then I sensed the other one flashing over my shoulder. My body tingled with terror and for the first time in my life I felt the hairs on the nape of my neck pricking and rising.

I could hear two of the sentries talking quite clearly. They did not sound at all excited and yet surely they must have seen me. My body began to flinch and cringe as I imagined a bullet striking home. My mind went numb, and I had no idea how long I lay there, but at last, one after the other, the lights swung away.

I sprung up. Instead of vaulting the low wall I passed along it, turning into the courtyard of an M.T. garage. I dropped behind a large oil drum as the first light swung back. Here I was not so frightened, for the low wall now shielded me completely from the one searchlight and the drum from the other. I must have been pinned there for all of ten minutes. It was uncomfortably cramped, and I was apprehensive lest some driver or late-returning guard should discover me.

But when darkness came I was able to slip over the wall and worm through the rubbish towards the outer ring of wire. There was no need to stop even when both lights were playing down the road, for there was sufficient shadow amongst the rubbish and small scrub to mask cautious movement. There was thirty yards of this cover stretching over to the outer ring of double apron barbed wire. This presented no problem with my wire-cutters. But I was surprised when I was through it to run into a wire-netting fence. Following it along, I came to a break covered by a sheet of iron, which I crawled through to find myself in a small cleared space littered with large boxes. I was just passing one of the latter when a movement somewhere near stopped me. I hugged the ground, my heart in my mouth. All was quiet for a few minutes then, just as I prepared to continue, again came the small movement, much closer this time. I placed it as just behind the box. I was becoming really scared when from inside the box came the unmistakable clucking of a disturbed hen. I was inside the guards' chicken run.

I crossed the run to the rear corner of the garage and cut a small square to let myself out. I found myself in a grass enclosure, bounded by two very high stone walls, which ran into a corner some two hundred yards away. Very clearly I could hear the rumbling of the trams on the main Salonika road.

The wall bounding the road was about ten feet high and I could see glass glistening along its length. But it didn't present any great obstacle— the Germans had attempted to make it more formidable by giving it an apron of barbed wire—thus making an ideal ladder.

I climbed up it carefully. The road was still very busy for that time of night. In addition to the trams and army vehicles there was a steady stream of civilians and soldiers on both sides of the street. I waited ten minutes and was thinking of retiring for a few hours to let things settle down when I fancied I heard a single shot from back in camp. I listened for a full minute. Although I heard nothing further and was almost convinced it was my overtaxed mind playing tricks, I decided to push on and take the chance of discovery.

With the glare from the lights of the prison camp there was quite a shadow on the road side of the wall, and as soon as there was a perceptible break in the traffic below I lowered myself so far as the lowest strand of barbed wire would allow me and dropped the remaining four feet, falling in a heap on the footpath.

My first reaction was one of acute pain. The jar was considerable. But almost immediately I became aware of two figures standing some fifteen paces away arguing volubly. They were both soldiers and I saw by the rifle he had slung over his shoulder that one of them was on duty. Yet as I picked myself up I knew I had not been seen. The second soldier was obviously very drunk and was abusing the sentry roundly.

I moved quickly up the street for two or three hundred yards, stopped and removed the spare pair of socks which I had worn over my shoes, and walked very quietly into Salonika.

The whole of the venture up to this stage had been cool and methodical. A desperate fear of risks had numbed my mind against any anticipation of success. But now at every step I felt welling within me a glorious exhilaration, an ecstasy so sweet that my eyes pricked with tears of gratitude. All the oppression, all the worry and boredom, which had so weighed me down, seemed to disappear as though they were taken like a heavy cloak off my shoulders. The air was pure and free.

For perhaps an hour I let my exuberance lead me drunkenly up and down strange streets. Every unsuspecting soldier I passed was a boost to my confidence. As each approached, I weighed up his size, darted a glance right and left for possible flight and then, as we drew level, either made a great play of blowing my nose or whistled the one Greek tune I knew in what I hoped was a nonchalant manner. But soon I realised there was no need to regard each as a suspicious enemy—each was going about his own business whether leave or duty; probably the last thought anyone had was that the stream of pedestrians might include an English officer.

Although there was some attempt at a black-out the streets were full of gaiety. From every restaurant and wine-shop came the laughter and music of the conquerors. Happy, and here and there inebriated, couples thronged the alleyways. At one street corner a lone violinist was playing old music rather sweetly. I felt wonderfully at ease, confident and vastly superior to all those in field-grey uniforms who had not the sense to recognise an enemy in their midst.

However, somewhere in the centre of Salonika, the exhilaration quietened and allowed reason to prevail. I turned reluctantly to follow my plan of being well clear of the city by dawn. With some difficulty I oriented myself. Striking south, I moved through a suburb full of cheerful chatter and houses that glowed with homely light until I came to the foot of the great Salonika Hill. I followed up the same zigzag path trod by many a conqueror, sitting down occasionally on the stone steps to rest and marvel at the beauty of the subdued lighting fringed by the sea below me. One by one the lights in the nearby houses went out as the city quietened down. By the time I reached the old Salonika wall with its massive gateways all was quiet.

I sat down fifty yards from the gateway and watched for a while. All the exits of Salonika were under guard. Occasionally every civilian would be forced to produce his identity card, but this particular gate divided the city from one of its more modern suburbs. From somewhere in the prison camp had come the information that, with the large numbers passing to and fro, the sentries had become very slack.

The sentry on duty moved out of the shadow of the archway and shifted his slung rifle from one shoulder to the other. A group of civilians, coming from a side street near the wall passed through quietly, so I braced myself and slouched through after them, blowing my nose noisily; indeed, so interested was I in appearing nonchalant that I almost collided with a sentry who was moving across the archway. But he hardly glanced at me. And so I went through the last suburb and down to the outskirts of the town. I drew my coat close around me, for the wind was bitterly cold.

Soon there loomed ahead of me a massive grey building, and the path I was following took me quite close to it. Just as I passed from the moonlight into its shadow, without warning and so suddenly that it froze me to the spot, a harsh order rang out and there before me in the dark I could see the glint of a bayonet some five inches from my throat.

Slowly I raised my hands to my shoulders, and as my fear was replaced by an overwhelming disappointment, muttered miserably, 'English—Englander—Englezi."

What happened then was typical of any adventure in Greece, the land 'you never know'. The rifle clattered to the ground, two hands reached up and grasped mine, and before my startled wits could register what was happening a bristly face had planted a kiss on both my cheeks. In the dark I could see my friend was in uniform. Looking again at the silhouette of the imposing building, in whose shadow we stood, some memory of a conversation in the camp convinced me that I had run into a Greek policeman guarding the civilian jail. It was the first indication, and a surprise after my experiences, to find that the Greek police were not necessarily pro-German.

However, after the first emotional outburst had spent itself fear seized him and immediately he fell to gesticulating violently and whispering urgent instructions. I gathered he wanted me to make myself scarce and also not to continue along the track I had been following. When I shrugged my shoulders in an expression of hopelessness he seized my arms and pointed to some lights in the far distance with repeated whispers 'Bon, kala, goot, bon, kala, goot.'

Half an hour, over a bare and stony hillock, brought me to the lights, a group of perhaps thirty poor houses. Most of them were in darkness and quiet, but the lights I had followed indicated that someone was still afoot. I moved in to try my luck, and knocked at the door of the nearest house.

We say an Englishman's home is his castle; so it is with the Greek. He won't let the drawbridge down at night until he recognises a friend. He peers furtively at you from the window on the left of the door, then from the one on the right, and finally decides through the keyhole and from your foreign jabber that you are no friend. After that no amount of noise nor knocking, no entreaties nor threats will affect him. You will hear urgent whispers inside, and movement near the door, but you are lucky indeed if it opens.

I tried every house in the first group whether lights shone or not, but always with the same result. I felt desolate and cold, and the unusual exercise was causing my wound to tug uncomfortably at my thigh. To make things more desperate, suddenly from one of the dark alleyways between two houses bounded a large village dog, fiercely growling and snarling. Three or four of its kind joined it and I was forced to move warily along one of the walls with my boots ready and my heart in my mouth.

At first the brutes showed a certain caution, would move back a yard or two if I made as though I had something to throw, but gradually, as their numbers swelled, they took confidence and started snapping at the cuffs of my trousers. The situation was ugly. There seemed no possibility of help from the dark, aloof houses, and I knew that to run would only bring them upon me in a ferocity far beyond my strength to combat. Yet in the end that is just what I did. Panic seized me and I ran full pelt down the rough street with them all at my heels, until, seeing a flight of steps leading up to a small house I ran frantically up and hammered on the door. The first of the dogs came half-way up the steps and paused, the remainder stayed snarling and yapping below.

From inside some order was called, then repeated, then footsteps padded over and the door was flung open. The smallest of men, about five feet high, smiled up at me and spoke rapidly in Greek. With a gesture I said 'Englezi' and indicated the bristling dark forms below. With that unique fluttering of the hand which is the Greek beckoning, I was waved into a tiny living room.

In the centre of the room, huddled round a tin of ashes on the top of which were a few live coals, were two more small people—an old lady and a young fellow. On my entry they both stood up and looked over inquiringly. The first one said something which I took to be an introduction of sorts, and the old lady, dear fragile thing that she was, reached up and patted my arm. She sighed deeply and suddenly I felt in that sigh all the sympathy I had been craving for so long. They indicated a chair, and as I collapsed into it, both body and mind relaxed into a relief that brought me almost to tears.

They fussed around me, talking excitedly to one another. A very stiff *ouzo* was followed by a meal they prepared from a cabbage out of their garden. They apologised in Greek, until even I understood that they had no bread in the house to give me. We all sat round the small tin of ashes, occasionally blowing on the four or five coals, and I tried to explain with my hands the adventures that led me to their door.

Finally they decided it was time for me to get some rest and ushered me into another equally small room. The smallness of the whole house was unbelievable. There were only two rooms and neither was more than eight feet square. I was given the only bed in the house and the brothers spread rugs on the floor beside me. As I stretched comfortably in the short bed the old lady came round and patted my forehead, sighing deeply. She then muttered something over me, crossed herself reverently and departed into the other room where I could hear her preparing a bed on the couch. Even after the house became quiet, I could hear her deep sighs as I myself lay, sleep impossible, and tried to consider my position and convince myself that I had really succeeded. Occasionally a half-moon broke cloud and shone wanly through the tiny windows. Outside the last of the dogs ceased its baying and left a peaceful stillness, made homely by the steady breathing of the two brothers on the floor.

Chapter Nine

Greek lessons by Cupid

The sky had just begun to lighten when the two brothers were about their household chores and preparing to depart. Before they left they came back into the bedroom, and tried vainly to tell me something important, but between the insistent jabbering and gesticulation of the two of them I was completely bewildered. After pondering over it all for a while I gave it up and dozed pleasantly on until nine or thereabouts, when I got up and gazed with glee on the hills, the sea, and the unconcerned lazy workers moving in the market gardens which formed the outskirts of Salonika. In the next room the old lady bustled around her household duties. My mind kept going over the adventures of the escape and carrying me through all the steps which had brought me to this haven. I gloried in my freedom.

The old lady prepared me a small meal of the same cabbage, and also gave me a little of their white goat's-milk cheese—very sour, almost acrid, but satisfying.

I relaxed and mused and made my plans. I was by no means out of the wood—I fully realised that the actual escape was only one step on the road which might eventually bring me to Egypt and freedom. With my wound as a handicap I could still see no alternative to the hazardous route through Bulgarian-occupied Thrace to Turkey-in-Europe.

About two o'clock the brothers arrived home. They came in with mysterious stealth (the Greek has a highly developed sense of drama), and after a careful look round the house, through all the windows, one of them went back, to reappear with another man. The newcomer was middle-aged, polished and well dressed, and the two brothers treated him with obvious deference as they gesticulated an introduction. My interest was immediately aroused. He spoke to me cautiously in Greek for a few moments, followed by French, to which I responded as well as I could.

He tried me in German and persisted until I sat down, wearily deciding it was hopeless to understand one another, and then he smiled and suddenly broke into perfect English. I was delighted. It was so unexpected.

We immediately fell into animated conversation, to the joy of my hosts who stood around us, eagerly handing on the interpretation given them. My new friend was a business man and, before he had launched out on his own account, he had been the Salonika agent of an English firm.

I told them my story. They asked where was I going and what were my plans? I briefly outlined the route I had mapped out, and they immediately began, all of them, to argue with violent gesticulations.

'My dear Thomas,' said my well-dressed friend very earnestly, 'believe me, the road you have chosen is quite impossible. Here in Salonika we have the Germans who, heaven knows, are bad enough—but in Thrace there are their jackals, the Bulgarians. And where the Germans lose some astuteness by their lofty self-satisfaction, the Bulgarian dogs are sly and cunning, and inherently suspicious. There are great rivers to cross such as the Struma on the new frontier. The bridges are closely guarded, so that no one may pass without correct authority. And it is said that there are large concentrations of German and Bulgarian soldiers on the Turkish border. Quite definitely you must abandon your plan.'

'But, sir,' I said, somewhat gloomily, for his picture was hardly encouraging, 'what alternative can there be?'

'We could hide you here in Salonika—it would not be for long. Surely any day now the English must return.'

I knew it would need at least two years before they could again set foot in Greece, but I did not tell him so. Throughout the land this great faith in England's might was the incentive which was banding the young patriots into forces of aggression.

'While I am more than grateful for your offer, which I well know could bring great danger on to your own homes,' I replied, 'I fear that I cannot accept. I must get back to my regiment as soon as it is humanly possible, whatever the difficulties.'

'Yes, yes, I understand that'—nodding approval and, I think, looking a little relieved—'my friends and I thought that would be your answer. We are sorry you will not stay, but if you must go, why then, we have a plan which, while it is still dangerous, is feasible compared to yours.'

He broke off and spoke to the elder brother who foraged around in the bedroom and reappeared with a large nationalistic calendar, which had, as one of its features, a map of Greece.

'Look here,' he said, bending over the map, 'immediately south of Salonika there are three large peninsulas, jutting out like three fingers from Thrace. Now this one,' he put his finger on the eastern-most one, the one nearest to Turkey, 'this one is a little kingdom on its own. It is called Agion Oros—The Holy Mountain of Athos.'

'Do you mean that it actually has a king?' I asked, intrigued.

'No, the only king they acknowledge is Christ. But they exist in every way as a separate kingdom. The whole of the peninsula is peopled by monks of the Orthodox faith.'

'When you say they are peopled by monks do you mean that there are a great number of monasteries dotted around the various villages there?' I asked, for there were certain villages marked on the map, including one which seemed quite large.

'No, I meant that there is no one there but monks. There are no laymen, and certainly no women. In fact,' he smiled, 'in fact, there are no animals of any sort of the female sex.'

'What!' I burst out, incredulous.

'It's true,' he said, 'there are nearly ten thousand monks on that peninsula, and not one female is allowed to cross the isthmus. And what is more,' he paused, to give effect to whatever was to follow, 'what is more, my boy, that has been the position for over twelve hundred years. When your country was still a group of warring kingdoms, long before your Norman Conquest, this little peninsula was organised as a sanctuary for monks against the temptations of the world.'

He went on to tell me something of the life the monks led there. It was interesting, but I was impatient to see how it all fitted into the plan.

Eventually I brought him back to the point.

'You must make your way as well as you can to this peninsula,' he said, putting a well-manicured finger on Mount Athos. 'They must give you sanctuary there: it is part of their creed. From them, or through them, for they are very wealthy, you may find someone who will take you by sea to Turkey.'

That sounded good. My thigh would be saved many painful miles, and the great risks of passing through two frontier forces would be avoided. We spent the remainder of the afternoon discussing the best roads, the dangerous villages and the enemy's habits in the area through which I would pass.

Unfortunately, it was necessary for me to go right through Salonika in order to start off from the east side of the large bay which formed the harbour. I was more than a little apprehensive of this, not so much of the chances of capture, but the difficulty of finding my way through the city. I would be denied any chance of asking directions. But my friends reassured me with a bold plan. I was to follow them at a safe distance into the centre of the city to a tram stop. There I could get a tram which would take me eight miles clear of the town. It would also take me through two of the German check posts on the road. They stressed that I must travel on the second trailer of the tram as the German soldier was too arrogant to enter them.

Just on dusk we set out through the village, the trio walking some fifty paces in front of me. In the village as we left there seemed many knowing eyes and whispered remarks, but as we made our way over the hill and once again through the old city wall, people passed with an indifference which gave me great confidence. Indeed, when we wound down into the streets crowded with soldiers, I found I was quite enjoying the unlikelihood of it all.

I have never seen a city so full of soldiers. They were moving up and down the streets in fours and dozens, all bent on their various errands and amusements, so that occasionally I had difficulty in keeping my guides in view. I had to dodge in and out of field-grey uniforms to keep up. These men must have been the new divisions on their way to reinforce Rommel in the desert.

At one stage I lost sight of my guides for over ten minutes. I began to feel frightened. At last, I saw them watching me furtively from across the street. I crossed over and the game recommenced until, after we had been away from the village for nearly an hour, they stopped and lit a cigarette under a tram shelter. Then I knew their part of the contract was complete. One of them came back and, in passing, silently gripped and pressed my arm.

I was alone again.

I took up a position under the one light in the shelter, purposely avoiding the shadow, so as not to create a suspicious appearance. At first there were only a few civilians in the shelter, and I felt quite at my ease but, as time dragged on, it slowly filled half with civilians and half with German soldiers. A Greek lad standing by me became curious and persisted in asking me questions in his own tongue. I kept an aloof and disapproving silence, but felt far from comfortable. In front of the shelter ran the footpath and road. And along the footpath, walking carefully and slowly in step, two German Military Policemen passed to and fro every five or ten minutes. But two hours passed and no trams appeared.

German and Greek alike were becoming restless, some left in impatience, and the remainder complained and conjectured in their two tongues. Things came to a head when a short and slightly tipsy soldier lurched against me and poured out some German abuse, finishing in an obvious question about the trams. I was petrified; my tongue, perhaps fortunately, seemed stuck to the roof of my mouth. But I managed to lift my wrist and with a gesture indicate an hour on my watch and point at one of the trams stationary nearby. This brought forth a torrent of angry questions and abuse in guttural jargon, and I think things might have gone badly had not one of the other bystanders volunteered the information required in hesitant French. The German immediately turned on him. After a few moments he broke away angrily and made off down the street. Some of his colleagues, and also quite a few of the Greeks, followed his example.

I, too, found that a new problem had arisen. From the French explanation about the tram I gathered that the city electric power had been cut off, as it frequently was, and it was doubtful if there would be any further service that night. If I waited too long I would not have enough darkness to get me clear of the city by dawn. Yet my detailed instructions only commenced from the terminus eight miles away. The situation was serious.

I left the shelter and crossed the street. Any elation the walk through the streets had built up left me, and I felt very sick at heart at the thought of eight extra miles. For my wound was still very much open, requiring at least three half-crowns of skin and flesh to heal over, and I knew myself to be ill nourished and flabby.

After gazing undecidedly through the window of a restaurant, where two German naval officers and some civilians were dining, I saw clearly that to wait any longer would be unwise. I must set off on foot. The sight of people eating reminded me that I had eaten but one small meal all day and, as I moved away, I felt uncomfortably hungry.

The tram lines took me through the very heart of the city, past the gay music of dancing, the raucous laughter and shouting of the wine shops and the subdued lit fronts of the picture theatres.

It was quite thrilling to pass in front of the prison again and to wonder what they were doing, what they were thinking of my escape. The brilliant searchlight played unceasingly along the wire in clear contrast to the semi-blackout of the surrounding dwellings. I could not refrain from chuckling aloud as I visualised the guards discovering first my absence and then the tell-tale door.

I knew then what a nine days' wonder it would be for all inside, but it was not until after the war that I heard from my friends what a terrible rumpus the Germans made of it. The whole compound was paraded for hours, the camp searched with a fine comb, the Senior British Officer bullied and abused. And the dread threat, which kept all prison commandants constantly fearful and alert, was carried out by the German Command. The Commandant was dispatched for combat duty on the Russian front.

I trudged on wearily through the suburbs, resting by the wayside here and there. Neither civilians nor soldiers took the slightest notice of me as they hurried past, and I felt far more tired than apprehensive. Suddenly, some two hundred yards ahead, appeared cement posts and a white-painted barrier across the road. On both sides were sentry boxes with armed soldiers moving around.

My friends had warned me of this and again I cursed the ill fortune which had denied me the opportunity of passing safely through in a tram. I drew in the shadows and watched for a few minutes.

Civilians trickling through were halted, their passes demanded and checked under a strong light. While it was obviously only a perfunctory examination I realised that I could not very well explain why I had no civilian identity card. Even the most casual questions would expose me.

I had decided to move back and round some side street, in the hope that there might be an unguarded way out, when a large party of German soldiers, mingled with girls and civilians, came laughing and singing down the road. The guards stood by good-naturedly and raised the barrier, allowing them to pass through with loud laughter at the hilarity of the party and the jests thrown at them. An idea presented itself and I waited impatiently until the next group of returning troops appeared. They arrived in half an hour and were mainly air-force men. They were well under the influence and were being egged on in their ribaldry by numerous civilians.

As they drew level with me I stood up and started walking slowly. They ignored me and the bulk of them passed me without a glance. I quickened my pace, so that I travelled in the rear, almost between two very drunken airmen. A Greek girl, who was assisting a third drunk, looked at me suspiciously. She said something to her swain. What she said was obviously connected with me, because she kept looking in my direction as she spoke. I wondered what I should do. I never could have managed to outstrip anyone if it came to a chase. But the airman mumbled some remark and began to abuse her in a thick, drunken voice. He looked over at me once only, and I could see that there would be no danger from him.

We approached the road-block. I felt naked and horribly afraid as we came under the strong light suspended over the middle of the road. I tried to whistle and look unconcerned.

The barrier swung up and the leading people in the party surged through, calling to the sentries in German. I was surprised how many of the girls spoke German. I arrived at the centre of the barrier and felt the eyes of the nearest sentry on me. I felt wretched. I was sure that I had been too rash, and had thrown away all my chances. At any moment I expected to be challenged. I felt myself walking mechanically, as though in a nightmare.

But, before I was really aware of it, I found myself approaching the darker area beyond the barrier. I had brought it off. I continued to walk with the airmen for a few hundred yards, dropping slowly to the rear. Then, when I judged it safe, I stopped and bent down as though to do up my shoe-lace. They all surged forward away from me.

I looked for a dark spot and rested for a few minutes before continuing. I was aware of no elation: I knew I had taken a foolish risk. I made a mental vow to be more careful.

By this time it was after midnight, and in my flabby condition I was near exhaustion as I pushed slowly through the outlying residential area until I approached the open country. I rested on the footpath outside a larger house and felt desperately homesick as I listened to someone playing a piano inside. I was tempted to try my luck for shelter, but decided I must be well clear of the city by dawn.

Mile after mile I travelled, over flat and rolling country, hedge-lined in places and with occasional farm buildings. The road remained wide and tar sealed, so that I was not at first in doubt as to my route. At last I reached the tram terminus. As the road was deserted I deemed it wise to take cover whenever the numerous German Army vehicles flashed by.

I must have done all of fifteen miles that night, when the sudden appearance of the sea on my right told me that I had taken the wrong turning. I hadn't the heart to turn back and so, in spite of the cold and a penetrating light drizzle of rain, I lay down on the wet grass on the side of the road and immediately fell into a deep sleep.

My clothes consisted of hospital trousers and singlet covered with khaki trousers and shirt, a civilian sports coat and cap. I had no greatcoat nor groundsheet for protection from the weather. So it was not surprising that when, an hour or so later, I woke up, I was frozen. It took a great effort to get up and under way, but I realised it was imperative that I get warm.

After two painful miles I came on a group of farm buildings. I made my way to the front door and knocked loudly. For a start there was no response at all, and then after some movement inside I was hailed from an upstairs window. Plead as I might it was to no avail, and after a few minutes of abuse the window slammed shut and the house settled down. There was no further response to my knocking.

I was determined not to go any farther that night. I was frightened to move away from the farm area in case I collapsed on a lonely stretch where no one would find me.

Not more than a hundred yards from the house, actually nearer the road, was a derelict barn. It looked very dark and cold, but I realised that it would at least give shelter from the rain. I approached it and looked around.

A large black dog appeared from the direction of the house, growling ominously. I threw a stone at it, and was fortunate enough to hit it. It kept a safe distance, but started a constant barking. I hoped it would get the farmer out of bed.

The barn housed some sort of farm equipment; it looked like a threshing machine. The floor was dry, but unbelievably cold. I lay down and tried to relax, but my whole body was shaking with cold. Outside the dog kept on barking.

At last dawn began to break. Through the open doorway I could see that it was still raining. Everything looked bleak and uninviting. I remained on the floor wondering what would happen.

After half an hour or so I heard footsteps approaching from the direction of the farmhouse. I sat up. Someone shouted at the dog and evidently threw a stone at it, for it ran off yelping. A figure appeared in the doorway. I tried to get up, but could not.

I was challenged in Greek and replied in English.

'English, eh?' said the newcomer. 'Where have you come from?'

I told him briefly that I had escaped two nights previously.

'Ah then, you are the English officer they are after. They have circulated all the police about you. Your name is Thomas, yes?'

This was a shock. I would have been alarmed had I not felt so utterly wretched. The farmer spoke with a strong American accent. He started to tell me how he had spent twenty years in the States, and then brought his money back to buy the farm. Then he saw that I was ill. The traditional hospitality and sympathy of the Greek asserted itself, and he made haste to help me to my feet. He begged me to come into his home and get warm.

Inside the house he put a match to an open fire and kindled a cheerful blaze. In front of this he made me undress completely and then draped me in a large blanket. I was made to sit in front of the fire, while he bustled to get me a large glass of *ouzo* to ward off chill. Soon the house began to stir and one by one the farmer's family came down to be introduced.

The lady of the house was a gentle woman with large, sad, brown eyes. She seemed about forty, but may have been older. Although she spoke only a little English she made me feel at home in a few moments. Her elder daughter came downstairs with her. She was a striking lass with beautiful dark hair and her mother's sad eyes. But her beauty was immediately eclipsed when her younger sister Maria came into the room. She was a picture of loveliness. To have been cooped up with men so long and then to see such a vision was too much for me. I must have appeared very ill-mannered, for I could not take my eyes off her.

The farmer seemed amused at my open-mouthed admiration. He filled up my glass with *ouzo* again and, as he passed it to me, I could see his eyes twinkling.

'Well,' he said, 'these are my womenfolk. Later I will show you my boys. They have all the family good looks, as you will see. Now what about you? Will you tell us something of your home and what you have been through?'

Keeping my eyes on the friendly fire in the hearth, in order to avoid staring at Maria, I started talking.

'My boy,' said my friend, when I had finished telling my story, my plight and my plans, 'you are my guest for as long as you wish to stay. We are patriotic and to us it is an honour to keep an Englishman. But,' he paused and looked embarrassed before continuing in his nasal American accent, 'but you will perhaps understand I must also consider my family.'

I knew what he meant. The Germans had cunningly instilled a deep resentment in many Greeks by a ruthless policy. If an Englishman was found in a house they would shoot the whole family out of hand—no trial, no difference for age or sex. But, and here they introduced their psychology, the escaped prisoner was not treated at all roughly while he was in the village. Of course, what might happen to him later was a different matter, but the village never considered that. Thus, the head of a Greek house, however patriotic, might well say, 'Why should I help you? I risk my all and the lives of my loved ones. You face no greater danger than return to a prison camp.'

I therefore replied very carefully.

'Gregorio'—for that was his name (in Greece only the Christian name is given and used)—'of course I understand, you have already been more than kind. Let me have my clothes and I must be on my way.'

'Oh, no,' he replied, genuinely shocked, 'that I could never do. But near here there is a German camp and the soldiers visit often to buy eggs and poultry. And also'—he looked venomous—'to insult my daughters with their filthy attention. You must stay with us until you are well and then I will find a more suitable home for you to hide in. But it will be necessary to hide you during daylight.'

Of course I readily agreed. When I was thoroughly warm I was taken, still with my blankets around me, into a large hay shed which formed a 'lean-to' on one side of the house. Here the boys pitchforked a hole deep down in the hay, and the girls laid rugs and cushions, and I lay down comfortably. Then, after a few minutes, just as I was getting pleasantly drowsy, the lady of the house appeared with a loaded tray, on which was arranged the most unforgettable meal of my life. A waitress in an English officers' mess in the First World War, she knew what would be appreciated. A large and delicious omelette with bacon and chipped potatoes, fresh home-made bread and sheep's milk butter, and a large glass of sweet goats' milk. All this was laid out neatly on the tray, with a napkin and, as a finishing touch, some toothpicks.

Silently she stood and watched me eat, and I am sure the gusto with which I tackled her cooking must have been a compliment in any language. I was surprised on looking up to see her brown eyes shining with tears as she turned to go. I asked Gregorio when he came in for a few minutes why she was so sad, and he explained that she had been thinking of my mother and what unhappiness this war was bringing her. True enough certainly, for home in New Zealand my mother's lovely hair was greying over the only news she had received for seven months, '... regret to inform you ... wounded and missing'. This spontaneous and generous sympathy, so very typical of the Greek, was too much for me in my weak state. When he had gone I buried my face in my hands, and let a stream of tears tumble into the hay.

About two o'clock I awoke from a most refreshing sleep, with the hay pressing warmly about me, and found two thoughtful brown eyes studying me through a thinner patch of the tent of hay above me. It was Maria. She climbed over the hay with a long glass of hot sweet milk, some fresh wholemeal scones, and some old American magazines.

When she had placed the empty glass and plate in safety she snuggled in beside me under the hay, we remoulded the tent over our heads, and then with exquisite determination she gave me my first lesson in Greek. We started with the pictures in the magazines—horses, dogs, men, women, and even after a while a few adjectives, so that at the end of a very delightful lesson I was able to tell her she had a beautiful nose. This amused her greatly, and her laughter left me wishing violently for a greater vocabulary. Few pupils wish to please their teachers more than I did then.

Evening came very pleasantly: I was invited into the house, fed on a tasty salad and potatoes and, after telling a portion of my story, I went to bed and slept deeply all night. In the morning the mother brought me my clothes freshly washed, and I spent the day in the hay again, most of it with Maria for company. We devoted a great deal of the time, but not all, to my lesson in Greek.

In the afternoon the sunlight streamed through the cracks and nail holes of the lean-to walls; that evening, as the last shafts of light reddened by the sunset, slowly faded, I realised how easy it would be to still my conscience and stay on indefinitely. But I knew that I should be moving on. The sleep and good food had refreshed me wonderfully, I decided to set off again that night.

The whole family rose up in protest when I told them my decision after dinner, and the mother was crying openly as she stuffed my pockets with raisins and bits of bread before I left. My teacher and her young brother accompanied me for the first two miles, and we all found it difficult to say goodbye. As the darkness closed round their waving figures on the track and their talk grew fainter I was sorely tempted to return, so touched was I at the spontaneous friendship they had given me. The thought of more Greek lessons in the hay was alluring. I pushed on, feeling lonely and sad.

Chapter Ten

Perambulations in occupied Greece

Keeping to the advice of the farmer, I followed a narrow track over rolling and very barren country until I struck a main road. According to him, this was the road I should have taken two nights previously, and he had saved me five miles by suggesting the track as a short cut.

There was very little military traffic on the road and the first three or four miles were uneventful. I sat down every half-hour for five minutes and ate a small handful of the raisins the good lady had given me.

In a few more miles I realised I was approaching quite a large village. It was after nine o'clock curfew, and I knew that I might well be checked. I made my way with some trepidation through the silent houses which lined the streets.

Before long, however, I found myself in the large square which formed the centre of the village. I was on the point of passing across it when I noticed a conglomeration of vehicles in the shadow of the buildings on the other side. Even without a second look I could tell that they were military transport. One, indeed, was marked with a brilliant white circle in which, even in the gloom, the hated swastika showed prominently. And as I slipped quietly behind the framework of a large village well, a sentry moved out of the shadows, obviously suspicious. I crouched in the shadow. Heavy steps approached. I took to my heels and ran full pelt back the way I had come, not pausing until I was well clear of the village. The sentry shouted at me repeatedly, as I ran down the street, but now as I took shelter, exhausted, in a ditch on the side of the road, everything behind was quiet. I rested for a while and let the panic leave me.

There seemed no alternative but to make a wide detour across country around the village and to rejoin the route on the other side. So I set off. For the first half-mile or so the going was good; ploughed ground broken here and there by deep washouts and small streams. But, as I began to climb the lower slopes of the hills behind the village I ran into brushwood, and it became increasingly hard to keep direction in the dark. Then it came on to rain. I floundered through the dripping bushes for about two hours until I realised I was completely lost.

It was a terrible night. There was something uncanny about that tall brushwood. I had a terrible feeling that it was holding me back all the time as I forced my way through. It was all so quiet and lonely my apprehension grew until at last I broke into a clearing and ran with relief into the open. Nothing, absolutely nothing, would have induced me to go back into that thicket. Even when the continued upward slope convinced me that I must be moving away from my route I carried on.

The rain eased off to an uncomfortable drizzle and the clouds broke occasionally to show some stars. I tried to keep a constant direction in what I hoped was south-east, but I really had no idea where I trudged throughout that long night.

Towards dawn I came over the summit of the gentle rise I had been climbing all night and heard the homely sound of cows being driven through the darkness of the valley below. I heard the lowing of the beasts, the striking of the hooves against the stone, intermingled with the unmusical tinkle of the brass cow-bells; I felt strangely comforted as though these pleasant noises were a signal calling me into a haven in the valley.

As the clouds above began to lighten, a small village cradled between two spurs loomed up ahead. I sat down on a large rock to consider the best approach. The first of the village dogs picked up my foreign scent and began to spoil the quiet of the morning.

The village was all in darkness, although a rattling of pails proclaimed that some were early afoot. There seemed to be twelve or fifteen houses grouped together. I decided to chance my luck with the first house which lit a lamp. Meanwhile, the village dogs gathered in numbers and filled the whole valley with their chorus of disapproval.

The lamp flickered and flared up in a house standing a little away from the others so, gripping my heavy stick firmly, I approached as confidently as I could. The dogs barked and snapped frantically, but withdrew before my brandished stick, and in a few moments I was hammering on the rough wooden door.

There was whispering, and peering from all the windows, and then the door was swung open and I was ushered into a small room. In the far corner a baby cried from a box on the floor. In front of a dying fire were five forms, two of which raised sleepily inquiring faces as the Greek and his wife motioned me to sit on the small wooden form which was the only furniture of the room. Very soon, the embers of the fire were raked up and enlivened, and a large piece of fresh pork set to sizzle and spit in a wrought-iron cauldron hanging from a chain in the chimney.

The house was that of a poor villager, typical of the peasants in Macedonia and Thrace. My host was lean and dark, tall in comparison with his fellows and perhaps forty years old. His wife was much shorter. The children, two boys and two girls, were strikingly attractive in spite of their rags and tousled appearance, and the adventure of having an English officer in their home was not lost on them. I was quite spoilt.

When the meal was ready the pork was cut into small chunks and put into a common bowl. We all sat round on the floor Indian fashion, with forks and fingers of heavy black bread. In between an animated conversation of gesticulations and guess work I enjoyed a highly satisfying meal, while my limbs thawed out and the steam rose like a cloud from my sodden clothes. This bulky meal of pork in a house so humble was not unusual in those early months of the occupation, when the redoubtable peasants were grimly eating all their stock rather than submit to the systematic 'theft by payment' of the hated German.

When I was satisfied, and when the children began to tire of persistent questions, to which no reply was forthcoming, I was taken into the only other room in the house and put into the only bed while my clothes were taken for drying. This idea of a second room, I later found, was quite common amongst these humble and hospitable people; it was generally used solely for guests, the husband and wife sleeping on the floor of the living room under the same rough rags that covered the family.

I spent the whole of the day in a small barn in the fields beyond the village, and was brought back into the house in the evening and fed again royally. They were simple people, but so bravely patriotic that I could not bear to ignore their growing panic. I decided against their protests to start off again at midnight. Before I left they pressed an old homespun blanket and some bread on me. Knowing just how much these things would mean to them I did my utmost to refuse, but they were adamant. I contented myself by insisting that they in return should accept a Bank of Scotland pound note which I had won off Rex King at cards in the Athens hospital.

The night was clear and starry; there was a cold wind, but I was grateful for the absence of rain and the comfort of the blanket wrapped as a shawl over my shoulders. I made good time down the valley and, keeping my direction by the light of the German vehicles on a road some miles away, I began to climb and move along a low plateau which ran parallel to the road.

It was a glorious sunrise that morning and it flooded a peaceful valley full of beauty. It refreshed me wonderfully and I stopped by a small stream to enjoy it to the full. All that day I made slow progress.

My way lay over a series of low hills which formed the foothills of more mountainous country. On my right, to the south-east, a fertile plain stretching to the sea was cut by a ribbon of road on which I could clearly see a constant stream of German motorised traffic. From this road numerous gravel and mud side-roads branched off into the villages in the hills.

About four in the afternoon, having skirted two small villages, I came over the crest of a hill to look down upon an unexpected scene. The other villages had seemed deserted, with their occupants in the fields, but here was a hive of activity. Outside a wine-shop in the small square below me was a group of nine or ten figures in light-green uniforms. They were gathered around a table on which an old-fashioned gramophone blared, encircled by the largest collection of dirty children I had ever seen. The sight of uniforms put me immediately on the alert, and I would have turned back to some other route had not one detached himself and come shouting and waving towards me.

There was no chance of running, so I took the bull by the horns and walked down into their midst.

What an enthusiastic welcome it was! All ten policemen, for such they were, saluted me and gravely kissed my hand, an old, bearded priest blessed me and kissed me on both cheeks, and generally I was made the guest of honour for the day.

No one spoke English, but I understood that I had stumbled on to an illegal gathering of loyal police who met to work out plans against the overlord as well as to drink in good fellowship. They gave me food and wine, slapping my back all the while and proudly showing an assortment of firearms, held for the day when it would be ripe to strike. All the time the tiny children pressed about my chair.

It was only after I had eaten well of olives and tasty salted fish, and refreshed myself with wine that I realised I was under scrutiny and discussion. Presently I was approached and in hesitant French apprised of their secret. In a nearby village, I was told, were two other Englishmen. Would I like to join them? They produced a notebook and showed me two names which, by their army numbers, I knew were those of New Zealanders. I immediately asked if I could be taken to them.

Accordingly, in about half an hour, I left with a policeman guiding, waving an acknowledgment to the now rather drunken cheers of the police, and the increased babble from the children. On the insistence of my guide I had put on the long field-grey overcoat of the Greek Police and their French type, tall, flat-topped hat. This camouflage was very welcome as the day drew to its end, but I felt a little uneasy about it. I was risking the fate of a spy, if the Germans caught me.

We made over some rolling foothills and then started up the side of a rough and forbidding hill. I had thought the distance was only a few miles, but now I found that the trip was likely to take some seven hours' hard walking. I was horrified. I knew that I was not up to such a distance, certainly not at the pace my guide set. However as the darkness closed around us we pushed steadily on.

After vainly trying to make him slow down and give me more frequent halts, I finally showed him my wound. It had the desired effect. He was aghast and, indeed, wanted straightway to return to the village. But, following an old maxim of mine never to turn back whatever the cost, I persuaded him to continue at a gentler pace and cover at least part of the journey.

There was no moon, and the night seemed unusually black, so I was not surprised that we continually lost the small track and spent long periods trying to find it again. Well before midnight I realised I would not be able to travel much farther, and even when we traversed the pass and began the more easy descent I had to drag my body along as though drugged.

As an unfortunate inspiration, it occurred to me that to eat a 'Bovril' cube would make some energy quickly available. I had a carton of six cubes from a Red Cross parcel which I kept as my 'emergency ration'. Accordingly, I broke the carton open and popped one into my mouth. Of course, it being so highly concentrated I had not the saliva to masticate it and swallowed it uncomfortably as a sticky and salty mess. This left me far worse than before with, in addition, a raging thirst. I drank at every opportunity, at small streams, from dirty dew-ponds, from water collected in the hoof-marks in the mud of the track—but to no avail. It was soon as much as I could do to make fifty yards in a spurt, and this only with the assistance of my guide.

At the foot of the valley we had entered, the occasional dimmed lights of military vehicles showed the presence of a fairly important road. My guide, growing perceptibly agitated, would now not allow me even a few minutes' respite, but dragged me along, keeping to the darkest routes. We crossed the road, which was tar sealed, in a lull in the traffic, and passed with great stealth through the outskirts of quite a large village. Then we struck the main road again and followed it along, sheltering in the ditch alongside whenever a German vehicle approached.

Then there came the time when I just could not continue. I sat down in the ditch and refused to budge.

My friend the guide was terrified. He made me understand that at daybreak the area would be alive with Germans. He pulled and tugged at me, but when he showed that we had to cross yet another mountain pass, I stuck to my ditch obstinately. Finally, in despair, he agreed to allow me to hide in the woods rising steeply from the side of the road and to stay hidden there until he could come and get me early the next night.

I climbed up into the trees and spent a miserable night. I was aching with exhaustion. Try as I might I could not find a place in the thick undergrowth where I could sleep. Everywhere I tried seemed too steep; if I started to doze off, I would feel myself slipping down the hill-side, and if I tried to lie at the base of a tree the weight of my body would soon become unbearable. I dared not light a fire, yet after my exertions the cold seemed to strike through my clammy, sweaty clothes to my very bones.

There was a continual furtive movement going on in the undergrowth all around me, which kept me in a state of fearful apprehension—not so much of wolves and poisonous insects as of the shapeless dark shadows my tired mind persisted in conjuring up.

Finally I gave up all thoughts of sleep and, propping myself against the trunk of one of the larger trees, clutched my stick firmly and stared balefully into the blackness around me.

The morning broke fair, for which I thanked God, and I climbed higher to find a small clearing which would allow the sun to thaw me. I found a flat rock and spent a desolate day aware of each minute that ticked by on my watch.

I had not expected the guide to return until dark, but about four in the afternoon I heard the agreed signal and answered as softly as I could. There was the sound of people breaking through the undergrowth and presently my friend appeared, together with a tall civilian who, to my pleasure, could speak quite reasonable English.

He was a doctor who had been approached by the guide to come and give some attention to my wound. He dressed it expertly and comfortably with some yellow salve and fresh-smelling lint, binding it all firmly with a large roll of crepe bandage which I knew would last me for some time. I felt greatly relieved by this unexpected stroke of fortune and really enjoyed the bread and olives they brought me, together with a large flagon of wine which we all shared in good comradeship.

Perhaps half an hour after dusk, the foot traffic on the road lessened perceptibly and, having made our thanks and farewells to the doctor, my guide and I clambered down on to the road and set off once again. We went along cautiously and much slower than on the previous night.

The road took us up and up until we passed through a narrow defile and came into a steep valley, heavily bushed and uncannily dark. Here my guide seemed a little lost for a while, and then suddenly discovered a familiar landmark and led me off the road on to a small mule track striking into the depths of the forest. We continued skirting the side of the great hill for some three hours and finally broke through into a clearing. We saw far below us a peaceful cultivated valley, with here and there in the distance the soft glow of lights from scattered farmhouses.

We wound and zigzagged down the mountainside, and in perhaps an hour came upon the outer fences of a farmhouse. My guide bade me lie low while he went forward to see if all was safe. As I watched, a light flared up in the upstairs windows and presently I was being warmly welcomed by an old farmer, while his wife fussed about the open fire preparing us a meal. The wine was brought out and we drank to the Glory of Greece and England, and then, with Greek vehemence, to the damnation of all Germans.

My guide and I had a strange bed that night. The house, although two-storeyed, was only two-roomed, one on top—the living room and bedroom of the farmer and his wife—and one below for the stock. Now we were taken below amongst a collection of cows, pigs and poultry. I chose what I thought was the largest space between two cows, and the farmer spread some fresh, sweet-smelling clover hay for me to lie on.

We settled down quickly; I was very tired. The farmer bade us goodnight and went upstairs, taking the only lamp. It was somehow very cosy in that strange bedroom. On either side of me I could feel the warmth of the two cows, and hear them methodically chewing their cuds. Up in the rafters the hens ceased their disturbed clucking and quietened down to an occasional drowsy chirrup. Across, near where my guide slept, an old boar grunted his disapproval and moved restlessly about in the straw. Once again the thrill of a strange situation crept over me. Nestling down in my hay, I felt unaccountably light-hearted and happy as I dozed off.

We were awakened early by the farmer who, after turning out the reluctant livestock, gave us a good breakfast of the same dried meat and some maize porridge. Then, while it still needed half an hour to dawn, the farmer and the guide took me across some fields, over a low, scrub-covered hill until, soon after sunrise, we came over a small ridge. Nestling in a basin formed by the head of a large washout in front of us was an almost circular enclosure some forty paces in diameter, made of piled-up scrub and brushwood. In one corner was built a shelter, also of scrub and brushwood, circular, about five feet high and perhaps eight feet across. A pale wisp of smoke hung over the apex and, as we drew nearer, a rough wooden door was revealed. I realised, with disappointment, for it was a miserable habitation, that this must be the hide-out of my two compatriots.

There was no sign of any one afoot as we reached the door, but my spirits rose at the thought of meeting my countrymen. I hastened the last few paces, and then stood impatiently, waiting for my two Greek friends to open the door and enter. But the Greek is unfathomable. The policeman who had made the long and tiring journey solely for me was now obviously worried about something. He put out his hand to restrain me when I made to open the rough door myself. The farmer rubbed his bristly face in silence.

I tried to understand them. In the absence of a common tongue, I asked by gesticulation whether the occupants of the hut were friends. They nodded an affirmative. Then, with no preliminaries and without a word in Greek or English, they both came closer and shook my hand warmly. It was an obvious farewell. Before I could try to thank them for all they had done, they turned about and walked quickly away in the direction from which we had just come. They turned to wave as they went over the rise. Then they disappeared.

I opened the small door and crawled in.

Chapter Eleven

I meet two countrymen

'Is there anyone in?' I called, rather unnecessarily, for in the haze of smoke and darkness I could make out two forms. They were lying one on each side of a small fire in the centre of the hut.

The response was immediate. The form on the left, the larger by far, sat up and demanded loudly and, I thought, a little fearfully, 'Who is that ... who are you?' then, struggling to sit up and face me, 'Where have you come from?'

He was quite agitated and uncertain for a few moments; I thought he had woken from a deep sleep. But when I had put him at his ease and told him briefly who I was, he seized my hand with both of his and welcomed me heartily.

'Well I never,' he beamed, 'I thought you were a blinking Hun when the door opened. Hey, Johnny, wake up Johnny, we've got an addition to the family!'

He prodded the embers of the fire, which was in a hollow scooped out of the ground, and the three of us burst into animated conversation. It was so wonderfully refreshing to speak English again. I felt like a schoolboy telling my tale, the words tumbling out breathlessly, and a feeling of repressed excitement making it all scarcely coherent.

The hut was so low that one could not even sit in comfort, while the smoke from the fire, having no exit but through the straw roof, hung low, stinging the eyes. Both of my new friends were in rags and even in that smoky gloom I could see that they were far from well. As we fell eagerly to exchanging news and adventures I gained an insight into the terrible privations these gallant fellows had endured and felt how tame my own adventures were in comparison.

The smaller of the two was Private John Mann, a genial fair-headed lad from Auckland. Captured near Olympus while serving with the 18th New Zealand Battalion, he had been free since July, five months, and had known both ups and downs in his travels.

Warrant Officer
R. H. Thomson, DCM

The Dominion

The heavily built and hearty New Zealander who had first welcomed me into the hut was Sergeant Major R. H. Thomson, D.C.M. A veteran of Wavell's first Libyan campaign, Thomson had been captured in Crete, while fighting as an infanteer in the 4th New Zealand Reserve Motor Transportation Column.

Both men, naturally, were in low spirits. They did not think it possible to leave the country and were beginning to believe, like the Greeks, that 'the English will be here any day now'. And so, with the first snow falling outside, they were prepared to wait where they could at least get food of a sort until either the winter passed or something happened.

The hut was re-arranged to allow room for me to put down my blanket, and we found that we lay in a close triangle, with the fire in the middle. This fire was both a necessity and a cause of worry; we were forced to keep it alive day and night because neither of my compatriots had any sort of blanket. But the smoke drifting through the framework revealed that the hut was inhabited. The Germans seemed distant enough, but we were afraid of the results of any idle gossip by the peasants.

Life in that hut was miserable enough, but it had its compensations.

There was quite a pattern of procedure, laid down by Thomson, for our daily existence. First, it was understood that, in view of the terrible length of the days, we should sleep on in the morning until the last was properly awake. Then we would wash in the small stream. Following this, we would make a cautious reconnaissance to commanding ground, each in a different direction, to see if there was any suspicious movement. This expedition also served the purpose of gathering wood for fuel.

Returning to the hut, we would unhurriedly prepare the first of our daily meals. This would entail boiling some water in an old iron kettle, and then heating an empty copper bowl. Into the copper bowl, when properly hot, we would put a spoonful of precious fat. This would be followed with a handful of fine grains of some meal mixture and we would stir briskly for a few minutes and then fill the bowl to its brim with boiling water. This stirred gently for some thirty minutes resulted in as thick and as appetising a porridge as I have ever tasted.

The food was saved for us, from their meagre rations, by the good folk of a small village in the foothills and brought out to us every two or three days by the Mayor, or by the village policeman, Gregorio. Evidently each humble home kept a bowl for some unknown English fugitive and put aside crusts, beans, small pieces of meat, salted fish and olives.

If it was fine we put our rags in the sun, took off as many of our clothes as we could, and spent long hours on one of the most revolting tasks in the world. For we were overrun with lice. The hut had been used by passing tramps and dirty shepherds, so it was not surprising that an active colony waited there to fall on our rags and weakened bodies. It seemed impossible to get rid of them; we washed our clothing piece by piece in boiling water, but after temporary relief they would reappear in force. In the sun we could search along the seams of each tattered garment, destroying the horrid grey-white vermin and their eggs. We even derived some amusement from it. A morsel of the more dainty scraps would be set aside for the man who finished with the greatest number in a measured time.

Towards evening we would sally forth for a quick look around the horizon again, returning laden with sufficient wood to keep the fire up all night.

As dusk closed we sat cross-legged around our fire, with our heads rather uncomfortably pushed forward into the smoke by the slope of the roof above, and prepared the evening meal. We tried always to have this in style, that is, in two courses. Our mainstay, the soup, was started with the water which had soaked all day in the copper porridge bowl. During the afternoon it had been thickened with any herbs we could find during our wood forays—together with any unconsumed bones or morsels. Now we added just a few grains of barley and some crusts, and stirred the mixture in turn, savouring with almost unbearable impatience the appetising odour which filled the hut.

We had no plates and only one spoon. The soup was consumed by passing the steaming bowl from one to the other; and each in turn took ten spoonfuls until it was empty.

Then the main course was prepared, often less in bulk and food value than the soup, but nevertheless the main course. We sometimes had potatoes, sometimes tiny salted fish. The main diet, however, was dried beans which we soaked all day in the water jug and cooked when the porridge-cum-soup copper bowl was available. Then as a savoury there would be olives, eaten one by one in real enjoyment, the stones only disposed of when they were as bare and tasteless as a piece of flint. Thomson and I would then be finished, both being non-smokers, but Mann would unravel an old handkerchief to reveal some precious fragments of tobacco, and carefully roll a cigarette, using the pages of a German-Greek dictionary for his cigarette-paper.

If we had visitors it was always a bright evening. When they had been made as comfortable as possible around the fire, they would produce a flagon of wine and set themselves to cheer us up. We understood very little Greek and they no English at all, but as the red wine chased the boredom and weariness from the hut we conversed freely, and told long stories, jokes and adventures, unhampered by the normal difficulties of language. They would always have some secret, whispered story that had come to them through mysterious but absolutely reliable channels. The Mayor of such and such a village had heard the thunder of Russian guns as they approached through Bulgaria, the British had landed a large force on this or that island, the R.A.F. had maintained a ten-days' attack on Berlin and the people of that city had demanded an immediate armistice. There was always news of a landing in France, either just about to start or already on the outskirts of Paris. The Russians were always advancing and destroying thousands of German planes.

As for the Western Desert, the British, now reinforced with thousands of Greek soldiers, were sweeping the Germans and the Italians into the sea. The King of England, on Churchill's advice, was to grant Eritrea, Abyssinia, the Dodecanese and Albania to Greece for their gallant part in this last campaign. It was never doubted that the Allies would be in Greece 'AVRIO, METHAVRIO'—'tomorrow or the day after'.

The stories about Turkey were particularly inconsistent. One day, because of a deep-seated hatred of the country, Turkey would be fighting with the Axis and therefore soundly thrashed by Australian troops advancing from Syria. The very next night the star news would be the fact that Turkey had declared for the Allies and were already advancing deep into Bulgaria to join up with the Red Army.

We were fully expected to be thrilled and excited at each morsel of news, and our guests felt cheated if we failed to hug them and one another in an ecstasy of thankfulness. But it was fully understood that it was not done to inquire at a later date about the progress of a previously reported Russian thrust. After all, it was never the Greeks fault that their stories did not come true.

Most of this time there was a somewhat hazy but plausible plan which, according to the Mayor, was to take us safely to a rendezvous with a Greek submarine called *Papanikolas*, which would take us to Alexandria. We were all dubious, particularly because the Mayor would excitedly maintain on each visit that the big day was 'AVRIO METHAVRIO'. As it turned out, nothing ever did come of it, although I was to be astonished many months later when Intelligence in Cairo showed that the worthy and patriotic little Mayor spoke with knowledge and authority. What he did not know, however, was the fact that the gallant submarine had at last met her fate in the Aegean.

I stayed with Mann and Thomson for nineteen days. I was loath to leave them. But I knew I must push on. I felt stronger, and the thrill of adventure was back to give new blood to my flabby and ill-used body. I found myself impatient to be winding over the countryside again, drawing nearer to my goal.

Chapter Twelve

On pilgrimage to the
Holy Mountain

The morning of 8th December 1941 broke fair and promising. I walked briskly over the light, crisp snow, turning at the crest of the hill to wave a last farewell to Thomson and Johnny, who were standing a little forlornly at the door of the hut. Then I turned my face to the mountains which made the eastern horizon and, gripping my heavy shepherd's stick firmly, strode forward to see what further adventures fate had in store for me.

It was a really lovely day, and I passed many peasants on the vague track I had chosen for my road. Some of them passed without a second glance, others eyed me curiously. Some also recognised my nationality and stopped me to offer what little they had—tobacco, olives or bread.

Later in the morning a horseman overtook me and, after regarding me for some minutes, reined and had me join him in an excellent repast he produced from his saddle-bag—new bread, cheese and olives, with the inevitable bottle of fresh-watered wine. The slopes of the foothills I was now traversing were thawed of their snow and it was wonderfully pleasant to enjoy the wholesome food while basking in the sun on the side of the track. My benefactor was an elderly farmer by his appearance, and did not seem greatly disposed to enter into conversation. Before he mounted, however, he wrote some Greek hieroglyphics on an old scrap of paper. He explained slowly and carefully that it was a note to a friend of his, a miller, in a village ten miles farther on. He himself was branching off to another route, but he was sure I would find food and shelter with his friend.

I pressed on steadily throughout the afternoon. Half an hour before sunset I wound up a steep approach and entered the village where the miller lived. It was not a large village, perhaps some thirty homes in all, and soon I entered a three-sided enclosure which I took for the village square described by my midday benefactor.

I sat down by the village well, from which flowed a steady stream of the delightful water known only to mountain villages. Children flocked around as I refreshed myself from the large stone bowl attached by a chain to the well. They soon guessed that I must be a fugitive Englishman, and all tried eagerly to show their patriotism. I was offered precious sweets and coveted morsels of food, and shown quaint little rag dolls.

When it was quite dark and the last of the children had gone home I followed the directions given me, and knocked quietly on the door of a small house built against the side of a large, barn-like building. It was obviously the village flour-mill.

The miller was short, fat and jovial. He waved aside the note and ushered me into his home, slapping me on the back and beaming with hospitality.

'Englezi—uh good! Ver good!' he wheezed, when he had sat me down. 'Alla Englizi ver good, alla brudder Yannos.' He hustled about the small furniture-crowded room and produced a bottle of *ouzo* with two small glasses.

'Noma?' he demanded, offering me my glass, 'noma—?'

'Thoma.'

'Thoma?' he seized upon it with delight, and demonstrated with his hands the sacred actions of St Thomas when doubting the resurrection of Our Lord, 'Thoma good. Me Yannos, you call 'im John.'

We shook hands. I felt very much at home and pleasantly tired.

Presently, down an attic ladder appeared his wife, a dark woman in her late thirties, with a surprisingly fair child of perhaps eighteen months in her arms.

Yannos introduced them proudly; the little child clung shyly to her mother, but dimpled her chubby face affectionately at her father as he took her hand to place in mine.

It all made a very happy and homely picture, and I readily understood and agreed with Yannos when in his stumbling English he explained that he had more than most men to live and fight for. The introductions over, the wife bustled about in her kitchen and prepared a lovely meal of pork and potatoes fried in olive oil, while Yannos told me in some detail of the other English who, earlier in the summer, had passed through the village. He always kept his eye open for them, he said, and on one occasion soon after the invasion had sheltered twenty-three soldiers and airmen in his mill whilst a German convoy of troops were bivouacked nearby. His face shadowed as he told of the terrible anxiety of those few days, for he well knew to what risks he was exposing his beloved family. I felt that I had found a true and great-hearted patriot, and with this feeling came the resolve that I must move on as soon as possible, so that no unnecessary risk would threaten his home.

After my meal, which satisfied me wonderfully, I was told to stretch out on a low couch in the main room, and a coverlet was pulled over me. In spite of the homely clatter of dishes being washed in the kitchen and the laughter of the child as she played with her father, I was asleep in a very few minutes.

I must have slept heavily for two or three hours, and when I awoke the room was filled with people, both men and women.

Yannos had called in all the members of the local resistance movement to meet me. They were all young; Yannos was at least ten years older than the eldest. They all seemed intensely eager to shake hands and tell of their plans and hopes.

Suddenly, there was an urgent triple rap on one of the windows. The same signal was repeated, and then Yannos, his face drawn and pale, spoke quickly to his friends, who began to file silently through a small door which opened into the flour-mill. I rose from my couch and made as if to follow, but was waved back.

When the last had disappeared into the mill Yannos closed the door carefully. He inspected the curtains covering all the windows, drawing them fully across, so that no one might peer in. He placed a chair against the door and then turned to me.

'Germanos,' he said quietly and seriously, with no trace of panic, 'Germanos b____s; we think they see you today, now come here.'

I rose again, and made to go immediately, but he restrained me quickly. He went into the next room, and came back in a moment with his wife who, though startled, tried to smile reassuringly at me.

The two of them placed themselves one on each end of a large, wide dresser which was against the wall of the adjoining flour-mill. Then they began to work it slowly forward. It came out easily, moving on two heavy wooden bars about three feet from the ground. Underneath these bars was a large cavity, newly constructed with fresh timber. It was, perhaps, five feet wide, and was set a good four feet into the mill building.

Yannos and his good wife bundled some blankets into the cavity and waved me inside. As soon as I was settled they worked the dresser on its two bars back flush with the wall, leaving me in complete darkness. For a few minutes I could hear their footsteps in the room and then all became quiet.

The unruffled calm of my host had taken away any fear. Now, in my 'priest's hole', I considered the situation and came to the conclusion that, provided all the patriots managed to sneak back to their homes, there would not be much chance of my discovery. For a few moments I panicked at the thought that I had left my stick and cap in the main living room. But then I considered the obvious resource of my friend and drew comfort from it.

The hide-out was well ventilated and, although it was too short for my long frame to stretch out, I found it snug and comfortable. Presently I fell asleep. But not before that pleasant and now familiar feeling had crept over me—the sensation of living a part in some great adventure story. The imagination of youth is considerable, but my wildest day-dreams had never carried me from my remote home in a little valley in New Zealand to this strange hide-out right in the midst of an enemy-occupied country.

Some hours later I awoke and, recovering from a momentary panic at the dense blackness, realised that someone was working the dresser forward again to release me. Presently the miller bade me a good morning as he and his wife gave me an arm each to help me on my feet. I found it quite typical of the Greek people that both my host and hostess were cheery and bright and that neither thought it at all necessary to volunteer any explanation as to the reason for the midnight panic. They talked trivialities. They fussed about me and made a comfortable dressing for my wound. They joined me in an excellent breakfast, which they enjoyed unhurriedly as though such things as Germans did not exist.

Finally, my impatience and curiosity could not be further restrained.

'Yannos,' I demanded, 'what happened?' Where are the Germans who were seen approaching last night?'

The miller paused in his contented munching, looked quite genuinely blank for a moment as though he had no memory of anything unusual having happened. Then his face relaxed in comprehension.

'Ah, yus,' he said, shrugging casually, 'ah, yus, Germanos.' He waved his hands in deprecation. 'Greco no scared Germanos! Greco fort, strong, kill 'um Germanos by'n'by.'

He resumed his breakfast.

I caught the eye of his wife across the table.

'Nix Germanos,' she said, twinkling. 'Nix Germanos,' and then in Greek, 'everything is good now, there was never any German in the village last night. One of our compatriots was told by his children that a strange foreign man had entered the village at dusk. He presumed it was a German spy.'

'But it was probably me!' I cried. 'I arrived at about sunset!'

'Of course, of course,' she responded, still amused, 'we know that now. But last night was a different matter. Our compatriot was alarmed and immediately came to warn us—you know the result,' she laughed merrily, and pointed to her husband.

'Yannos is therefore not very pleased with himself this morning, are you, my husband?'

Yannos looked up from his plate and grinned a little sheepishly.

'Oh, well,' he replied, 'one must not take risks—and it was a good test for our organisation.'

It was still very early in the morning. When we had finished our breakfast the sun was just rising. I told them that I must be on my way again.

While his wife prepared some food for me to eat on the road, Yannos explained the route I was to follow in my pilgrimage to Mount Athos. He showed me on my road map where the German camps and control posts were, and cautioned me to keep clear of certain villages where Bulgarian agents mixed with the people. A young friend of his would act as a guide for me.

Half an hour later I had made my farewells to them both and was following, as fast as my leg would allow, a lanky, merry-faced youth of sixteen years. He was obviously thrilled with his mission and darted from house to house, corner to corner, glancing furtively this way and that as though he half hoped to find some German lurking in ambush. All the while he clutched with theatrical tenseness a large meat knife which was hung in a rawhide sheath from his belt. A redoubtable warrior, Niki. He led me in this manner through the deserted streets and then down a narrow, hedge-lined lane which opened into the fields below the village.

Here Niki drove into a corner, and finally secured, a small donkey. On this, despite my protest, for it seemed so tiny that my weight must be too much for it, I was made to ride.

We continued in this way for over two hours, winding first in a wide circle round the village, and then up to a rough track along the side of a mountain. Niki took me as far as a narrow pass over a ridge between two mountains and, when I had dismounted, bade me farewell.

The track took me down into a steep valley. There was no sign of any habitation. The sun beat warmly down from a blue sky. I spent a pleasant hour by a sparkling mountain stream at the foot of the valley, and enjoyed bread, olives and salted fish for my lunch. There were dozens of small birds in the trees, and their songs and chatter filled the valley with music. It was all so serene and restful that I was quite loath to push on, but reflecting that it would be cold and desolate by night, I rose and began to climb the opposite side of the valley, in the direction of a mountain town called Arnea.

As the afternoon wore on there was a gradual change of weather. It did not seem to get any colder, but heavy grey clouds drifted across the sky from the north and hung low over the hills, leaden and ominous. As the first shadows of the evening gathered in the valleys, it came on to snow in the hills. By the time I had crossed the last ridge there was already a fine white dust on the ground, and the bright lights of Arnea shone through myriads of soft flakes.

I walked down into Arnea with every confidence of a sheltering roof and food. Things had gone so very well so far that I was certain I would land on my feet again. But Greece was always the land of 'You cannot tell, you never know'. How often in those days and nights of travel was I to find luck change swiftly and inexplicably to disaster, and back again! Now, as I swung jauntily into the one street of Arnea, I felt that I was terribly unwelcome. People passed with averted heads, and when I spoke to them, shrugged, drew their cloaks closer around them in fear or disdain and moved away.

At first I could not understand this rigid aloofness, and thought that my ragged appearance must be the reason. I continued down the electric lit streets, however, and found the unmistakable cause—a German truck was parked right up on the narrow footpath of the street, whilst around it and milling in and out of an adjacent wine-shop were a dozen or perhaps fifteen soldiers. They appeared quite uninterested in the awed population about them, so that I felt suddenly more relieved than afraid.

The Germans ignored me. They seemed to be having fun with one of their number who had obviously misjudged the effects of the heavy Greek wine. So many of the conquerors had been used only to their light lagers and beers; these local red wines, drunk without the water which was customary to the Greeks, drove them raving mad. As the danger faded behind me I felt very jealous of their freedom and, even more, of the warm-looking greatcoats they all wore.

I set off in the gloom along the ill-defined track to the next village. A party of older children, some dressed still in the nationalistic uniforms of the Metaxas regime, accosted me before I had gone very far. They were all wildly excited to recognise me as English, and clamoured for me to return with them to Arnea. At least, they all clamoured until I told them of the presence of the German soldiers, and then only a few of the more rash pressed the invitation.

However, they assured me that the next village, some five miles distant, was a patriotic community, and would certainly grant me asylum. And before they left me, after some prompting from one of the older boys, they went down on their knees and chanted a blessing.

It was an unforgettable picture. Soft snow falling all the while, they knelt in a semi-circle around me on the road, their small hands cupped on their chests, their baby-like faces raised into the tumbling snowflakes, and their eyes shining. When they had finished, solemnly and in perfect unison they made the sign of the cross.

I entered the next village about ten, just as the restaurants and small wine-shops were closing at curfew-time. I looked eagerly around for a friend. But even amongst this mellow crowd, hearty and happy with wine, there was no-one who showed anything but a swiftly ruffled composure when they realised I was English. Each, as I accosted him, jabbered some urgent but unintelligible information and then scuttled off.

At last, as the streets quietened down, the door of a café opened into the street, and silhouetted by the orange glow of the lights behind them, two men emerged and crossed the street in my direction. They were youths, of about eighteen years of age. Turning towards them, I held out my hand to the taller of them in greeting.

'Kalimeris,' I said, as friendly as I could make it. 'Kalimeris io Englizi theles speti apopsy Paragalo,' which was, as near as I can write it, my version in Greek of 'Good day to you, I am an Englishman and seek a house for shelter this night, if it pleases you.'

(Strangely enough, this phonetic Greek of mine, together with the expressive gesticulations I learned from these demonstrative people, was intelligible to the average Greek. From this stage forward, adding always a word here and there to my vocabulary, I was able to converse well enough with the people I met.)

The two youths stopped dead in their tracks. With no attempt to take my proffered hand, they bustled me into the shadow.

'Where have you come from,' they demanded, after a few moments, 'and for where are you bound?'

'From Salonika,' I replied, 'and I make for Egypt and the English Army.'

'Do you know there are Germans here, here in this valley, in this village?'

'Yes, I saw them in Arnea. But they are not in pursuit of me, nor searching for prisoners. They are here to purchase cattle and tobacco.'

'How is it you know their intentions?'—this came suspiciously from the shorter of the two.

'I was told by some schoolchildren whose parents had been forced to sell some of their stock.'

'What schoolchildren?'—in unbelief and with open hostility—'Where have you spoken with schoolchildren?'

'Two hours since, on the road from Arnea. It is as I say. The children were returning into Arnea, and turned back to accompany me for a while.'

They considered this for a few moments, and then, after an obvious difference of opinion, told me to follow them at a safe distance. They walked off swiftly up the unlit streets, and I kept them in view from about twenty paces. They were still arguing, but their speech was so fast and fierce that I was unable to follow. I felt a vague mistrust of them.

Presently we branched off from the main street and followed a narrow alley between two houses. They led me round the back of a farm building and under a low eave where, although it was still cold and wet underfoot, we were at least out of the snow.

'Why are you going to Egypt?' demanded the short fellow, who did nearly all the talking.

'To join the English Army again!'

'Why,' vehemently, 'why, why?'

'To fight the German,' I replied, 'and to help towards the liberation of Greece!'

'The English are already finished, broken and finished. They will never help Hellas. If they come back here, it will only be to smash our bridges and to be hounded out again by the Germans!'

This was delivered harshly and with contempt. It was something new, something I could partly understand, but had not heard of before. These lads, I thought, were bitter in defeat. They felt deserted, firstly by their politicians, and then by the English when the northern hordes had engulfed their peaceful valleys.

'You must not lose faith,' I remonstrated. 'Hellas will be free again, and it will be England who will destroy her enemies. You must have faith. O THEOS EINAI MEGALOS, God is great.'

There was a burst of horrible curses from them both.

'To hell with faith, and to hell with God!' spoke the tall one for a change, emphasising his utterance by spitting at my feet, 'and to hell with the Englizi.'

'We would be paid well to hand you to the German,' from the shorter, 'you are of the same cursed breed, Germanos and Englizi. You must be ever conquering at our expense.'

I was not really alarmed at this threat. In the large towns citizens collaborated with the enemy and informed on their erstwhile friends and allies with some security. But in the mountain villages peasant hearts beat more warmly and loyally. To play Judas with me would be to have the whole of the loyal community on their tracks; to be hounded from the mountains.

Suddenly I looked at my wristlet watch. It was nearly eleven, an hour after curfew. I turned away from them furious, but also acutely aware that my one chance of refuge had gone.

'Don't go, Englizi!' called the shorter, 'don't go, we are your friends, yes, your friends! We will give you shelter.'

'Yes, yes, Englizi!' chimed in the taller, laying a hand on my shoulder. 'Perhaps we have been impolite. You must forgive us. You must share a bed with us!'

'Well,' I said, slightly mollified, but still distrustful, 'you certainly did not sound friendly. However, I will gladly and very gratefully accept your offer of shelter. I am wet through and frozen.'

My mind was racing madly. I did not like them, but shelter was imperative. I think I would have accepted refuge from a mountain bear that night, rather than stay out in the snow another hour. I tried to reply in kind to their change of manner and, talking quietly, we moved along the back of the village.

'What is the hour, Englizi?' said one of them.

'Ten past eleven,' I replied.

'Surely not! It is only just after curfew! Let me have a look!' said the tall fellow, swinging in towards me and stopping.

Foolishly unsuspecting, I extended my wrist and exposed the brilliant face of my watch from under my sodden coat sleeve.

In an instant my wrist was seized, the short fellow kicked me savagely in the groin and I was thrown, groaning with pain, into the snow. It was all over in a moment. As I clambered to my feet and painfully tried to straighten my back I was aware of their harsh laughter ringing louder than their snow-muffled footsteps as they ran back towards the village.

What could I do? My watch was gone. It was useless to run after them, too dangerous, even if my leg and the excruciating pain in my groin had allowed me. Thus my one real possession, the last personal belonging I had to comfort me, was lost forever.

Standing in the snow, forlorn and wretched, I felt a rising bitterness and anger. It surged over my pain, rose chokingly in my throat and pricked hotly in my eyes.

In a flash I saw my watch, nicely engraved, being presented by my old headmaster, as president of our small country social club. Through the tumbling snow in front of my eyes I could see all my friends gathered for the occasion in the drawing room of my father's house, and hear their farewells (for on the next day I left for overseas).

No one could ever appreciate what that watch, the loss of that watch, meant to me. And, as my rage burnt out, I realised like a child the final crushing, overwhelming thrust; there was no mother, no understanding brother, no friend, not even my old sheepdog, to whom I could turn for sympathy, to whom I could confide my misery.

All round the snow billowed and swirled in the darkness, the village stood silent and unfriendly.

I felt unbelievably tired and miserable, but more tired even than miserable. I was tempted to lie down there and then and go to sleep. But I knew of the danger of sleep in the snow and forced myself forward, not caring greatly where I was bound.

Presently I came to a rough wooden farm gate. On the far side I could make out some buildings. The first turned out to be a milking-shed and the second a store-shed. This last I entered. I felt about in the darkness, hoping to find some hay for warmth, but was unsuccessful. I decided to get down in amongst some corncobs which were piled in one corner. They had still their sheaths on them, were dry and I hoped would be warm.

My clothes were so hopelessly wet that I took them all off, in case they froze on me. But after a cold half-hour on the corncobs I fumbled in the dark and put them all back on again. However wet they were they still kept some warmth in.

The night dragged painfully on. It was impossible to sleep from the cold. With no watch to aid me, I peered into the gloom of the doorway and prayed earnestly for the first glimmering of dawn.

When at last a furtive greyness crept into the shed it was only to show that snow was still falling heavily. To push on was out of the question; my bad thigh and leg were stiff as a board. So gritting my chattering teeth, I counted off the minutes one by one and waited for a change. When it was fully light I saw on a raised platform at the far end of the shed a large pile of dry hay. After a terrific effort I rose from the lumpy, uncomfortable corncobs and, clambering up, made myself a fairly snug nest.

All that day I remained in the shed. Two old women discovered me and brought me food. The warmth of my body had partially dried my clothes. I passed a peaceful night in the hay.

In the morning the sun streamed in through the open door of the shed. Feeling rested, but very hungry again, I set off over the crisp snow. In front of me the road rose over the last ridge I would have to traverse before dropping to the plains which swept down to Mount Athos.

The village was already stirring as I made a wide detour around it. It looked very picturesque, with lazy spirals of smoke rising from the nicely rounded white roofs.

As I rejoined the road, on the other side a lanky figure walked out alone from the village. With a start I realised that it was the scoundrel who had stolen my watch. My bad leg had not yet thawed sufficiently to allow me to move fast with ease but, spurred on with a sudden anger, I overtook him in no time.

'You blackguard,' I spluttered, out of breath, and furious that I could not think of any angry Greek words, 'you thief and despicable rogue— where is my watch?'

I closed in to grab him, but he slipped away and ran a little distance back towards the village.

'Ah, the Englizi,' he taunted, sure of himself now that he realised he could easily outrun me, 'the stinking, vermin Englizi, you want your watch, eh? You want your watch—well, if you want your watch, come and get it! Come with me and find it—do you know where it is? The police have it! Yes, the police! I gave it to them! We will get it from them, they are in the village square now, talking to the Germanos!'

He turned away, pleased with himself, and with an exaggerated swagger made towards the village.

A large jagged piece of granite in the shingle of the road caught my eye. I picked it up and, running towards him, I threw it with all my might. It was not a good shot, too low, but it caught him on the calf of his leg with tremendous force. He gave a terrific bellow of pain and rage, almost crumpled to the ground, and then collected himself in a headlong rush to the village, half running and half hopping.

I felt some satisfaction as I turned away to press forward to Athos. One day, I resolved, as the village fell farther behind, one day, however many years ahead, I would return and make the police produce my watch from the culprits.

The road wound across a wide basin, through a narrow gorge, up and along the side of a forest-clad mountain. In spite of the snow I found myself enjoying the fresh briskness of the air, and the lovely colouring of the clear-cut peaks against the early morning sky. There were small groups of houses off the track on either side, some almost hidden by the forest. I considered the desirability of calling into one of them and trying my luck for a meal, but with the village I had left still visible in the distance behind me I deemed it wiser to push on.

Presently the track ceased to climb and dropped quite steeply. Through a small clearing in the forest I caught a glimpse of low hills below the snow level, and beyond them, far in the distance, was the blue of the sea. Half an hour and the grass began to show through patches of snow, and I began to follow the course of an ever-swelling mountain stream as it wound down to the valley.

It was a long day. I must have covered all of twenty-five miles. There was no doubt that it was too much for my leg. As I approached a small fishing village, it was swinging and flopping against my good leg. I found it almost unbearable when I was poorly received by the first three houses

I approached. It was late, after ten o'clock, and quite dark. No one would even come to the door in answer to my summons; there was the usual furtive whispering and patter of feet, but after a while silence.

Tired and sore, I sat down on the road and rested. Just as I was feeling drowsy and wondering if I could find some sort of outhouse, someone almost tripped over me. It was a Greek soldier, or rather an ex-soldier, still in what remained of his uniform.

When we had made ourselves known to one another, and I had explained my plight, he exclaimed:

'Come with me. Perhaps I can help you.'

He led off down a narrow street and out into the open country running down to the sea. We followed a rough track through the dark until the last houses of the village were over a mile behind. Then out of the gloom a small shack appeared. We approached this cautiously and, after listening carefully at the door for a few minutes, my friend knocked quietly and whispered:

'Papa, Papa, open the door, Papa. It is I, Lazarus, your son.'

There was a sound of footsteps, the door was thrown open, and a very old man waved us into the single room of the shack. The two Greeks embraced warmly, as though they had been long parted, and then Lazarus turned to me.

'This, Papa, is an Englezi. Will we help him tonight? He is ill and hungry and has no one to go to for shelter.'

The old man did not answer immediately. He went over to the open fireplace and prodded the embers there into life. He threw some more wood on the fire. Then he lit a taper from the flames and took it over to the far side of the room, from where he emerged presently with a lighted hurricane lamp. He held this up to my face and looked at me from every angle, all the time muttering into his beard. Finally he said in English:

'God save King George of England!'

'God save the King,' I agreed, wholeheartedly, 'so you can speak English, eh?'

The old fellow, evidently satisfied that I was quite harmless, purred at the thought that I could understand his English, particularly as his son was deeply impressed and was staring incredulously at him. However, he did not put it to further test and the rest of the conversation was in Greek. He told me how he had worked for the English in the First World War, and maintained that he had seen King George in Salonika ... he was referring to King George V, and I did not feel it necessary to tell him of his decease.

The son, Lazarus, did not stay with us long. He and his father went into a long whispered discussion near the door and then, after saying goodbye, he slipped off into the night. His father stood listening at the door for fully five minutes. I felt certain that Lazarus was a hunted man come down from the hills for this visit and was now, at some risk, on the way back to his hide-out.

We stoked up the fire, and made a hot drink from some dried leaves, which looked like and indeed smelled like a weed that grows on New Zealand river beds and is called 'lambs' ears'. After a brief talk I made my bed on a large pile of dry bean-pods in a corner of the room and, pleasantly warm from the fire, fell asleep.

The old man woke me before dawn, gave me some more 'tea' and asked me to be well away from his house before daybreak. He apologised for the lack of any food to offer me, but assured me that I would be well treated by the monks on the Holy Mountain. At the door, as I made my farewell and thanks, he drew himself up in military fashion jutted his chin and beard out in front of him, and chanted, 'God save King George of England!' He was still standing thus as I turned to wave from a hundred yards away. It was a lovely morning. The sun rose into a clear sky with tiny, rose-tinted wisps just above the horizon. The air was bracing and full of the strong tang of a fishing village.

There was no sign of any German vehicles, and the people I spoke to along the foreshore showed no alarm at my presence. There were some fine-looking boats drawn up on the sand and my hopes were high as I moved down to approach the fishermen who were preparing their nets for the day.

But, one by one, they all gave me the same answer. They shook their heads emphatically and said, 'You must see Salos. We cannot help you unless you see Salos.'

Salos, they told me, was the mayor. I found his house without much difficulty and knocked at the door. Mayor Salos was a large man with a dark but pleasant countenance.

He was not pleased to see me. He seemed to guess immediately that I was English, even before I had spoken a word. He closed the door behind him and pulled me into a closed courtyard on the side of the house.

'What do you want?' he said bluntly.

'A boat,' I replied, a little ruffled by his manner. He looked such an honest, pleasant fellow that it was somehow incongruous. 'A boat to take me to Turkey. I can pay a certain amount and will give you a cheque for the balance.'

'We don't want your money,' he replied testily, 'already I have sent over a hundred Englizi to Turkey and Imbros. For nothing. But now it is impossible. I cannot help you. You must go away from here.'

I could feel there was something behind his abruptness and, although my first thought was to turn and leave him, I asked him if he would explain why he had helped others, but would not consider helping me.

He frowned for a moment. Then he sighed, his face relaxed a little, and he motioned to me to sit down on the stonework of a well in the courtyard. He called up some instructions to a window above, and then turned to me.

'Very well,' he said, 'I will tell you. And then you will understand and go away as swiftly as you can. I alone of all the mayors along this coast rallied my people to help the English when they came defeated to us and asked for help. Many villages turned them away, but I could not. We fed every man who arrived here, though we ourselves had little enough. And we sent over a hundred on our own boats to Turkey. We lost four of our best boats, but we accepted this loss philosophically, as we knew we were doing a loyal and Christian deed. We expected no thanks, and certainly no money. It was enough for us to think we were saving the lives of these fair-haired lads, and sending them back to their homes.' He paused and his face worked as though he was finding it hard to continue. Then it came out in a rush, the words tumbling over one another and his voice rising.

'But then *they* came. They came in here one morning, two hundred of them, all armed to the teeth. The swine were all round the village before anyone was out of bed. They soon had us out. They went through every house, smashing, looting and striking anyone who got in their road. At first I was not very worried. We had never kept the British in the village, but in a hide-out up in the hills and, in any case I knew that the most recent batch of fugitives had left some days before on their way to Turkey. I was not worried, I say, I was not frightened. I treated them scornfully and told my people not to be worried. But they are devils ... devils! When they had finished their search the officer sent for me. He demanded to know where the English were. At first he played with me, and then he said he knew I had sent them to Turkey. He said he knew I helped all the

English who passed through. He demanded that I give him the names of at least five of my young men who had been taking the English to Turkey. I refused, but he said that by noon he would have the names or would shoot every man in the village. We talked it over. Some of the men, the single men, volunteered. I gave their names, together with my own, to the officer. The German laughed when he saw my name. He said it would be a better punishment for me not to be included.

'Later in the afternoon the officer ordered us all into the field by the church where the children play. We went quietly as we did not know ... the officer knew that all the boys were innocent of any crime, they were too young for the long trip to Turkey ... but when we were all in the field they took the boys ... one by one ... in front of us all ... in front of their mothers ... and shot them ... with their backs against the wall of the church ... one by one they killed them, shot them so that each tumbled in a heap over the first one. We tried to stop them, but they held us back with their bayonets ... old Mother Xanus pushed between the two of them to reach her Filipos, he was only seventeen. They swung her back at us by her skirts ... and they laughed. They laughed while two of our boys lay squirming in the grass and the other three were being lined up to follow.'

The poor fellow could go no further. He buried his face in his arms and, still standing, allowed sob after sob to shake his big frame. How shrewd the Germans had been! This mayor was suffering the death of those boys every day; no torture could be worse than the agony he was going through.

'You understand ... you understand,' he implored me, 'you can see now why I cannot help you?'

I could hardly bring myself to answer, there was such a lump in my throat.

'Of course, Salos, of course, I understand. Such a thing must never happen again. Thank you for your confidence ... and if it be of the slightest comfort to you, please be assured that I will do all in my power to bring those devils to justice. It may be a long time before I am in a position to do this, but I will never forget your story.'

We shook hands rather awkwardly over the framework of the well, and I made to go.

'You must go on to the Papas of the Holy Mountain. They will help you if they can.'

'Which is the best approach, Salos, along the northern shore or the southern?'

'There is little difference, but I think the southern is better. If you follow a small track which runs along by the village church it will take you through the great canal, and by midday you will be under the mountain.'

We shook hands again and I left the village. I found the track easily and was soon in a wide depression which I took for the remains of an historic engineering feat. Xerxes, with hundreds and thousands of slaves, had made the peninsula into an island, so that he could manoeuvre his fleet in battle. Even after so many centuries the steep sides were still visible, although fertile silt now replaced the water of the canal.

Presently the sea reappeared in front of me, and I swung south-east along the fields which ran down to the beaches below.

The sun was low in the sky as I approached the village of Pyrgos, the last before the Holy Mountain. Beyond the village the land began to rise steeply. Ahead of me, away up in the billowing clouds, a majestic peak towered over a long line of lesser peaks. All round its base and scattered up to its very snow-line were groups of strange-looking buildings, shining white in the rays of the setting sun. There was an atmosphere of serenity and peace.

I pressed forward eagerly. Already, I felt an excited premonition of the discoveries and adventures I was to have on the Holy Mountain. Warming me also, as I passed into the cypress trees, was a deep satisfaction at having reached my first goal.

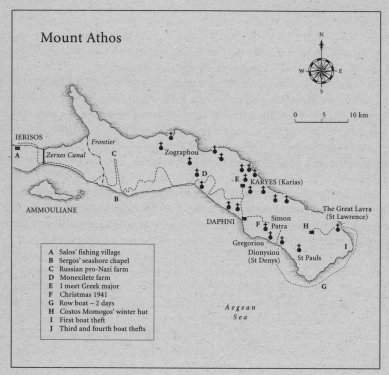

Map of Holy Peninsula

Chapter Thirteen

Life with the monks

Mount Athos, the Holy Mountain of Greece, is the easternmost of the three fingers which jut south from Macedonia. It consists of a rugged razor-back of mountains, rising at its apex to Mount Athos itself at 5,800 feet. From this chain great ridges sweep into the Aegean, dropping so steeply that large ocean-going liners and yachts in calm weather can come safely alongside its rocky base, although their anchors can never find bottom.

The history of this gaunt and forbidding mountain can be traced back beyond biblical days, either as a haven for brigands or, after the second century, as a hermitage and place of repose for the Byzantine religious orders. Tradition has preserved the legends of the foundation of the old monasteries and convents from the Byzantine Emperors, and also the colourful story of the visit of the Holy Virgin to the Mountain. Because of this, Mount Athos was dedicated to Her name, and under Her patronage.

In 845, during the reign of Theodora, the monks of Mount Athos took an active part in the restoration of their ruler, and accordingly in 855 Basil I, the Macedonian, assured the liberties of the various orders and the autonomy of the peninsula for all time. At about that time the few convents disappeared, and from then on no woman, indeed no female creature, was to walk across the isthmus for a thousand years.

Basking in the benevolent regard of all the great Orthodox monarchs of Russia and the Balkans, the peninsula flourished and wanted for nothing.

With their riches from the monarchs, and the slaves despatched from far-scattered kingdoms, they terraced the barren mountain and gathered fertile silt into the small areas where it could be held. When the slaves were gone the monks themselves continued industriously to build, stone by stone, the imposing, castle-like monasteries which have lasted to this day.

With the decline of the great empires and kingdoms, the monasteries also suffered. But in adversity they grew more spartan, more determined and more certain of their role in the changing world. Now today there are twenty-one large and small monasteries on the Holy Mountain and no fewer then eight thousand monks there have dedicated their lives to meditation and prayers, denying themselves the pleasures which the outside world find so important.

From the moment I crossed the line of cypress trees which marked the frontier of the Holy Mountain I felt I was stepping back hundreds of years. When, after climbing for half an hour or so, I looked down on a small bay, it was hardly a surprise to see a long narrow craft moving swiftly over the water, with ten or twelve tall, bearded figures capped and robed to their feet in black cloth, standing at long oars and chanting some weird rhythmic dirge in deep, resonant tones.

Presently, in front of me, another of these black-robed people appeared, winding down the track towards me, sitting side-saddle on a small donkey. As he drew level I found him to be a young boy, probably of fourteen years with, nevertheless, a sparse, fluffy down on his cheeks and jowl.

'God be with you, stranger,' he called, reining his donkey, 'and for where art thou bound?'

I felt tempted to reply in old-time speech, he spoke with such Elizabethan grace and charm.

'Good evening. I am an English officer and I seek shelter and sanctuary with the good monks of the Holy Mountain. Could you, perhaps, put me on the correct route to the nearest monastery?'

'I am very honoured to have met you,' said the youth gravely, 'I have a great regard for the English and will find it a pleasure to help you. But from where do you come, and which monastery do you wish to approach for sanctuary?'

There seemed nothing incongruous about explaining everything to a youth of fourteen, so I told him enough of my story to satisfy him. He sat all the while on his donkey, nodding his head wisely and courteously asking me to repeat the various parts of my story that he could not understand. I told him I was indifferent to which monastery I went that night, provided they were friendly and able to take me in.

'You are Christian ... yes? Orthodox?' he inquired, when I had finished.

'Certainly Christian, but not Orthodox. I am of the English Protestant Church,' I said. I was a little afraid that this young man might disapprove, might be intolerant of other religions.

'Yes, the English Protestant Church is almost as good as Orthodox,' he rejoined, 'but, of course, it makes no difference at the moment what your religion is. Only I am very pleased that you are not a Roman Catholic.' He slid down from the donkey. 'God is always watching and guiding those who love him. If I had not met you on this track I think you might well have run into great danger this evening. At the top of this hill is a small monastery maintained by the Monks of Zogafrau. Therein I study as a learner, a cadet. I and most of my colleagues are Russian and, with a very few exceptions, we see the English as in the right in the war. But we have some senior priests who have promised the Germans that they will advise them instantly when we give sanctuary to English fugitives. They have already denounced one noble man of your race who used to fly in the heavens in one of those strange things we often see now. You understand that by law now we may only give sanctuary for one day and one night ... and the Germans, if warned, might be waiting at the gate when you left.'

'What, then, do you advise?'

'Let us thank God for His providence in that I was here to stay you, and then you will follow me.'

We knelt down by the donkey and both prayed silently for a few moments.

Then the young monk led me along the track for a few minutes, until we came to a fork. We branched to the right and started to descend again on the other side of the spur I had been climbing. Presently we came into a clearing and were able to look down on to a small, sheltered bay. We could see a tiny stone cottage perched on a cliff above it. Adjoining this cottage was a small marble cross showing clearly through the gathering gloom. We tethered the donkey under an olive tree and scrambled down a steep and stony track.

As we approached the two buildings the door of the chapel opened and allowed a beam of soft candlelight to outline the figure of an old man standing in the doorway. He came to meet us. His flowing white beard reached a foot below his waist.

'God's blessing be ever with you, my friends!' he greeted us, little waves rippling down his beard as he spoke. 'Can it be that Providence has granted me company tonight?'

'God be with you, Father,' replied the youth. 'I am afraid that I may not stay with you more than a few minutes for, as you know, I must return to my senior. But this is Thomas, a fugitive Englishman, who seeks your hospitality and sanctuary.'

'Welcome, Thomas, welcome to whatever I have here in my keeping! It may be small and frugal, but it is all yours tonight! Come you within and join me in a meal.'

The young monk made a serious and stately farewell and disappeared into the darkness. I followed my venerable host inside the small cottage and sat down on the wooden bench he offered me. He at once prepared me a meal of tasty salted fish, spring onions and olives, which I ate with heavy maize bread and white wine. Sergos, for that was the old man's name, ate little and, as soon as I had finished, insisted on taking off my shoes himself and putting my feet in a bowl of warm water. Then, to my embarrassment, although it was also wonderful relief, he commenced to bathe and massage them gently, muttering and protesting over the small blisters along the toes and on the heels. When he had finished he dried them carefully and dabbed them all over with olive oil. The long walk, the thrill of having entered this strange kingdom, and the relief at having found such a homely haven combined to make me luxuriously tired, and when the old man showed me a small but impeccably clean guest room I curled up on the wooden bench there and fell immediately into a deep and restful slumber.

The sun was well up when I awoke next morning and when I arose and went in search of Sergos I found him washing my socks.

'Good morning, my young guest,' he beamed. 'I trust that you have slept well, yes?'

'I cannot remember such a wonderful night,' I told him. 'I honestly think it is the first time I have really relaxed for nearly a year. I feel wonderful now. But, Sergos, you must not wash my socks for me ... let me do it, I beg of you.'

'Indeed ... and you my guest! Certainly not!' replied Sergos, properly shocked. 'Kindly sit yourself in the sun and rest. We will have a meal presently.' And not only did he finish washing them, but later in the day he also darned them neatly and mended my shoes.

It was a glorious morning; the sun beat warmly down as I sat, completely tranquil, and enjoyed it all. The sea stretched wonderfully blue from a clear horizon to the frothy little wavelets surging to and fro on the bright sand of the beach below. How tempting it was to forget about the war for a while, to forget the Germans and the need to push on to Egypt.

After a while I took off my trousers and the bandages from my wound. I clambered down to the beach, and waded waist-deep into the cool, healing sea. All the time I had been in hospital I had longed to be able to do just this; it had seemed the ideal way of helping the shredded tissues to knit. Now, after the surfeit of walking I had forced upon it, the wound was inflamed and discharging freely ... the clean salt water lapping over it cleansed and soothed it wonderfully. It was a happy and restful morning.

We had a meal at midday as we sat at our rough wooden table in the sunlight and Sergos asked me to tell him of the outside world and the war. He was amazed to hear of the many things I told him, and would scarcely credit that men were able to drop from the skies by parachute with lethal weapons. He had been living on the Holy Mountain for sixty-three years, forty of them in his cottage, and he had only a hazy memory of life in the outer world. I tried to tell him of electricity and wireless, but realised that the credulous look he was trying so hard to keep up as a host was becoming a little fixed, so I desisted. I tried also to jog his memory of his early life under the Tzars of Russia, but he could only remember the magnificence of the Cossacks' horses and uniforms and the grandeur of the buildings in Moscow.

I bathed my wound in the sea again just before sunset, and Sergos was waiting for me on the beach as I waded in.

'Oh, my boy, my boy! What terrible thing has happened there? Who could have done such a thing?' His long beard rippled with his agitation. I told him as well as I could how I had been wounded and how the doctors had cut away so much dead flesh to save my leg. I also explained that it gave me little pain, the nerves being dead. But he refused to be pacified.

'We must take you to a doctor, and that as soon as possible,' he cried. 'Now come along with me, and straight to bed with you, come along!' and he assisted me up the slope as though I had just been wounded, and practically put me to bed. Then he prepared a wonderful dressing of cotton wool sodden with olive oil, with which he filled the cavity of the wound, covering it with my own freshly washed bandages. I passed another peaceful and contented night.

Though he protested, I was up very early in the morning and we went together to the tiny chapel to pray. Strongly made with hewn stone, the interior was no more than six feet across. It was full of rather too ornate brass and gilt work and framed pictures of haloed saints, with small oil lamps suspended from the roof by fine chain in front of each. Sergos genuflected before the picture of the Mother and Child, and then donned a stiff heavy surplice, laden with gilt-thread woven into patterns and pictures. He then pulled a heavy black cowl over his fez-like cap and shoulders. Solemnly and with the greatest of dignity the service commenced, a heartening example of true and earnest worship that seemed to fill the little church with a serene peace.

We had our breakfast in the early morning sun, enjoying the fresh air and the sparkling waves below.

'My boy,' said Sergos, as we pulled our chairs away from the table, 'my boy, I am not satisfied with your wound. We must see a doctor today.'

'I assure you, Sergos, that it is nothing to worry about. Indeed, every day I see some improvement. But if you wish I would like to show it to a doctor; sometimes I think that it discharges overmuch for a healthy wound.'

'Then, my boy, it is agreed. We will go up yonder this afternoon to the main monastery, where I know of a brother monk who has knowledge of medicine.'

'But Sergos, our young friend who brought me here warned that there are those at the monastery who would inform the Germans of the presence of any English. Surely it would be unwise therefore to show myself there?'

'Nonsense, the child should be soundly thrashed for such a suggestion. No Christian would behave in the manner you speak of, and certainly no member of the Sacred Monastery of which I am a member.'

Accordingly, after a small meal at midday, we locked the cottage securely, snuffed all the lamps in the chapel, and set off up the steep track to the monastery above.

After an hour of hard climbing we found ourselves on a flat plateau of some ten or fifteen acres, at the far side of which a high stone wall encircled some massive domed buildings.

'There it is,' said Sergos, pausing while I regained my breath. 'There is the monastery. Actually, it is only an annex to the main monastery, which is several hours away up the coast. These buildings were originally constructed for a hospital when there were many thousands of monks more than there are now. Today, however, it houses some fifty of our Brotherhood who tend the monastery farms in this region.'

In about half an hour we were at the great iron-studded gates that towered twenty feet above us. Sergos jerked an old and very rusty chain, and we could hear an answering bell from within. Presently the gates divided and were swung slowly inwards. No gatekeeper appeared from the lodge above the gateway and we proceeded unheralded into the wide courtyard enclosed within the walls. All around, black-robed figures moved in and out of various arched doorways, industrious and quite uninterested in our arrival. Sergos led me to the grandest of all the buildings and into the stone-flagged entrance hall. A young monk answered his deep summons and presently took him away, obviously to some senior priest or official. Ten minutes, twenty minutes passed, and I began to feel more and more uneasy when he did not re-appear, particularly as I could hear angry words and shouts in the distance.

After half and hour Sergos returned, looking terribly sad and crestfallen, his chin buried in his beard. He did not say a word, but took me quietly by the hand and led me out of the building, across the courtyard and under the great archway. Only when we were half a mile from the monastery and in the trees again did he attempt to speak.

'Ah, my boy, what a pitiable thing is war! That it should so warp the minds of men, even the Lord's followers in high places! That it should defeat the very principles of godly men, and make them forget the meaning of our blessed Christianity!' He sighed and shook his old head slowly, 'Thomas, my boy, they have been possessed. They have lost sight of our role on this Holy Mountain. They are frightened and will not help you ... they are very angry with me for the little the Lord allowed me to give you, and they say the Germans might destroy our monastery because of it.' He paused and muttered, half sorrowfully and half indignantly into his beard. 'And,' he added slowly, 'they have forbidden me the right, and my desire, that you should continue to stay with me. I must abide by their ruling, my boy.... You must go on your way and hope to find better men.'

Poor old fellow, he looked so terribly miserable. I took his hands in mine and pressed them warmly, thanked him earnestly for his hospitality, and asked him where best I should go to find shelter that night.

'You must follow this path,' he replied, pointing to a track winding away through the trees, 'until it reaches the end of this plateau. You will come to a smaller path there which will drop down into a long steep valley to the sea again. On the beach there are some monks in a small monastery farm, but I cannot say whether they will help you. I fear, Thomas, that it will be necessary for you to walk a further four hours to one of the greater Greek monasteries where, or so I am told, the English are always well received and the Germans flouted.'

We made an awkward and rather embarrassed farewell, and I set off into the olives. I looked back after a minute or so and saw that he was walking slowly back to the monastery.

After two hours of steady walking I could hear the waves breaking on the beach. Rounding a corner, I came out of the forest to see a group of houses in a clearing on the foreshore. It was already dusk and I decided that it would be out of the question to attempt to reach the allegedly friendly monastery that night. Accordingly I approached the gate in the wall which enclosed the houses and pulled the rusty chain.

A rather scruffy-looking monk answered my summons, peering suspiciously through an aperture in the gate before emerging.

'You are English,' he said, before I could introduce myself. 'You cannot come in here. Go away ... go away!'

'But surely,' I remonstrated, taken aback by his surly manner, 'you will not turn me away so many miles from the nearest shelter? It is almost night and I am very weary.'

'If you are here in the morning we will send for the Germans!' was the answer, and the door began to close in front of me.

I walked slowly along the beach. I found an abandoned boat-shed. It had no roof, but its three sound walls made a good shelter from the wind. I collected some small leafy branches and made a bed, and then carried in all the dry driftwood I could find on the beach. Then, with great care as I had but three matches, I kindled the flame and was soon warming myself in front of a cheery blaze.

I had just warmed a large stone to keep the cold from my back as I faced the fire, and was quietly whistling 'In a Monastery Garden', when I heard a movement near the open doorway. Two monks entered.

'Quiet! Quiet!' they remonstrated. 'You will have the Germans on all of us if you behave so foolishly. Why are you still here in our bay? You were told to move on!'

Furious at being spoken to as though I was a disputable tramp, I did not even stand to greet them.

'Now look,' I said, as aggressively as possible. 'You—sworn monks of the Holy Faith—have already shown yourselves to be un-Christian. Understand this and then go.... I am not moving from here tonight. Now please leave me and go back to your warm beds and comfort.'

'You must put out the fire; you cannot have a fire on this beach, it is dangerous; some German boat might see it and come in to investigate.'

'Oh, go away,' I replied. 'You act and talk more like old women than men. I have no blanket and therefore, if I am to stay alive outside your stone-hearted hospitality I must have a fire.'

They argued for a few minutes more, then left reluctantly, using language which one would have thought unheard of on the Holy Mountain.

I rewarmed my stone, stoked up the fire, and lay down to sleep, with the stars above for a roof. I slept spasmodically, awaking every half-hour or so to throw more wood on the fire.

I rose about five in the morning and, as the first rays of dawn were lightening the sea on the horizon, set off along the coast in the direction of the next monastery.

The track swung inland after a while and then began to climb steeply. Soon after sunrise I rounded a bend to behold a sight more in keeping with my first impressions of the Holy Mountain. Approaching me through the trees was a handsome, black-bearded monk mounted on the finest horse I had ever seen. It was a white Arab, perfectly poised and beautifully groomed. Black, highly polished harness and saddlery twinkling with silver and jewels completed the picture. I bowed as they drew near. The lovely stallion threw up its fine head and mane, nostrils quivering, as the monk reined.

'May God bless you and guide you, stranger,' said the monk, his white teeth flashing in his beard, 'and for where, may I ask, are you bound?'

I liked the look of him immediately. I told him of my hopes of sanctuary and ultimate escape to Turkey. He dismounted and led me into a sunny clearing some distance from the track, where he tethered the horse and sat down on the trunk of a fallen tree.

'My friend,' he said, when I was comfortably seated next to him, 'I am very glad to have met you. I would like you to do me the honour of joining me in a small breakfast while you tell me of your adventures.'

Mt Athos at sunset

Ralph Brewster, *The 6,000 Beards of Athos*

I was particularly hungry and enjoyed the meal of bread, olives and cheese he produced. I told him of the kindness of the old monk Sergos and then of the inhospitality of the monks of the nearby bay. He was furious at this, and held up a well-kept hand in front of my face in some signal or gesture I could not understand. I asked him to explain.

'Why, surely, you know what that means,' he said, repeating it. 'I show to you the fingers of my hand ... you see that although all are fingers some are shorter than others, some thinner also. It is the same with men. We are all men, but some are good, some are evil. It is so with every race, whether English, Greek, or even German. But I am sorry, my young friend, that you have been treated thus, and it will be my duty to bring those white-livered scoundrels in front of their seniors for discipline.'

When we had finished he cut the remaining bread into two portions, giving me the larger. Then he mounted, and made to continue on his way.

'*Au revoir*, Thomas,' he said. 'I will see you again before long. Continue on your way and you will find better men and true Christians at the end of your day's march. In the meantime, God be with you.'

'God be with you, Father,' I responded, and we parted on our different roads.

My way led me along the lower slopes of one of the lesser mountains, always climbing and looking down steep inclines on to rugged but attractive coves and bays. Ahead of me were the steeper and bush-clad ridges of Athos itself, with small clearings dotted with olive and cypress trees, which showed the monastery farms and vineyards. Soon after noon I dropped down to the beaches again on a very steep and rough track.

I realised that my leg was more troubled than usual, so I took off the bandages to bathe it in the sea. I was horrified to find it a revolting yellow colour, the cotton wool sopping with an unusually foul discharge. I rinsed the bandages carefully in the sea, waded in to bathe it, and then re-dressed it as quickly as possible. With some panic I realised that it had taken a turn for the worse, that perhaps I had used some infected bandage or cotton wool, and that I must press on with all haste to find someone who could give me treatment should gangrene develop.

In my hurry I did a very foolish thing. The track ahead was visible, and I could see that it followed the coast with steep climbs over the numerous ridges that enclosed the bays and coves. I decided, therefore, not to follow the path chosen by those who lived on the Mountain and knew their land, but to try the possibly shorter route around the rocks of the foreshore. Indeed, for the first hour or so I found it a great saving; the tide was as far out as was possible in the Aegean, and from one sandy beach to the next there was only about three hundred yards of rocks to negotiate.

But I soon found myself in difficulties, having to slide down steep fissures and to leap across alarming gaps with the waves surging angrily underneath.

I had just come to my senses and resolved to make the present obstacle the last before I rejoined the track, when I trod on an unstable rock, lost my balance and fell heavily on my thigh. My wound was forced against a rough, mussel-covered rock. Everything went black for a moment or two and I felt weakly sick; I vomited a little before I was able to get to my feet again. My thigh felt absolutely numb but, before I had gone more than fifty painful yards, I could feel the blood squelching in my shoe.

I stumbled off the beach, found the path and pushed slowly on, horribly frightened that I had opened such a haemorrhage that I would not have the strength to reach help.

My progress had degenerated into desperate spurts of no more than ten yards between long rests when I rounded the extremity of a ridge and saw below me a large stone house with a church attached, nestling on a small plateau overlooking a wide sweeping bay. Several figures in black were seated on the wooden benches arranged around the edge of a large stone-flagged courtyard.

I stumbled down the track which led to it, and, mustering all my determination, mounted the dozen or so steps which led up on to the courtyard. All the monks turned towards me, and I made my way over to their obvious senior, an old, white-bearded dignitary seated in the corner. Some emotion, or some involuntary urge, prompted me to act a part in this serene picture. Before I knew what I was about I was on my knees and kissing his proffered hand. No one seemed to find this in any way unusual. The old man tilted my forehead gently back with his hands before he spoke.

'May God bless you and allow us to help you, my child,' he said quietly. 'I can see you are in some need. From where do you come and what would you have us do?'

'Oh, Father ...' I had commenced to reply, when one of the younger monks gave an exclamation and pointed excitedly to my trouser-leg.

'Look, look!' he cried. 'There is blood. This man is sorely wounded ... look at his sodden clothes and the stains on the stones where he kneels.... He is wounded, I tell you!'

There was a flurry of horrified comments and instructions, and in a few minutes I had been rushed inside, undressed, and a firm pad of clean linen bound tightly round my thigh. Two of the younger monks watched me anxiously from either side of the wooden bed on which I was lying. We exchanged names and I found that one was Nikolas and the other Leonides. I told them of my adventures, very briefly, and asked them to which of the great monasteries they belonged.

'We are student monks of the Holy Monastery of St Denys,' replied Nikolas, the elder of the two, 'and we are sworn to this monastery farm for the two years of our apprenticeship before we take the final oath of renunciation. Here we have the famous vineyards of Monexilete, this farm producing the wine which bears its name and which graces His Hellenic Majesty's table in Athens.'

Nikolas spoke quite fair English. He told me he had studied many years before in the American University in Salonika. He was a small quiet man, with a short dark beard and, in contrast, soft blue eyes. He was intensely interested in my story and I could see that he was bubbling over with questions. His friend, Leonides, also seemed more alert and curious about the outside world than the average monk I had so far met. Leonides was taller than Nikolas by some five inches and wore a longer beard than the older man. When he smiled, which was often, he displayed strong attractive teeth marred by too much gold.

When I had rested they brought me a satisfying meal of shell-fish, stewed in olive oil, and fresh bread. Then, with great pride, they produced a large stone flagon of their famous wine. This wine, they told me, was too strong, too wonderfully rich, to be drunk undiluted. They poured perhaps two inches into my pewter pot and filled it to the brim with fresh water. It cleansed and pleased the mouth, quenched thirst, tickled the palate and sent a warm glow coursing through the veins. I drank deeply, enjoying it to the full, and feeling that somehow this wonderful soothing fluid would replace a little of the blood I had lost.

That evening all the monks except the Abbot came into the room in which I lay on my wooden pallet. There was a large open fireplace on the side, and they all gathered round it on roughly hewn wooden benches. Four of them came in later with the trunk of a great tree; it was at least two feet six inches through and five feet long. Everyone crowded around and jockeyed it across the room and into position, at the back of the fireplace, where it slowly began to burn. They told me that such a log would burn as a 'backlog' for several days; every morning it would require only scraping and a little fanning, and it would spark up again.

My adventures and news of the outer world formed the early part of the conversation, but after a while it became general and I was amazed at the zest and good fellowship that came with the telling of simple stories of the day's happenings. The various speakers were an extraordinary mixture, both of age and type, but as each of the eleven told his tale the remainder listened with genuine interest and pleasure. One told of his strenuous efforts with the fishing-nets in the bay and the disappointing results, another of a peculiar knot with the appearance of a human head he had found while pruning the grapes, another on the insistence of his mule on having a nibble of grass at the end of each row of tilling. The broad-shouldered fellow with the thick oily curls hanging two feet down his back told of a drunken rat he had caught while inspecting the great wine vats below the building, and the tired-looking monk-cook revealed how very nearly he had sent the Abbot a potato for his supper without noticing that it had a large grub in its centre. And so they continued. These men were content in their own little world.

They left early and I settled down to sleep. The panic and worry I had felt in the afternoon was replaced by a marvellous sense of comfort and security. Outside I could hear the splashing and gurgling of a small mountain stream, and in the distance the call of some night bird to its mate.

I was sleeping deeply some hours later when a light tapping came into my dreams to disturb me. I was reminded of schooldays when we youngsters would make music on the desks with rulers to the exasperation of the teacher. When we tapped the ruler on the desk close to our hand there was a deep sound, and as we tapped progressively down to the end of the ruler the sound took a higher pitch, so that we could simulate a tumbler being filled with water or any simple tune. Now in this strange old-world land the same sounds of wood on wood played on my consciousness, a queer stirring sequence of notes rising and falling all the time. I woke to find that the noise was there in fact. In the darkness outside the window someone was tapping a frenzied tune.

Presently, one by one, the various monks shuffled into the room and stirred the fire into being again. They told me that the strange music outside was their summons to Midnight Mass, and when they had tidied their tousled clothes, in which they had obviously slept, they passed out again. In a few minutes the wood tapping eased off on to lower and softer notes, and then finished with three distinct raps. As I dropped off to sleep again I could hear voices blended into a low monotone as the monks chanted their prayers and hymns.

I felt much better in the morning, although I still had quite a headache and a heavy listless feeling. The wound, which was after all the main consideration, was comfortable and warm in its firm bandages. I thought that I could have got up quite easily, and taken things very quietly, but the monks would not hear of it. Indeed, for five whole days, I was kept in bed and treated as a star patient and a guest of honour, fed on the best food they could provide and fussed over as though I was desperately ill.

One morning a cheery voice was heard outside and a clatter of horse's hooves sounded on the stones of the courtyard outside. Both Nikolas and Leonides leapt to their feet and bounded outside. I could hear them enthusiastically welcoming someone. Presently they all entered and I was quite thrilled to find the visitor was the handsome monk who had given me breakfast when I had met him on his white Arab horse some four days before.

'Ah, Thomas, my English friend of the road!' he exclaimed striding, hands outstretched, across the room, his long black robes swishing as they flowed behind him, 'how nice to see you! God is indeed good that He has arranged for us to meet again so soon.'

He hugged me as I sat up in bed, and kissed me on both cheeks. Nikolas and Leonides stood back, smiling at his exuberance.

'So, you have met our noble colleague,' laughed Nikolas. 'It is amazing that he knows so many, that he has so many friends!'

'And what is more amazing still,' put in Leonides, smilingly bantering the well-dressed newcomer, 'is that all who meet him out on the road like him immediately ... yet in places I know of he is not always popular. Eh, Simonos, am I not right?'

All three of them joined in hearty laughter. I asked Nikolas to explain the reason for their mirth.

'Well,' replied Nikolas, glancing with amusement at Simonos, 'our friend here is, as you see, a man of some means as compared with us humbler people. He can afford the finest mount in Macedonia, wear the best clothes on the Sacred Mountain. For Simonos comes from a wealthy and famous Greek family, indeed, has Royal blood in his veins. Most of us on the Mountain are proud that he has chosen the life of the monk when so much was open to him, but there are those who do not always like him. In his monastery he sometimes holds high posts, because of his accomplishments, but more often his unruly tongue gets the better of him and he is either relegated to minor posts or punished otherwise. At the moment he is serving a sentence of banishment. He is denied the right to enter his monastery for three months.'

'Good heavens, how terrible, Simonos!' I said. 'Whatever will you do?'

'Ah, do not worry yourself, my friend,' he replied, his eyes dancing with amusement. 'I always look forward to my periods of banishment. It makes an excellent opportunity to visit all my friends on the Mountain. Remember that there are twenty-one great monasteries here as well as countless rich farms I may visit and enjoy. I have no complaints!'

The three of them gathered around my bed and fell to discussing the best way of aiding me to freedom. To my surprise they all knew about the submarine *Papanikolas*, and said that it had taken some Greek officers from the lonely coves of the Holy Mountain on quite a few occasions.

Simonos had, in fact, seen its long black form in a certain bay one moonlight night.

They had a plan to make contact with the captain, and late that afternoon Simonos left full of optimism to execute it. He was to have returned in two days, but I never saw him again. A series of messengers arrived from him during my stay; they all slunk in with theatrical secrecy, but brought the same negative news. My hopes fell again to the frustrated despair I found normal now that the winter gales were threshing the Aegean.

After my five days in bed I spent a further five at the farm getting my strength fully back. They would not hear of my helping them in their daily work, but would allow me to go with them when they went out into the fields to work. The weather was not too bad and I was able most days to sit in the sun and watch them. We always took our meals out with us ... there was no breakfast, the first meal of the day was bread and olives with wine at midday.

The work at that time of the year was the close pruning of the now leafless grapevines. The monks remained in their long robes and black caps, although I cannot imagine a more unsuitable dress for such work, particularly as the ground was soft and, in places very muddy. They had old-fashioned saws, with long, curved blades, and they approached each vine with a slow deliberation. I have no doubt that their work was of the highest order, but I had never seen a task approached in such a laborious and uneconomic manner. One rather simple fellow had a fez or cap some sizes too small for him. Every time he bent down to prune it fell off, and his long hair tumbled over his face. It did not seem to occur to him to leave it off for a while; time meant absolutely nothing to him, nor to his fraternity. He just patiently picked it up each time, readjusted the bun of his hair, and put it on again.

I greatly appreciated the monks' hospitality and the insight they gave me into their simple and happy life. When at last I made my farewells to them, early one morning, I left the farm with quite serious thoughts about the merits of a monk's life on the Holy Mountain.

I travelled a good fifteen miles of rugged mountain country that day. At nightfall I arrived at the gates of a large monastery and was admitted on my presentation of a note from Nikolas. This was Simonos' monastery and when I told the monk who brought my meal into the small guest room that I had recently seen him, he bristled with interest and demanded all the news I could give of the miscreant. Simonos was obviously quite a legend amongst his fraternity.

My path on the following morning took me up the side of the mountain through acres of gnarled olive trees, until I looked down on the wide blue horizon of the Aegean Sea. In the far distance the island of Lemnos rose out of the sea in a hazy outline, while in the foreground the white sails of the various fishing and trading craft tacked to and fro. Soon after midday a large German transport plane, its black crosses showing clearly on its ugly fuselage, lumbered slowly over the saddle under the peak of the Holy Mountain and out of sight into the haze over Lemnos.

Late that afternoon I arrived at the highest point of the road which wound over the saddle to the capital of the little kingdom, and approached the gaunt-looking monastery there for shelter. But they would not hear of it. To them the fear of the Germans was much nearer than at the other monasteries, for both soldiers and sailors on patrols and visits often traversed the pass from one side of the peninsula to the other. And it was rumoured that there was a large party of Germans in Karias at that time, searching all monasteries for escaped prisoners. I was advised to try the houses farther up on the mountainside, above the pass. After hours of climbing to seemingly inaccessible crags, I tried my luck at a series of small houses, but always with the same result.

Becoming apprehensive, I hurried down the mountainside again, winding through the silent forest fearfully; I heard the mournful yowling of wolves in the distance. One of those horrible creatures actually brushed past me in the dark, and for half an hour or so I imagined that it had turned round to follow me, for I could hear twigs snapping close at hand, and the shadows thrown by a waning moon seemed to move into life.

My heart in my mouth, cold and lonely, I had started into a frenzied run through the trees, when out of the shadows came a small donkey bearing a heavy-moustached man. I grasped the stranger's proffered hand eagerly.

'Well, well,' said the stranger, dismounting by standing firmly on his feet and allowing the donkey to walk out from under him. 'So I meet an Englishman. And for where are you bound?'

'I had intended to stay in one of these farms for the night and to push on to Karias tomorrow,' I replied, 'but these people are very frightened and tell me that there are soldiers in Karias.'

'Well, you would not make Karias on foot tonight. You don't seem very well; are you all right?'

'I have a wound which has done enough for today. Where do you think I might find shelter? I think it is going to snow shortly and there are too many wolves around here for my liking.'

'These people should take you in, but I know what old women they can be at times. Ah, well, you had better come with me.'

With that he turned the donkey round, insisted that I should sit on it, holding my legs off the ground, and we set off. We wound down mile after mile through the forest.

In some strange manner, I felt at home with this big, confident stranger. Walking by the side of the donkey with one of his large hands steadying me, he told me that he also was a fugitive, but with a difference. He was not trying to leave Greece, he was endeavouring to organise forces of resistance within the country. A Major in the Greek Regular Army, he had studied for years in the French Military Academy. He had been captured by the Germans north of Salonika, had escaped, and after the capitulation organised a successful sabotage of an important bridge over the Struma. Because of this there was a price on his head and he was lying low for a while.

After three hours the track evened out, and we came to the sea, where houses appeared in the weak moonlight. The Major tethered the donkey under a tree. Then we crept with the greatest of caution through some bushes and undergrowth, climbed through a window, and found ourselves in a dark but dry room of a fairly large house.

The Major was quite at home and, when we had closed and securely locked the window, he lit a candle which was stuck on to the surface of a rough table. There was no other furniture. He explained quietly to me that this was one of the many hostels maintained for monks on pilgrimage to this or that sacred chapel, and for the wayfarer generally. He did not intend to tell the monk in charge that he was harbouring an Englishman that night, but would collect some blankets which we would share.

In addition to blankets he brought back some hot broth and bread as well as some cotton wool and clean rags for my wound. We slept on the floor.

In the morning the Major smuggled me out of the building into the nearby trees and there brought me a good meal to set me off for the day.

I thanked him heartily and left him, winding up the mountain again towards a monastery he had recommended—the monastery of Simon Petra. After climbing for perhaps an hour I came on to a sort of plateau contained by steep cliffs on three sides, and having a weird quietness broken only by the sound of falling water. This last came from a fifty-foot waterfall tumbling over the lip of the centre cliff and falling on great boulders below. I made my way over to it and had a good wash and clean up. It was the morning of the 24th December 1941, and I wanted to be well spruced up for Christmas Eve.

With a contrariness which I found quite in keeping, the Holy Mountain did not consider that the next day was Christmas. They lived by the old time, the Bible time, which had been good enough for their forerunners. Their dates were thirteen days behind those of the outer world and they still had a further fortnight of fasting before the great celebrations of the birth of Christ. Still I had high hopes that I would find a comfortable haven for the night and the morrow.

Presently I came over the ridge of a spur, to see the monastery in front of me. I had never seen a building so awe-inspiring. It was perched on the very lip of a sheer hundred-foot cliff, below which the ground fell away at a steep angle to the sea thousands of feet below. My first impression was that it looked terribly insecure, as though the slightest

Monastery of Simon Petra, Mt Athos   WBT collection

puff of wind would send it toppling down on to the rocks. As I gazed at the great ramparts towering above, with their background of billowing white clouds, I thought how near it all was to my childhood conception of a fairy castle.

From the spur it appeared to be quite close, a matter of no more than a mile across the deep, intervening valley, but to reach Simon Petra I had to cover all of eight long miles, around the head of this valley and then down a narrow and rocky spur. At the end of this spur a slender neck of rock supported a track which made the only access to the outcrop on which the monastery was built.

There were the usual tremendous double doors, studded with bolts and wrought-iron designs. They were slightly ajar, so I pulled the bell rope and waited just inside.

After a while, as there was no response to my repeated ringing, I meandered along a cobbled alley between high walls until I arrived in a large courtyard, completely enclosed by four or five storeys of old stone buildings. There was still no one in sight, so I made my way over to the finest in appearance and walked down the high corridor.

As I went on, the furniture and drapings grew more and more splendid, until a turn in the corridor revealed as fine a sight as I had seen in any castle. Both walls were hung in magnificent tapestries at least twenty feet high and fifty in length, while the deep red carpet on which I walked in my muddy shoes was inches thick and springy. Old-fashioned plush and gilt chairs, severe and high-backed, were placed at intervals between the Gothic archways of the windows, and these archways were draped in splendid curtains. The view outside was enchanting. The outer wall seemed to be built flush with the edge of the cliff, and one looked as though from an aeroplane down on to a limitless expanse of sea over a mile below.

Confused at all this splendour, and feeling out of place in my rough clothes, I was on the point of turning back when two monks approached me from the end of the corridor. They were only mildly surprised to find an English officer unannounced inside their monastery and, after welcoming me civilly, they led me along to meet the Abbot.

The Abbot was very charming. He sent for coffee, and we had it together on a wooden balcony hung precariously from the outer wall. He explained that it was quite out of the question for him to consider harbouring me for any period in the monastery.

'We have been threatened,' he said, seriously, 'that to succour English prisoners is forbidden. A Major from the *Wehrmacht* was here not more than a week ago and he said we must choose between continuing our peaceful mission and annihilation. The officer said that were we to be discovered flouting their commands he would send an aeroplane with bombs and topple us into the sea below.'

I glanced involuntarily over the edge of the balcony down on to the foam-fringed rocks far beneath. It was not unrealistic to imagine the fiendish delight of a Stuka pilot at such a spectacular target. However, I hastened to reassure the Abbot. Surely no one, I reasoned, would be so dastardly as to destroy the age-old sanctuary, and in so doing kill utterly defenceless men? The Abbot, however, had few illusions in regard to the Nazi.

'Child,' he said, 'do not try to teach me anything about those men. Years before you ever left your far-off country I had people of all creeds here who had been hunted from their peaceful homes in Europe by these people. Were you to know even some of the tragic stories that were brought to me by fugitives, you would understand that these Nazis stop at nothing.'

I asked him, therefore, whether it was impossible to give me shelter.

'I am not unaware,' he replied, 'that tomorrow is your Christmas Day. Germans or no, I will not have anyone spending their Christmas in the open. I cannot risk the monastery by allowing you our guest room, but I would be pleased if you will permit me to make you comfortable tonight in one of our houses just outside.'

Presently I found myself in a large stone building some little distance from the narrow spur leading on to the monastery. There were two men there, also wayfarers, sitting by a large open fireplace. They made room for me without much enthusiasm, and after a while a monk brought the three of us a meal. As it grew later we all stretched out on the floor in front of the fire and after a desultory conversation settled down to sleep. I did not get much sleep, however, as my colony of lice had appeared again and, no doubt liking the unusual warmth from the fire, they held a field day on my chest and back.

The 25th December broke clear and cold. As part of my agreement with the Abbot of Simon Petra I left just before daybreak for another house, where I was to be permitted to spend the sacred day. After I had been walking for an hour the sky over the Holy Mountain turned a soft salmon-pink. It deepened steadily into scarlet, diffusing lighter shades into the clouds around the peak and into the snow-covered crags. It was so beautiful that I caught my breath. I moved off the track a little and found a natural altar of rock. Here I knelt facing the Mountain, allowing my thoughts to dwell on Christmas, and on my home so far away, where my mother and father would be rising early on the farm to reach our village church in time for Communion.

As I had been told, there was no one in the tiny, single-roomed house when I arrived. But there was a large pile of wood placed in readiness in front of an open fireplace and a jar of wine together with a parcel of food on the small table. I felt myself well served in the circumstances, lit the fire and settled down to a lonely but quite comfortable Christmas. Most of the afternoon was profitably devoted by going inch by inch over each article of my clothing and reducing the colony of lice.

The next morning, Boxing Day, I continued on the track which wound up and down the ridges along the south coast of the peninsula. Evening found me at the gates of the small but renowned Monastery of St Denys. I approached the gate-keeper's lodge, which was opposite the main gates, and told the old man there that I had been friends with his fraternity on the farm at Monexilete. He was pleased to have news of them and asked me to join him in a cup of coffee. Presently he went into the monastery to seek permission for me to enter. He returned in a few minutes, quite agitated.

'You must lie down!' he said, hurriedly. 'Lie down here on my bench. You really look quite ill, you know, yes, quite ill!'

'But, Papa,' I remonstrated, 'I feel well today. I had a good sleep last night and my wound feels comfortable!'

'Your wound ... you have a wound ... where is it; is it at all bad?' He seized upon the fact of my being wounded with such an obvious relief that I had guessed what his predicament was before he said, somewhat lamely, 'You see, my boy, I wanted to make quite sure that you would be admitted into the monastery ... and I told a little untruth. I described you as ill to my Abbot, and he is sending out our hospital monk, Demetrius, to see you. But, as you are wounded, I have really spoken the truth and all will be well.'

I laughed at the blunt admission, and found I liked this old fellow immediately.

In a few minutes a younger monk arrived with an important look about him and a medicine bag in his hand. Quickly and seriously, he felt my

Monastery of St Denys

forehead, took my pulse, and looked at my tongue, all in a business-like manner.

'He has a wound,' said the gatekeeper, 'have a look at that, for I am sure it is troubling him.'

The younger man undid the bandage around my thigh and stood back in astonishment. I always enjoyed the incredulous look people assumed when they first saw the ragged gash. The gatekeeper peered over the shoulder of his compatriot, mouth agape and speechless.

Thus, my wound again turned out to be the admission card to safety and comfort. In a very few minutes I was hurried into the monastery and put to bed in the room they reserved as a hospital. The Abbot came down to see me as my leg was being comfortably dressed. He was a giant of a man, much younger than I would have expected, and he entered, beaming a warm welcome, his large wooden staff of office held across his chest.

The monks on the Holy Mountain were fasting for their own Christmas, thirteen days after that celebrated by the west, and in St Denys they ate only at midday, and then only of olives and dry bread, with water. They adhered to this diet rigidly and cheerfully. But, with some amusement, the Abbot ruled that as a Protestant guest in their midst I should eat of the food they were denied.

Thus, I had fresh fish, mussels and even octopus. Cooked in a satisfying stew, this was very like a good mutton. The monks of St Denys lived as a community, as opposed to other monasteries where they lived properly *monos* or apart from one another. Because of this, I was told, they were not permitted red meat in any form. Christ, they explained, lived only on the fruits of the soil and the white flesh of the fish of the sea, and they as his followers did likewise. Thus octopus was a real favourite with them, and their faces were very long when one was caught during the fast.

One evening soon after my arrival, a short, middle-aged monk came in and spoke to me in English with a terrific American twang. This was 'John' or Yannos, who had been in the States from his early boyhood until some years before the war when, on the death of his wife, he had come to the Holy Mountain for peace and seclusion. From him, in many pleasant hours of conversation, I gained an insight into the monastic life.

After the initial three days in bed I was permitted to get up provided I did not do too much, and I used to make my way up to John's small room. He had sent to America for paints and curtains and had decorated it to look like a cabin in the *Queen Mary*, in which he had voyaged to

Europe. The walls were painted white and blue, his wooden bench or bed was built in behind curtains to appear like a bunk, and the window had been replaced by a slab of timber in which was cut a large porthole. As the room faced the sea, and no land was anywhere visible from it, the effect was amazingly realistic.

'Good day, how are you today?' he would demand, when I arrived to see him. 'Come into my cabin, it is warmer than up on the deck,' and he was right. His 'cabin' as he called it, was by far the warmest spot in the monastery, and with a deep fall of snow outside I found it a comfortable retreat. We spent hours discussing the history of Athos and the merits of the monastic life.

'There have been learned men on this Holy Mountain since before the memory of man,' he told me. 'Before the advent of Our Lord there were philosophers who lived here as hermits and studied the wonders of nature and the blessings of the Lord. They had certain premonitions that the Master was coming.

'Then, years later, after Calvary, great men of the Church and the Disciples of Our Lord came here to found the great monasteries which to this day stand on the peninsula. As you know, there are now twenty-one monasteries and perhaps ten thousand monks in all scattered around the Holy Mountain.

'Each of these monasteries is ruled today as it was eight hundred or a thousand years ago. Twelve of the most worthy monks are appointed and these represent the twelve disciples of Christ. They all assume the names of these disciples, changing each year. They sit in Government round a table at which a thirteenth place is left vacant and thus decide for the Master what is best for the monastery.

'From each of the monasteries a representative is nominated for the Central Government at Karias, and from these twenty-one representatives the "Twelve" for the whole peninsula are chosen. The Holy Mountain is an autonomous state, a theocracy, whose existence is recognised by the Athens Court and by all the great powers. Except, of course, the Nazis and their like. But we pay no taxes, nor is there duty as the world knows it on any articles which come in or go out.

'At one time the monasteries were wealthy beyond imagination. The Tzars of Russia and all the Orthodox Royalty of the Balkan countries gave annually such fabulous sums that each monastery has gold plate enough to feed a great city. In those days, too, there were many, many more thousands of us, and we owned nearly the whole of Thrace.

'Gradually, we have been driven into the peninsula by wars and revolutions. The Turkish hordes fought in these mountains and we resisted, building ramparts and walls around our churches and fighting the Ottoman with sword and fire, with pitch and boiling water until we drove them off. But we lost many priceless relics to their looting, and some of our old churches were razed to the ground. You will see their ruins to this day.

'After the Great War, which finished for you people in 1918, but for Greece not until 1922, we gave the whole of the rich wheat-land which lies between Salonika and here to the refugees from Greece-in-Turkey, which was ceded to Turkey by the Great Powers. These refugees from Smyrna arrived destitute, and only the charity of the Holy Mountain sustained them from starvation and oblivion.

'From that time we have lived on our own resources, on the olive plantations and vineyards, and from the small acres of wheat we are able to grow. The Russian Revolution denied us our greatest source of revenue, for the Tzars were always most generous.

'But, as you have seen, we lack none of the essentials for a simple life of prayer and devotion. I sometimes think we are better now that we must work for the food we eat and the wine we drink.'

One day I asked him where all the monks came from, what prompted them into a life of seclusion, and what their vow of renunciation involved.

'We come,' he said, 'from the outer world for a multitude of reasons. Some for sanctuary, some because of great grief or disillusionment. Some of us awoke in the night, or paused in the execution of some simple task and suddenly, inexplicably, thought on the meaning of our existence on this earth. We saw for the first time that our pursuits which seemed important before were futile, worthless. Straightway, we quitted everything wherever we were, America, Australia, or home in Greece and, like the prodigal son, came humbly to the Mountain to ponder further.

'But by far the greater number of monks come at an earlier age, from good families of the Orthodox Faith scattered through the world.

'For many years, indeed for many centuries, it was the custom to give the second son to the Holy Church; some even gave their first and only child. These youths, or children, for they were and are often still only ten and eleven years old, come into the monasteries much as apprentices come into trades in the outer world. They are schooled in the ways and teachings of the Master. When they reach their majority they are catechised, and if they are suitable they are invited to renounce all the pleasures and whims of the outer world and to enter into the peaceful Brotherhood of the monastery. Very few fail to do so.

'What does this vow of renunciation mean? ... well, it differs according to the man who makes it. Certainly one is rigidly denied access to the temptations of the world, but one is also given a large measure of choice how one will serve the monastery and the Master.

'You know of the family arrangement we adopt, where annually domestic duties are divided among us? In addition to this each monk is to decide himself, according to his desires and abilities, whether he will be a warden of the game in the Mountain, or a worker in the vineyards, or a fisherman ... or whether on the other hand he will become a painter, a theologian, or an historian. Others show by their devotion that they were intended to serve at the Master's table and they are given careful tuition to aid them on the difficult road to priesthood.

'To all of us comes the satisfaction of a life devoted to Our Lord and of working together as He intended, in a happy community. And when we grow old and cannot be of much use we graduate to the Old Monks' quarters, where the aged are looked after with due veneration and respect by the younger monks.'

On one occasion John took me to see the Old Monks. Twenty of them were seated in a room which was, to say the least of it, greatly overheated. They ranged in age from seventy to the oldest, a toothless veteran of ninety-five. Two or three of them were quite querulous, one indeed was crying bitterly when we entered, but for the most part I could not help being impressed at the contented atmosphere of their room.

They were of all classes ... two old priests, a cultured astronomer, some obviously well-educated men, and also the ex-fisherman, the ex-cook and the ex-gardener. But they all seemed to get on famously. One tall and rather angular old fellow of at least eighty was most interested to hear that I came from the under side of the globe. From a large cupboard in the wall he produced a rough sphere on which the continents of the world had been painted. He demonstrated to the less well informed where Greece was and then asked me to show them New Zealand. To my chagrin it was not shown on the globe at all, nor was Australia, and I thought they all looked a little dubious when I maintained that their globe was some centuries out of date. However, the tall fellow stood by me stoutly. He had been overseas in his youth and had always thought on entering the monastery that the globe was not quite complete. Australia and New Zealand, he explained to his audience, were little places and, like many other small islands, not shown on all the maps.

I stayed at the Monastery of St Denys for nine days in all. I knew that the Abbot was more than willing that I should spend most of the winter with them in spite of the ever-present danger of discovery by the Germans; but he was also very worried about my wound. One day, he told me that he wished me to go to the great Monastery of Lavra, or St Lawrence, where an old friend of his was a qualified doctor. Demetrius was a little hurt, I thought, but supported his senior. I was told to prepare myself for the journey, which would be by sea to save me many miles of difficult country.

I went up to John's 'cabin' to say goodbye. He was very sorry that I had to go, for I think he quite liked to talk English. I asked him seriously before I left how best I could go about getting a boat to Turkey just as soon as the weather abated enough to be able to put to sea in any safety.

'The monks of Lavra are very wealthy,' he said, 'and have many boats. I think they will help you. I will give you a note to the same doctor our Abbot has recommended, and ask him to do all in his power to aid you. And remember that if all else fails you will always be welcome here again.'

When I had gathered up my few belongings all my friends came with me out of the main gates and down the steep steps which wound down to the sea. There, waiting to make his farewell, was the Abbot himself, wooden mace in hand. Held away from the hewn rock landing stage by two monks was a large rowing boat, pointed at both ends. Before clambering aboard I knelt with my ankles on the fringe of the swirling waves while the Abbot placed a hand on my head and blessed me.

The two monks stood shoulder to shoulder, facing the direction in which we were travelling, and rowed long oars which rested in wooden forks two feet above the side of the boat. I sat in the seat enclosed by the pointed stern.

It was a long trip, two days in all. On the first day we rounded the end of the peninsula and travelled under the steep and forbidding cliffs of the main Athos ridges. For over three hours we traversed the face of one of the largest landslides in the world, where a tremendous slice of the Mountain had tumbled down into the sea. Great slabs of rock jutted out of the sea at its base, but there seemed to be many millions of tons more above which looked loose and dangerous. I was astonished to see, high up on this loose, boulder-jumbled landslide, a well-marked track running right across.

Late on the second afternoon we rounded a rugged cape and came into a large bay which ran up into the most fertile and cultivated valley I had seen on the Holy Peninsula. In the centre of this valley, only some few hundreds of feet up from the rocky beach, was a walled monastery. It was surrounded by perfectly terraced vineyards and luxuriant olive groves, with here and there stately cypress trees, which must have been several centuries old.

'The very Great Lavra!' announced one of the boatmen, resting on his oars to enjoy the sight the more. 'Over a thousand years old and still the most impressive building on the Mountain.'

As we drew in to the natural harbour, a stone-flagged path became visible winding up through the olive groves. My interest was suddenly centred on three figures in grey-green hurrying down to be on the stone jetty when we pulled in.

'Great Scot, Germans!' I exclaimed in English, jerking forward in the boat to arrest the oarsmen.

'They are not Germans,' said one, amused at my alarm. 'They are police. And good police. Yonder are Philippas and his two assistants. They are good friends of the monks and of the English, too. Have no fear, you are in good hands.'

Presently I was introduced to Philippas, a large, handsome Greek in a smart uniform. He shook hands firmly and said with a laugh, 'Well, Thomas, we are pleased to see you. We have heard that you were in our area and wondered when we would meet. But I do wish you would not row so openly into my very headquarters. Surely the Abbot of St Denys has more discretion. Had you arrived after dark I would have been much happier but, nevertheless, you are welcome. Come along with me and join my police in a small meal and a drop of wine.'

I said goodbye to the two boatmen, who were anxious to get back as soon as possible, and then followed the police into a stone building. Two other police sprang to attention in deference to the Sergeant and we all arranged ourselves around a large wooden table. It was so like barrack life that in a few minutes I was entirely at my ease with them all. Before the meal appeared one of them was sent up to the monastery with a written message from Philippas asking that I might be allowed to enter.

The Great Lavra

'By all the Saints!' exclaimed one of the younger police when the meal was eventually brought in by one of their number, 'I will be glad when the monks go off their fasting. The food has got progressively worse ever since they started it. Just because they have to go without is no reason why they should make us go hungry, too!'

'If you were a good Christian, Nicos, you would not mind, you would be pleased to go without,' said Philippas, smiling.

'That's probably true, Sergeant,' replied the youth, 'but I have to cover forty kilometres of this mountain every day on my round, and I claim it is a different matter for a monk who only has to meditate.' He turned to me. 'Thomas arrives at a good time, anyhow. For him there will be feasts and wine parties!'

In about an hour the messenger arrived back, bringing with him a large mule. With Philippas holding the reins I set off up the time-worn stone track to St Lawrence.

The sun was sinking into the sea, and the great bells sounding the end of the day, as we turned into the high archway under the outer wall. The gatekeeper challenged Philippas from the balcony of his lodge, and when he was satisfied bade us enter. Behind us, as we made over the large courtyard, gates at least twenty feet high slowly swung together. The bells announced that no one might enter or leave the monastery until dawn.

Chapter Fourteen

A close shave

'I have thought over the whole thing,' said Pavlides, the quietly spoken and cultured monk-doctor of St Lawrence, 'and I will have some suggestions to make to you later. In the meantime, let us enjoy the meal that God has provided.'

We were seated at a small table in the good doctor's quarters and in front of us was arrayed a tasty meal of macaroni and white cheese. I had been in the monastery for over ten days and this was the first time I had been 'invited out' for a meal, normally being required to live and eat in the monastery hospital. The monks of St Lawrence differed from St Denys in that they lived *monos* or to a greater degree singly. Thus, they did not dine together as a community. On the other hand, they were permitted two great privileges. Firstly, they were permitted in between fasts, to eat red meat and, secondly, they could bring into the monastery and still retain their worldly wealth. This enabled some of them to live in well-furnished quarters, with paid lesser monks for servants.

'Well now, Pavlides,' I tackled him when we had finished our meal, 'what is the news you have for me? What are the suggestions you mentioned which will help me in my one great desire to get to Egypt?'

'Do not expect me to present to you a simple plan or any sort of answer to your prayers. I can only try to show you the possibilities.

'You realise that a boat on this coast or anywhere in Greece today is the livelihood of several men. Particularly now that we have lost so many.

177

Therefore, you cannot expect anyone, however patriotic, to give you a boat for nothing. A great deal of money will be involved, and I presume you have no more than a few drachmae.'

In actual fact, I had some eight thousand drachmae, most of which I had won on that highly successful game of pontoon the last day in the prison camp at Salonika. I told him so.

'That is at least something,' he replied imperturbably, 'but it would not go far these days. To you eight thousand drachmae represents some fifty pounds of sterling, but here now it has perhaps only a hundredth of its previous value. You must understand that the German has flooded the country with paper money. For a while everyone went mad at the wonderful prices they paid for everything, and then we found that it was only a highly organised way of looting the country. Now it would take a hundred thousand drachmae to buy even a small boat.'

This seemed a terrible blow, and Pavlides must have seen my crestfallen look. He filled my glass again and said, 'However, do not worry over much. You are not without good friends in the monastery. I myself will help you with what little I can raise, and Papa Gregorio has intimated to me that he will stake all his money to assist. And I think that Papa Gregorio has a great deal of money.'

That was good news. Quite apart from the money side of it I was very pleased to think that Gregorio had some confidence in me. He was a giant of a man, dark skinned and heavy featured, with penetrating brown eyes, which were the fear of the lesser monks. From the first day of my arrival he had been more than good, sending his servant-monk, Philippas, down twice a day with tasty dishes to supplement my quite adequate rations in the hospital. In his youth he had been to America, where he had learnt some English, and at the same time made a tidy fortune on the wheat market. Drawn to the Church in his thirties, he had brought all his wealth to St Lawrence, bought a fine monastery farm nearby, and settled down with determination to study theology. Now, after years of perseverance, he was a fully fledged priest and one of the most respected in the monastery.

'When, then, do you think I might be able to leave?' I asked, for there seemed to be no other obstacle.

'Two things govern that,' replied Pavlides. 'First, there is the weather. No Greek who knows the Aegean would put to sea in this weather. Remember that all you can expect is a small fishing boat, large enough for perhaps only four or five men, and such a boat would not last a night. Secondly, we must find someone who will take you over, for it is no mean feat to sail from here to Turkey.'

'Have you anyone in mind?' I asked.

'There are many civilians who work in various capacities for us. One of them is a good friend of mine, Costos Momogos and, while he is not a sailor, I hope he will be able to put us in touch with one.'

'Where is he, is he in the monastery now?' I asked, eagerly, for I would quite willingly have sought him out there and then.

'No, he lives some three hours from here. But he visits me regularly once a month and I expect him any day now.'

We rose from the small table, for it was getting late. I started to make my farewells and thanks. Pavlides, however, was in no hurry to retire. He drew me out on to a small balcony.

'This is the most restful place of my apartment,' he smiled. 'Here I work on my hobby of bookbinding when it is not too cold. Don't you think it is a beautiful view for an old man to look on for his last years?'

A three-quarter moon was shining through scattered clouds, laying a silvery path from the horizon across the sea to the snow-covered shores fringed with black rocks. All the olive and cypress trees from the shore to the monastery were evenly rounded by soft blue-white snow and threw long shadows towards us. Everything was perfectly quiet, although from far below the faint sound of the waves rose and fell with the breeze.

We stood for a few minutes in silence.

'People of thought and faith have stood like us on this balcony for nearly a thousand years,' said Pavlides presently, 'and no doubt they, too, have talked of means to aid some fugitive across these seas. I think that things will turn out as we wish, although for you a great deal of patience is necessary.'

I thanked Pavlides and made my way down the long, narrow corridors, strangely lit by long shafts of moonlight, down the steep steps into the courtyard and across to the monastery hospital where I lived.

My friend, Chrysostomos, was waiting up to see me as I walked into the cleanly kept room reserved for the sick. He had been thrilled when I was asked to dinner by the doctor, who was one of the 'upper ten' of monastery life, and was now agog to hear all about it. He pressed me for details—what had been eaten, how had it been served, was the soup better than his own?

Chrysostomos answered exactly to my idea of a monk before I came to the Holy Mountain. Fat and jolly, his robes tied around his ample waist with thick knotted cord, he even had a bald pate to complete the picture. And, like 'Friar Tuck', he was an accomplished cook as well as a sound trencherman. Although his portly form and healthy appetite made him the butt of many jokes, he answered all with his deep and ready laugh, and he was most popular amongst all classes in the monastery. Everyone spoke of him with affection.

He had been wonderfully kind to me since I arrived in the hospital, which was in his charge. I think he was delighted to see someone who enjoyed good food in plenty as much as he did, particularly as it was generally frowned on at St Lawrence for two monks to dine together.

I told him everything I could remember about the excellent meal and wines I had enjoyed with Doctor Pavlides and then, tired and well satisfied, I was soon asleep and dreaming pleasantly of the fruition of my plans.

Fate, however, had something exciting in store. Late next morning I was sitting in the sun in front of the only window of the hospital, intent on studying some of the niceties of the Greek language from the books Papa Gregorio had provided for me. Everything seemed much the same as any morning, but I was conscious of a vague premonition that something important was about to happen.

Chrysostomos was waddling around on his various duties and indulging in his favourite pastime of cursing his assistant, Isitheros. Poor Isitheros was willing enough and always irrepressibly cheerful, but he was, without a shadow of doubt, quite mad. He would do anything for Chrysostomos, except at meal times, when he would become quite uncontrollable. His eyes would bulge out of his bewhiskered face in blatant greed, and he would begin slobbering and moaning in anticipation. There was always plenty of food for him; indeed Chrysostomos would give him much more than the ration provided, but he would whimper until he was given his bowl, and then wolf it down in great gulps in spite of the fact that he did not have a tooth in his head. He must have had a stomach of cast iron. On rare occasions when he had been particularly good, Chrysostomos would allow him to have some giant red chillies which were hung on long strings from the heavy wooden rafters of the hospital kitchen.

Isitheros would go all a-twitter with excitement and, falling over himself with anticipation, would cut down ten or a dozen of them. These

Monks, Lavra, taken on 'thank you visit' 1946.
From left: Isitheros, Chrysostomos, Papa Gregorio, Dr Pavlides,
Demetrius, 'Micro' Philippas

WBT collection

chillies were as big as tomatoes and one alone would last a normal family's requirements for a month, but this simple fellow would break them all into his soup and in a matter of minutes consume the lot. I could not understand why he did not go up in flames, as even a small piece of the scarlet skin made a meal almost unpalatable for me.

This particular morning, however, Isitheros was very fractious and Chrysostomos lost patience with him. After warning him several times, he finally gave way to his exasperation and threw a loaf of bread at his head. Isitheros screamed his disapproval, retrieved the loaf of bread from under one of the beds and scampered off outside into the snow. Chrysostomos settled down to his work and I carried on with my studies.

There was perhaps half an hour of peace when we heard Isitheros's unmistakable jabbering in the distance—presently he stumbled through the doorway, greatly agitated. He rushed across the room trying vainly to tell us something which seemed to him to be very important. Incensed by our incomprehension, his agitation increased. He grabbed me as I sat on the edge of my bed and tried to drag me to the door. When I resisted he buried his food-sodden face and beard into the nape of my neck and moaned as though in great mental anguish.

Chrysostomos, who alone understood some of his jargon, stood back perplexed for a few moments, and then suddenly galvanised himself into action.

'Now I see it,' he cried, rushing to the door and bolting it. 'There are Germans coming, German soldiers. Isitheros has seen them, is that right, Isitheros?'

Isitheros, overwhelmed that he was at last understood, nodded his head vigorously, and pointed across the courtyard to indicate that they came from the sea.

I immediately started to get things together for a quick departure, while Chrysostomos ran across the courtyard to find out if Isitheros was, in fact, right and if so, how near the enemy was. He ran surprisingly nimbly for one so fat and in a few moments was back, puffing and out of breath.

'You must fly!' he gasped, 'there are at least ten of them, and they are within half a mile of here, all armed to the teeth. Make up into the forests above the monastery, and I will search you out when things quieten down.'

With a loaf of bread under one arm and two blankets under the other I raced headlong out into the courtyard. My heart was in my mouth and I cursed myself for the placidity which had led to such a situation. Of course I should have been prepared for such an emergency, should have had someone always watching for approaching German craft. However, I was determined that if speed could save me I would get clear of the monastery before they arrived.

The great gates of the outer wall were open. Stumbling over the rutted and frozen snow, I made to pass under the archway. The gatekeeper, jolted into action by my commotion, began to close the gates as a precaution until he could inquire into the cause, but I was well through by the time they clanged together.

I had not gone fifty yards, however, when a dishevelled and exhausted figure emerged around the bend in the track which led down to the sea. It was one of the police and he was obviously straining every muscle to reach the monastery. As I paused, undecided whether I should wait for him, he sighted me and immediately waved frantically. He tried to shout some message, but was too much out of breath. In a few moments he was alongside and, in spite of his spent condition, dragged me backwards towards the monastery.

'Too late ... can't get away now ... they are coming from three directions,' he panted, gulping for air all the while. 'Philippas says you must hide within the monastery!'

'But that will be fatal. I should be caught like a rat in a trap!' I objected, trying to resist his persuasion. 'Surely I would be better off in the woods up yonder?'

'Must obey orders ... Philippas knows best ... cannot hide in woods when snow on ground ... easily found. Look up there!'

I followed the direction he indicated and my heart missed a beat. Above the thin line of bush I had been making for were three figures, their uniforms and square helmets standing out unmistakably against the background of the snow. And a quick glance at the only other exit into the mountain hide-outs above showed two more figures less than a thousand yards away. Convinced, I turned to assist the gallant policeman in his hammering against the now closed gates. Presently the gatekeeper came abreast of the urgent situation and we were allowed to enter.

We went straight back to the hospital, where our entrance, naturally enough, acted like a bomb-burst. No doubt they had gathered to conjecture on my chances of escape, and now to see me back in their midst was a great shock to them. Doctor Pavlides, Papa Gregorio, Chrysostomos and their henchmen were all there and from their open mouths and blank looks I thought at first that the situation was beyond them.

None of them, however, appeared in any way frightened for his own skin. There was consternation but no fear, although each of them must have known what my capture in their midst would mean for them.

The policeman who had been sent to warm me threw himself into a chair and mopped his streaming face and forehead.

'Philippas says... Thomas must stay here ... the monastery is surrounded ... he said ... underneath the old dungeons perhaps ... Germans would not look!'

'That is the very place they would go first,' interrupted Papa Gregorio, decisive and now obviously the dominant figure in the room. 'You must go somewhere less conspicuous. In the meantime, we must make you as unlike an Englishman as possible. How long have we got?'

'Perhaps ten minutes,' responded the policeman. 'I asked the gatekeeper to delay them for as long as possible while he sought permission for them to enter.'

'Good! That will be ample. Now, Chrysostomos, we must dress Thomas as one of us. Go up to my rooms and bring down some of my robes. In the meantime, Thomas, my young friend, strip off all those tell-tale clothes. And as for you,' Papa Gregorio turned to the policeman, who was sitting back in admiration of this towering and dominant man, 'you have done your duty nobly. Thomas may well owe his life to your effort and we are all duly grateful. But you must pull yourself together and appear to be in the monastery on some errand. You must realise what these dogs would do to you if they were to discover your complicity in aiding the escape of a British officer!'

Papa Gregorio gave his instructions calmly but forcefully. In a very few minutes the policeman was out in the courtyard with Isitheros, making a check of the personal belongings of the latter, Doctor Pavlides was away with all my clothes to conceal them somewhere, and Chrysostomos was putting the final touches to the fitting of the long black robes of a monk which I now wore. Papa Gregorio placed one of their black skull-caps on my head and then pulled the black cloth cowl over so that it draped down on to my shoulders and partially hid my face.

When he was satisfied he led me unhurriedly away from the hospital, down a long corridor, and then up a series of winding stone steps. The standard of the furniture and drapings diminished as we climbed and presently I realised that we were in the very attics of the four-storeyed main building. Rafters at least two feet square and running the whole length of the roof were only inches above our heads and, indeed, on occasions we both had to duck to get under them.

We passed along a line of small Gothic arches in stone and, glancing down, I saw that we had travelled round two sides of the building which contained the main square, and that we now looked on to the main gates. Even as I looked, they began to open slowly, and both Papa Gregorio and I stopped involuntarily to see what happened.

Three square-helmeted figures sprang through the half-open gates, their sub-machine carbines aggressively at the ready, and rushed to take up positions to cover the windows and archways overlooking the courtyard. A minute later, two more followed and aligned themselves on either side of the gates, while a fifth rushed up the narrow steps over the gateway to emerge with the gatekeeper. The position under control, one of the sentries at the gate shouted some message, in response to which a young *Unter-Offizier* entered, followed by the remainder of the patrol.

In all, there were fifteen of them, overladen with machine-guns, rifles and grenades, as though they were expecting to meet a small army. The *Unter-Offizier* began to shout guttural orders to the uncomprehending monks who were gathering at the doorways.

Papa Gregorio and I hurried on.

I could see that we were now in a part of the monastery where no one had been for many years. In contrast to the rest of the buildings which were kept spotlessly clean, the floors of the attic were thick with dust and two or three large rats scampered in front of us. There was also a fusty smell which pricked the nostrils unpleasantly.

At last, Papa Gregorio arrived at the place he had chosen for my hiding-place. We came into a line of small, cell-like rooms walled into the eaves. Some of their doorways had been bricked up, some had iron-studded doors and some had no doorways at all. They all looked singularly bleak and uninviting, but I could not have imagined a more suitable hiding-place, particularly when Gregorio demonstrated that they were all inter-connected in that one could climb up on the roof through the heavy skylight of one and then drop into the next.

'Now it is up to you,' he whispered urgently, pressing my hand to give me confidence. 'You must climb up on to the roof and find one of the walled-up rooms which has a loose skylight. No one will find you there provided you keep absolutely still. I will go back and act the part of the aggrieved host!'

'Thank you, Papa Gregorio, I think it should be quite safe. But they are damnably efficient, these Huns, and if they have definite news from someone they might keep on until they find me. What then?'

'I think it is unlikely. However, you are in our robes and it will be given out that you are a dangerous mute. If you are found you must act the part, even to putting those manacles on your wrist and ankles.' He pointed to some rusty old chains fastened to the walls. I realised that they had been used for centuries for the custody of maniacs. A horrible thought crossed my mind and, in spite of his obvious impatience to be gone, I asked, 'Papa Gregorio, why are some of the rooms walled up, and others not?'

'Because, eh, well,' he began, with some loss of his usual composure, 'many years ago there were unhappy incidents which warranted the sealing of those rooms. But nothing to discuss at the moment. I will tell you one day when we have more time. Now, move quickly and get settled!'

It was not at all easy to clamber up on to the roof through a narrow skylight with the long, black robes draped around my legs. And the first time I succeeded was in vain because my cap and cowl slipped off at the last moment and fell back on to the floor. However, finally I found myself on the stone-tiled roof of the monastery in a saucer-shaped corner which prevented any view of me from below.

Moving gingerly over the heavy stone tiles, I peered down the second skylight. I had marked it as belonging to one of the walled-up rooms. The rusty iron frame of the skylight seemed at first to be firmly stuck, but to my relief it responded to my efforts and swung open. A nauseating stench of foul air and rat droppings rose up into my face and I jerked back, half imagining that it was from the remains of the centuries-dead monk I quite expected to find in the chains below. However, in a few moments I had lowered myself as far as possible and dropped to the floor. A terrific commotion in one of the dark corners set my heart pounding, but frightened squeaks revealed a large brown rat which I soon sent scurrying off down one of the numerous holes.

A quick search of the room failed to show any sign of skeletons or skulls, and as soon as I got used to the gloom I chose a worm-eaten stool and sat down to consider my chances of discovery. After a few moments I closed the skylight in case it might be spotted. There was little enough air, and it was unbearably stale and foul, but I was prepared to put up with some discomfort if I was to retain my freedom.

At first it all seemed very quiet outside. I could occasionally hear shouted orders in the distance and faintly the sounds of heavy feet tramping along corridors below. I did not know until later that the *Unter-Offizier* had ordered every monk outside into the main courtyard and that they were now making their first perfunctory search of the building to ensure that their order was obeyed. Evidently, when he was satisfied that all were present, the young *Unter-Offizier* had all the six hundred odd monks searched for firearms and briefly questioned. This took all of three hours and it was apparent that the soldiers were disappointed with the lack of results. When this was completed the *Unter-Offizier* addressed the gathering pompously, telling them that the *Wehrmacht* expected them all to co-operate in the New Order in Europe, and that they must desist from aiding English prisoners and political fugitives. He said they had heard from reliable sources that many of the monasteries were giving succour to prisoners, indeed, he quoted the fact that an English officer had been sheltered in the hospital of St Denys for over a month. They had arrived only a day too late to capture him, he declared, and they were now searching every monastery in case he might be there. He called on any one of the monks to denounce the English pig should he be at St Lawrence, and offered all sorts of inducements. When there was no response he gave his orders for a thorough search.

Here he made a foolish mistake. Instead of holding all the monks in the courtyard during the search he dismissed them peremptorily. In a few minutes all the corridors and main rooms were filled with excited and curious monks, who unwittingly hindered the searchers at every turn.

As Gregorio had foreseen, they first went carefully through all the dank dungeons and cellars under the monastery. There was a considerable network of these and it took them over an hour. They visited each cell and room, even insisting on entering the vaults where the bones of countless hundreds of monks were kept.

After the dungeons they visited the chapels, the hospital and all the ground floor, working up stage by stage to the attic where I was waiting in the gloom.

When at last I heard the heavy tread of half a dozen men coming down the corridor towards the cells, it was six hours since they had arrived and the sky was darkening as the evening drew in. They entered each of the cells which had doors and I heard them in the two which adjoined mine. They paused outside the walled-up entrance behind which I waited, scarcely daring to breathe, and I heard a discussion going on between three of them. I gathered that they did not like to leave such a possible cubby-hole, and when I felt them hammering against the brick and mortar I rose apprehensively to escape through the skylight. But to my relief they desisted, evidently satisfied that the mortar was centuries old, and tried tapping both of my walls from the outside, no doubt hoping to find a hollow panel to denote a secret entrance. In a few minutes they tired of this and I heard them clumping off down the corridor. I relaxed.

No one came near me that night. I slept fitfully, stretched out on the floor, constantly having to chase away large rats which scampered boldly around the room. I was also afraid that large spiders might drop on me from the ceiling. While it was light I had seen that the roof was almost hidden by a mat of cobwebs undisturbed for countless years ... and I had always been frightened of spiders. I was very happy when I saw the first lightening of the sky in the morning.

The next day past uneventfully, although soon after midday I heard a shot fired and wondered what could be happening. Late in the afternoon I heard footsteps approaching and presently was relieved to hear Papa Gregorio calling softly at a room some three to four doors away from mine. I tapped quietly on the wall and he moved nearer.

'Are you all right, my boy?' he called. 'Come out now for a while; I think it is reasonably safe and I have some food for you. Only be very quiet as they are still in the monastery.'

I was ravenously hungry and terribly thirsty, so I took only a few moments to traverse the roof between the two skylights and join him in the corridor. He had a bowl of steaming stew, some bread and a large flagon of wine. With him to carry this food was his manservant, Philippas, who was called 'Micro-Philippas' to avoid confusion with the police sergeant. I took a long draught of the wine. Then I sought news from my friends.

'Yes, they are still here,' responded Papa Gregorio, in quite an offhand manner, 'but they are not up to much at the moment. Come and have a look at some of them!'

I followed him to one of the Gothic arches which looked on to the courtyard. Cautiously peering down, I beheld four of the '*Herrenvolk*' desporting themselves in the snow below. They were blind drunk, almost incapable of standing. Even as I watched, one of them waved a Luger revolver aimlessly in the air and let off a burst of shots which spattered against the stone walls, ricocheting dangerously into the open arches.

'The *Unter-Offizier*, he is also drunk?' I asked, for if he was, there would be little to fear from him.

'No. He was tipsy last night, but today he is trying to get his men sober. They, however, are past taking orders from a young stripling, and he has a lot of trouble on his hands. Serve him right, in my opinion he needs taking down quite a bit. He had the effrontery to tell our Abbot that he was displeased with him and ordered that all the monks should bow to him when they passed. They are all the same, these strutting toy soldiers, they are drunk with power.'

Gregorio and Micro-Philippas left when I had fully slaked my thirst and had a hearty meal. I did not try to get back into the same ghostly room, but passed a peaceful night in the corridor, kept warm by blankets brought up by Chrysostomos.

About noon of the second day, that is at six o'clock by the Holy

Mountain time, Chrysostomos and Doctor Pavlides came up to see me with some food. While they were with me, Micro-Philippas arrived with the news that the patrol was moving out. We hastened to the Gothic windows and looked down on the square.

Responding in a slovenly manner to the furious order of the young *Unter-Offizier*, the patrol was drawn up on the snow-covered courtyard. Two or three of them were reasonably sober, but the remainder appeared to be in a sodden stupor, dropping their weapons which were handed to them and draping their arms around one another for support. I thought about the stories I had heard of iron German discipline.

'Good heavens!' I mused aloud. 'Fancy all this fuss over such a rabble. Why—with any luck I could clean them up on my own!'

'Now, now, Thomas!' cried the doctor, horrified. 'This is a House of God and not to be defiled by needless violence. I do believe you are as bad as they! You soldiers are all the same!'

At last, the *Unter-Offizier* was satisfied and he gave the order to march. The crooked file lurched forward awkwardly towards the main gates. The *Unter-Offizier* looked up and around the watching faces at each archway and window, looked a little ashamed, then flushed angrily and strode after his men. The gates closed behind them.

That evening all who had been concerned with my successful seclusion gathered in the hospital. We had some wine to toast those who had played the greater parts. The police sergeant, 'Megala-Philippas', was there with the policeman who had been sent to warn me, as well as all the monks. There was great mirth at my robes and a certain amount of leg-pulling at my lack of a decent beard. It was a very happy gathering.

Before we broke up, however, Papa Gregorio announced that the 'Twelve' who ruled the monastery had ordered that it would be unwise for me to go on staying in the hospital. He, himself, was one of the 'Twelve' but his objections had been over-ruled. He was very sorry, but I must go as soon as the weather permitted.

Chapter Fifteen

Costos Momogos

The wet, sleety snow swirled around us as we climbed. My clothes were soaked to the skin, and my shoes squelched water at every step. But I was not at all cold; on the contrary, my face and body were streaming with perspiration.

Ahead of me, almost hidden by the heavy fog, was the small figure of Costos Momogos. Exerting every muscle to keep up with him, I found I hated this unusual dark Greek who had dragged me away from the comfortable Monastery of St Lawrence that day.

'How much farther? Surely we must be there soon?' I called, hoping he would pause long enough for me to regain my breath.

'It is not far. Perhaps only three hours,' came back from the still-moving figure.

A wave of hopelessness swept over me. Surely he had said the whole journey would take only three and a half hours, and we must have been fighting through this blizzard for over two hours already. Perhaps he was trying to tire me out so that he could easily betray me to the Germans. I clutched my stick in rage and considered creeping up behind him.

Costos Momogos had appeared in the monastery some three days after the big German scare. He had come into the hospital in his imperious manner, ordering Chrysostomos about and turning his back impatiently on poor Isitheros. Then he had sat down uninvited on my bed and talked in an unnatural and affected way, as though he was addressing a formal gathering rather than an individual.

I realised immediately that he had come in to sum me up, to see whether I was worth having anything to do with, and I did not like it. He asked me questions as though he was some sort of investigating officer, discussing my replies scornfully as if he did not believe them.

We had talked thus for nearly an hour when he suddenly got up and said, 'All right, let us go. We have over three hours to walk and the sooner we get away the better.'

'What! Where am I to go?' I cried, alarmed at this abruptness, yet concerned lest I annoy him, as he was my only contact with possible boatmen for Turkey.

'Doctor Pavlides has told me to take you away. It is too dangerous for you to stay here. We will leave immediately.'

'But ... it is snowing heavily! ... I have no coat ... and, besides, I must say goodbye to my friends who have been so good to me.'

'We will leave immediately. If you ever want to see your native land again you must come now. This very instant, for I can wait no longer! I want none of your so-called friends to know where you have gone!'

I had thought quickly. There was no doubt that Costos represented the only chance of freedom. It seemed that I had to choose between comfort and following this strange man. I decided very reluctantly to go with him, come what may, but not until I had at least made my farewells to Chrysostomos. As it happened, however, a detailed search failed to discover his whereabouts so, with no coat, and in a very bad temper, I swung out of the monastery gates behind Costos and followed him through the swirling blizzard.

We had followed a snow-covered track down on to the rocky shore, had crossed mountain streams swollen into flood, and were now climbing the steep face of a ridge. I was in no way fit for such a climb and every step was an effort. However, at last we stood on a small plateau and when the fog lifted momentarily Costos pointed out a small group of houses on the mountainside.

'Ten minutes,' he said briefly and we pressed forward.

The house was a two-storeyed building of rough stone and was absolutely frozen when we entered. Even a half-finished bowl of soup on the one table in the main room was frozen into a solid block. Anything more uninviting I could not imagine. However, we busied ourselves and kindled a fire in the large stone stove in the centre of the room.

I had never liked this type of stove during my stay in Greece. It had only a small opening for fuel and the heat was supposed to be contained within and passed out through the stone and mortar of the stove itself. As the stove was invariably painted white with some sort of decoration on it, the general appearance was a cold and comfortless one, with none of the homeliness of an open grate. It took long hours to heat up, one could not feel any warmth in the stone at all for the first hour, but when it was properly under way it was fair to say that it warmed the room most satisfactorily and was very economical.

There was only one bed in the room and only one rug. To my astonishment, when we made to settle down, Costos firmly insisted that I should have it. This gesture was the first of many which followed in the next few days and, little by little, I discovered the true worth of this strange, abrupt little man. Before I had been with him for a month I realised that he was the most unselfish and gallant individual I had met during my adventures. With the exception of two major sorties on the mainland, I stayed with Costos Momogos for the rest of the winter. Snow heavier than the oldest could remember fell day after day, overloading the gnarled old olive trees, so that their branches twisted and snapped with the weight. Down below us the Aegean Sea thrashed and stormed in its winter fury.

The days were painfully long. Most of the time we spent huddled against the stone stove, wondering if the snow was ever going to stop. Costos drew his rations from the main monastery; he would collect them once a week, leaving me on my own for a day and a night. It was interesting to observe that the monks had been employing for centuries almost exactly the same organisation for all provisions which the army used in war-time.

I grew very fond of Costos Momogos but he was, without a doubt, a most unusual character. He would keep me hidden in the house all the week, and then when I pressed him he would agree to take me for a walk. We would dress up with the greatest of care; I would wear a monk's robes and cap and a pair of waist-high sea boots. As we emerged from the house, Costos would look suspiciously from left to right as though the snow-covered trees were concealing hundreds of Germans, and we would proceed with the utmost stealth along the mountainside.

As we approached a house, Costos would hold his hand to his lips for silence, and whisper that it was a particularly dangerous hotbed of enemy intrigue. We would circle it widely, ploughing off the track into the deep snowdrifts with the maximum of discomfort. Only when we were well past would Costos permit me to unwrap the black cowl from my face and talk freely.

In this manner we would pass a series of eight or nine monastery farmhouses. Anyone who watched us would have taken us for Red Indian scouts or thieves slinking past a police station.

I would not have minded this stealth normally; after all, it was in my best interests to be careful. But Costos was so terribly inconsistent. When at last we had arrived at the house we had set out to visit he would accept the wine and hospitality with such enthusiasm that he became slightly tipsy in a pleasant way. He would entertain us with his wit and antics. Then, after two or three hours, he would suddenly decide that there were other friends to visit and, dragging me behind him, he would call one by one *at the very houses we had so carefully circumnavigated*. It was in vain that I remonstrated with him.

'But Costos, surely that is the house where this morning you said a German agent lived?'

'Shertainly not,' he would reply indignantly, having some difficulty with his tongue. 'Thatsh the home of a great friend of mine. Very patriotic. Mustn't call him an enemy agent, wouldn't like it at all. Come on, let's go and meet him!'

And, chuckling with merriment, which was quite out of keeping with his normal dour and abrupt manner, he would strike a crooked path to the door of the house. And, sure enough, we would be well received by hospitable monks who showed a real regard for Costos in spite of his merry condition. The inconsistency of it was beyond me, and I suffered the outward voyage each week, concealing my exasperation as we circled various houses, and looking forward only to the return home.

Throughout this period there were negotiations almost weekly with boatmen on the possibility of a passage to Turkey, or even to Imbros, a small Turkish island near the Dardanelles. I had a long series of promises and agreements which came to nothing. Not all the money which I could raise from my rich friends of St Lawrence would make the slightest difference to these people. When the promised day came I would approach them, always to be told either that the weather precluded all possibility of reaching Turkey safely, or that there were too many German patrol boats around.

'Not today. Perhaps tomorrow or the next day!' they would say, and when I tried to get something more definite they would shrug their shoulders, in that expressive Greek gesture which means, 'What can I do, it is beyond me.'

It was particularly galling when the weather began to ease and we would get two or sometimes three clear days between storms when the sea would subside to a greasy swell and make the chances of a quick trip across seem good. On these occasions I would visit one Lazarus, who had an excellent sailing craft, but although at times he seemed to waver and almost agree when I showed him my roll of notes, he never went beyond that.

As the first hint of spring appeared early in March, Costos and I moved to another small house nearer the sea, so that I could be in more constant touch with the fishermen. This house had an open fireplace and was in many respects more homely than the other. Here we lived well on fish and strange food such as snails. These snails were as big as small potatoes and were collected by the bucketful in the early morning after each rain. We would break the point of each and then stew them in vegetable water with a little olive oil. Eaten with bread and wine, they were delicious.

Another unusual meal was of flowering bulbs which grew in profusion in the bush. We would collect large quantities of these and take off their outer covers. To all intents and purposes they were the same as garden bulbs such as daffodils, they smelled as bitter and no doubt would have been unpalatable if cooked the ordinary way. But Costos showed how they could be made into a really tasty dish by boiling them more than five times, using fresh water each time. This took out all the bitter and, I think, poisonous flavour and left a white bulb which tasted like a spring onion.

The great danger of being down near the sea was the number of visitors we had. Scarcely a day passed without two or three people, monks or civilians, calling in, either to pass the time of day or to ask for refreshment. Consequently, I was not greatly surprised when the police sergeant, Philippas, arrived one day with his deputy Zachas. He brought the grave news that he had received orders from the Germans in Salonika to search for an English officer known to be in the area. It was obviously time to be on the move again. Philippas and Costos discussed where I could best be hidden until some plan could be evolved to get me to Turkey.

'I have it,' said Philippas at last. 'He must go up the mountain to Elisais! No one could ever find him there, and if any Germans approached, they could be seen for miles before they reached the house.'

'M' yes,' agreed Costos doubtfully, 'but I don't like Elisais very much. And he wouldn't like to have anyone staying there, would he?'

'He will do what he is told,' said Philippas firmly.

And so it was arranged.

The following morning, laden with gifts of food from my friends, I set off up the mountainside. It was a glorious morning and I felt loath to have to walk away from the sea which was looking particularly inviting. As I rose higher the horizon extended, and in the distance I could see the Turkish island of Imbros lying low between Lemnos and Samothrace.

I climbed steadily all day. Late in the afternoon I entered the tree-line and followed the track through tall and stately trees until, just before dark, I came to a small clearing. I saw, perched on a rocky outcrop on the very edge of the snow line, a large stone house with a chapel attached. I pressed forward and was soon hammering at the massive door.

Elisais was not pleased to see me. He had lived alone in this secluded spot for over fifteen years and he never liked visitors, whether on pilgrimage or in hiding. He grudgingly showed me to a room of sorts and gave me some bread and olives for a meal.

The room I was to stay in was indescribably filthy. Apart from the damp mud of the floor, the walls were covered with animal skins in progressive stages of curing. They all combined to produce a nauseating odour which was almost unbearable. And under each skin investigation showed whole colonies of horrid little vermin, while the roof was covered with spiders' webs.

I passed an unhappy night, homesick for the clean comfort of Costos's small home.

In the morning, I set to and made some progress towards making the room habitable. I scraped the mud, pulled down all the skins and generally emptied everything outside into an outhouse. Having got so far, I lit a roaring fire in the stone stove and dried the walls and floor. By the time evening came again I had a snug, clean corner, which was in every way satisfactory. Elisais watched the whole of my activities with silent disapproval, but I observed that he came into my room in the evening to warm himself before turning in.

He was not a bad man by any means. As I got to know him I realised that he was just a simple hulk of a fellow, not essentially selfish, but used to living completely on his own. He lived for his hunting, at which he had great skill, and the fact that he was a monk as well was merely incidental. The only times he entered the chapel during my stay were the occasions when we saw a priest climbing up towards us from the monastery; then he would rush in to dust the altar, sweep the floor and light all the various candles in front of the saints. When the priest arrived I would answer the door and have to take him along to the chapel where Elisais would be heard praying loudly.

He went off most days with his loose-limbed deerhound into the forest, and I never knew him to return empty-handed. Sometimes he brought wild poultry, sometimes a fox and, more rarely, a pig or deer. If the beast was too big we would harness up an old mule and drag it in that way.

With all this game we lived on practically nothing but meat. There was bread available at the monastery, but Elisais never bothered to go down for it. Consequently we had three heavy meals each day of pork, veal or wild birds, and I found my wound discharging freely with such an unsuitable diet. We did not eat the best parts of the various beasts, which were salted or sent down to the monastery, but we had the livers and other entrails and the heads.

On one occasion four of the police joined us in a day's hunting and, in spite of the fact that they all had modern rifles against his muzzle-loading flintlock, Elisais was the only one to bag anything. He dropped a young boar in the forest some miles from the house, and the party brought it back for a feast.

I watched them clean it, or rather watched them prepare it for eating, for they certainly did not clean it as we would understand the term. I was revolted to see the head hacked off, dipped very briefly into the stream running near the house and then straightway placed, tongue, bristles and all, into a large pan.

I was, however, more revolted when some hours later this same head was put in front of me to eat. I protested in vain; they were all adamant that it was the best part of the pig and that I was to eat it. I had always said to myself during my travels that I would eat whatever was put in front of me, but this seemed too much. Embarrassed at their insistence, I picked up my knife and gingerly cut out the bristly cheek. Two glassy eyes stared balefully at me, almost daring me to continue. And then the tongue slid out from the side of the mouth. I felt quite sick, but persevered. Elisais came to my assistance and cut the bristly outer skin away to reveal some quite palatable and tasty meat, but my initial feeling of gratitude passed quickly when he gouged out the two eyes and put them in front of me to eat. I was horrified. But they would not let me get away with not eating them.

'It is good ... it is *very* good ... it is wonderful!' said one of the policemen. 'Why, it is without doubt the best part of the pig.'

'Then by all means have it,' I cried in mortification. But they baited me until I popped one of the unsightly things into my mouth.

I did not attempt to swallow it, but made as though I was chewing it, and to please them did my best to assume an expression of enjoyment. But at the first opportunity I slipped it out into my hand and dropped it on to the floor under the table.

I thought it very unfortunate that the large tomcat, usually quite peaceful and too bored to enter into any games, should choose that moment to look for something to play with. There was a roar of laughter from one of the policemen and soon the whole room was in fits as the cat patted the offending eye from side to side. After that I was not pressed to eat pigs' heads.

Then there was the matter of the pigs' trotters. On one of Elisais's excursions he had left me four of the most revolting-looking trotters, still largely unclean and solid in a thick jelly of brawn. Certainly good enough for food for a fugitive, but I could not face it. I had made friends with the enormous, loose-limbed deerhound and as, on this occasion, Elisais had left it behind, I gave it the trotters. Of course, the big dog wolfed them down and chewed the bones contentedly all day. But I did not get away with my deception, for the next morning, when required to go hunting, the dog just sat down on the doorstep and refused to budge. Elisais was perplexed for only a few minutes.

'You have given the dog food?' he inquired—the first conversation he had made for some days. I told him what I had done and he left in high dudgeon to hunt without the dog. Evidently, cruel as it may seem, hunting dogs had to be kept as near starved as possible if they were to be any good. However, I had made a good friend in the house; for the rest of my stay he was always at my heels.

I stayed with Elisais for about a fortnight. Most of that time was spent inside because of bad weather, but on fine days I would go out into the forest and bring in loads of firewood with the old mule and then cut it into suitable lengths. One day I spent with my sullen host building a new framework for his grapevines which were beginning to bud. This little farm, on the snow line, had a name for producing a particularly fine wine in seasons when the frosts allowed a good growth. Underneath the house itself were cellars containing vats in the form of barrels as large as a living room in a modern home. They were all brim full of the maturing wine. Elisais often had me help in the evenings in distilling *ouzo*, a clear distillate tasting like aniseed, from the fermented residue of the pressed grapes.

Just after dusk one evening, one of the policemen from the harbour of St Lawrence arrived at the house. He had an urgent message from Costos Momogos for me to return forthwith, as there was a favourable chance for a trip to Turkey. I was elated beyond anything I had known before. I wanted to leave right away, but Elisais pointed out quite rightly that I would never find my way through the forest in the dark. I hardly slept at all that night, and was up and dressed well before dawn.

Elisais was, I thought, quite moved when I expressed my thanks and said goodbye. He was a lonely man by choice, but may have appreciated having a fire going and a warm house when he returned from hunting. I had quite a task in preventing the deerhound from following me when I set off. Dawn was just breaking as I wound through the great pines.

I did not call into St Lawrence as I passed. It was a perfect day, and the sea was as calm as a millpond, so I pressed on with the thought that I might be leaving that very night. Indeed, I found myself running at places, so desperately keen was I to get to Costos and find out what the good news was. On one occasion I saw a sizeable sailing craft some miles from the coast heading away east and with panic wondered if I was already too late.

Soon after noon I climbed the small rise which led up to the clearing on which was Costos's house. He greeted me very warmly and took me inside where he had prepared a bowl of broth for my arrival. I was terribly tired after the long walk and the broth put new life into me. With no little impatience I waited for Costos to tell me when I was to go.

'Well, now, I must tell you the news,' he began much later, when his Greek flair for the dramatic was satisfied, and I had reached an intolerable peak of curiosity. 'There is a boat on the coast of the Holy Mountain now which is hiding forty Greek officers who wish to escape to Egypt. They want to join the Sacred Brigade there for service under the King. One of these officers is an acquaintance of mine. He came here to seek news of German patrol boats and he has agreed that, if possible, you should go with them. In fact, he thought that an English officer would be an asset for negotiations when they all reached Turkey. Now, is that not good news?'

'Wonderful, Costos,' I replied, without much enthusiasm, however, as I detected a certain vagueness in the story which was only too familiar. 'But where is this Greek officer now? I would like to speak to him. And where is the boat? And when do they intend to leave for Turkey?'

'Slowly, slowly, Thomas my friend. You must have patience. He will come again in the course of the next few days. Why, he may even come tomorrow! Tomorrow or the next day.'

As soon as Costos said, in all seriousness, those fatal words 'AVRIO METHAVRIO' or 'tomorrow or the next day', I knew that this wonderful plan would come to nothing. Costos remained optimistic to the bitter end, and exasperated me for days by remarking each evening, 'Well, he should be here tomorrow or the next day.'

But this story at least had a sequel, unlike the majority of my disappointments. Philippas called in after I had been back with Costos for a week with the grave news that the Germans had effected a major scoop at the small fishing village of Pyrgos. They had found over thirty Greek officers and some English escapees preparing to embark in a large fishing caique. There was no doubt, Philippas said, that the Germans had followed their plans from the beginning and had smugly waited until the various would-be voyagers had been collected from their various hiding-places before they had swooped down on them. Only a few had managed to escape.

With all the Greek aptitude for inconsistency, Costos listened to this news with satisfaction, turned to me and almost beamed.

'Are you not glad I did not put you in touch with them?' he said. 'Remember that you wanted to go out and find them and were impatient to see them. But I thought there was something wrong. You should be very happy to have escaped capture.'

Philippas had something else on his mind that afternoon. I could see that he was worried and wanted to tell us something, but I was not prepared for the bombshell he blurted out just before his departure.

'Thomas, I have some terrible news,' he began, his strong face suddenly charged with feeling. 'The Japanese have had some frightful victories in the Pacific. A lot may be German propaganda, but we are told that your two great battleships, *The Prince of Wales* and the *Repulse*, have been sunk by the Japanese Air Force and, worse still, that Singapore has been captured with half a million prisoners.'

'Singapore!' I exploded, incredulously. 'Why, it is impossible, Philippas! The British have a base there like Gibraltar. It could never fall. I think this all sounds like Doctor Goebbels!'

'Maybe, we certainly hope so,' answered Philippas wearily, 'but the newspapers have been full of it these last few days. They forecast that nothing can stop the Japanese, that Australia will capitulate very soon and that ... and that your New Zealand is already under siege.'

I turned away and left Costos, who was also stunned, to see Philippas on his way. I tried to convince myself that it was all nonsense, but something within me argued that it was the truth and I felt dread, almost panic, that my people on the other side of the globe were in dire straits, perhaps even now fighting for their lives whilst I rotted on a monastery peninsula. Costos was curious to hear about these Japanese and I told him something of their ruthlessness, their cold and unnatural way of life. We sat mostly in silence staring into the fire for that evening; my own mind was racing as I reviewed every possible way there remained to get to Turkey.

Long after Costos had gone to bed, I quietly slid back the heavy wooden bars of the door and slipped outside. The night was still and peaceful; there was no moon but a clear sky of twinkling stars. I walked along the track, looking down on to the sea and then up to the stars, trying to change my despair into inspiration.

After perhaps two hours I turned back with a firm plan in my mind. Now that spring was here and the sea more amenable it might not require any great seamanship to sail to Turkey. So if one final attempt at buying a boat was to fail, I would persuade my conscience that it was within the scope of my duty to steal one and attempt the trip either on my own or with anyone I could find who would go with me. If necessary, I would row there.

I crept into the small house excited at the prospect of action once again. I could foresee lots of difficulties, but beyond them was the certainty of success and the imperative need to get in touch with my home again.

Chapter Sixteen

The rogues gather

'Well, it's certainly nice to be able to speak English again,' said the tall, fair lad as he came in the door, holding his hand out to me in greeting. 'My name is John, Sergeant John Coote, of the Middle East Commandos, and I am very glad to meet you, I'm sure!'

I introduced myself and Costos, and in a few minutes we were drawn up in front of the fire talking 'ninety to the dozen' like a couple of old friends. In the background Costos bustled about preparing some food and talking in Greek to Philippas who had brought John in.

It was three days since I had decided to force the issue and if necessary resort to theft in the matter of a boat. Costos, to my surprise, had guessed my intentions and had been of the greatest assistance. Quite rightly, he had pointed out that it would be almost impossible for me to effect this plan on my own, and he had suggested that Philippas the police sergeant might know of other would-be escapers who would make up a suitable force. Philippas had, with some reluctance, exposed the whereabouts of at least ten others, both Greek and English, and we were now gathering some of them in to make a plan of campaign.

John was not in favour of any more attempts at purchasing a boat: he was a man of action, and his training with the Commandos had given him an aggressiveness which I found most promising. With this stout-hearted fellow, I thought, as I settled down that night, we should be able to accomplish anything.

Costos was now working with great enthusiasm to help us. He was worried that neither of us could sail, cautioning us against the unbelievable fury of spring storms in the Aegean. Accordingly, he made inquiries the next day, and that evening a third member of the party arrived.

This was Alexis, a Russo-Greek, whose family had fled to Athens after the Revolution. He wanted to get to Cairo for reasons of his own and claimed to have a sound knowledge of sailing. We were all doubtful of his capabilities from the start, for he was only a lad of about eighteen, but we allowed his tremendous enthusiasm to sway us. He was irrepressibly cheerful. All that first night he kept us amused with highly improbable accounts of his life in Athens, where it appeared that every beautiful woman was his mistress.

The three of us made our farewells to Costos on the next morning. I, myself, felt quite emotional as I thanked the old fellow for all he had done for me. I knew as I waved a last farewell from the track above the house that Costos was one Greek I would seek out after the war.

In order to keep off the more normal routes, we struck high into the forest and traversed several ridges just below the snow line. We passed quite near to the lonely house of Elisais, but thought it wiser not to call in. That night we spent in a small empty shack in the forest, eating the food given to us by Costos.

Soon after noon of the next day we dropped down to a small monastery village, and while John and I concealed ourselves in the trees, Alexis was despatched to offer the large wad of money I had collected to a prospective seller for a small boat. As we had anticipated, he returned in about half an hour with the story that the owner wanted food or gold for the boat and had no use for the 'paper' we were offering.

We held a quick council of war. Costos had told me of a large boat-shed owned by some Russian Orthodox monks not far from this village. As a sop to my conscience I remembered that these White Russians were said to be collaborating with the Germans in the hope of seeing the old order restored by a German victory. A reconnaissance showed that this particular boat-shed was guarded by two monks who lived in a stout house built over it. But the area was lonely, and if we could somehow get the monks away we would be able to break in without much trouble. I would not countenance the suggestion that we should harm the monks in any way.

The ideal time for a theft had been explained to me by Costos. He explained that during Easter there was one night when every monk would go to church, when they would all gather together for the great Saturday night service. It seemed despicable to take advantage of this fact, but there was so much at stake, it was so imperative that I should get to Egypt at the earliest, that I decided it was warranted. John and I worked out the best approaches and tactics we should adopt on the presumption that the building would be left securely locked but empty. In conference with Alexis we came to the conclusion that we would need two more men at least, both for the quick seizure of the boat and for the long voyage. Alexis pointed out that the sails were a heavy task for three and that with five or six a steady speed could be maintained by rowing if the wind failed.

Accordingly, it was decided that I should remain on the spot to observe the habits of the monks in the boat-house while John made a trip to try to find an English Corporal he had encountered recently, so that he could come along also. Rather against my better judgement Alexis went off in another direction to seek the assistance of a monk friend of his who was a great sailor. We arranged a rendezvous at a house on the outskirts of the village, where evidently some rogue of a monk lived who would assist us to steal from his fellows. We were to meet there after dark on the following night, the Saturday of Easter.

When the other two had gone I made my way over to a small group of houses apart from the others, which were not Russian. I knew these belonged to the Monastery of St Lawrence. Here I introduced myself and was well received. I gave them no inkling that I was not on my own, nor that we were bent on stealing a boat from their rival monastery.

As it was Good Friday, all the monks were making their way to the all-night service and I was persuaded to join them. The church was a large one and had a special space with alcoves all round. Heavily gilded stone pillars led up into a glittering ceiling of polished brasswork. All along the main face were pictures of the saints, in front of each a tiny olive-oil lamp suspended by a fine chain from the ceiling. A large circular chandelier of tallow candles flooded the interior with soft light.

Each monk, on entering, kissed first the Virgin and Child, genuflecting several times, then his especial saint whose name he had assumed. Then he knelt for a few moments in front of the altar and lit one of the myriads of small lamps in front of the saints. After that he was given a long candle by one of the priests and led to a position in the church according to his grading. I found myself near the seats of the numerous priests, where I was gravely asked to make a sign of the cross after each prayer and hymn.

Gradually the hall filled up. Along the far side the boys could be seen with their too-sad girlish faces, and on the near side the older monks and junior priests. At the signal from my host, who was the Head Monk of the community, the lights on the great chandelier were one by one extinguished and the church left with a hundred flickering candles throwing weird shadows on the walls and pillars. According to the Orthodox custom, no one sat down at all throughout the long night service, although it was permitted to rest one's arms on wooden ledges built for that purpose. Many monks, I perceived, had cultivated the art of snoozing while standing thus, and I watched with amusement one old priest next to me who kept dozing so that his head would fall forward on to his candle and the black cowl over his cap almost catch fire. He was saved each time by one of his servants who would nudge him only, however, to be rudely reprimanded for his pains.

I excused myself soon after midnight. I was a little unhappy at the thought of avoiding the remainder of such a service in order to gain some rest for a very unrighteous enterprise, but slept well nevertheless.

'Pay Costos Momogos the sum of Ten "Pounds" Sterling.' Drawn by 9234 Lieutenant Walter Babington Thomas, Prisoner of War, Greece. (Agion Oros, Salonika), to procure funds for escape to Turkey. Address 'Dehra Doon' Riwaka, Nelson, New Zealand.

Cheques such as these were returned to the home bank after the war, and later reimbursed by the New Zealand Government.

Chapter Seventeen

Divine intervention

When I arrived at the agreed rendezvous just after dark the following night I was at first a little alarmed at the large gathering I found there. The owner of the house was a tall, thin fellow with as greedy a face as any villain ever had. I took an immediate dislike to him and his constant nagging for more money for the food we sought from him. We paid him at the rate of over five pounds per head, which was nothing short of blackmail.

John was there, in good spirits, in spite of a slight attack of malaria. With him was a short, dark lad who was introduced as Corporal Frank George. He had escaped from a working party in Salonika by sweeping the rubbish from a German Officers' Club down the stairs, into the street, and along the street until he could make a dash for it. He had met a wealthy Greek family in his travels and had stayed with them for two or three months, so he was dressed in a smart city suit which looked extremely odd amongst our rough clothes. The Greeks had dubbed him 'Nicki', as his small face was the image of the pictures in every church of St Nicholas.

Also with these two was a dark, heavily built man—Demetrius—a Greek Artillery officer who had befriended Nicki and now wished to join his monarch in Egypt. He was a well-educated and charming man, and I thought would probably be of great help on the voyage.

Alexis had with him an untidy figure of a monk. He presented him enthusiastically as Simonides, a champion sailor, who wanted to come with us, as he was now tired of being a monk and wanted to see something

Outline map of northern Aegean

of life. I looked at him. He was a giant of a fellow, perhaps six foot four tall and heavy to match. He had a mass of bright red hair, which hung untidily around his shoulders and down his chest almost to the length of his beard. I did not like the way his eyes lit up at the mention of Cairo. This man was not prompted by any thought of service to come with us: he was out for his own selfish ends and wished to avoid the sacred oath of renunciation he had made. However, I realised that we could probably put his knowledge of the sea to good purpose and welcomed him as a member of the team.

We removed the host from the room and had a quick conference. It was agreed between us that I should command the operation for the seizure of the boat, and that Alexis should be the master of the vessel while at sea. About nine in the evening we set off in groups of two down the steep hillside, around the monastery village, and then down into the small rock-enclosed bay where the boat-house was.

We were nearly caught out at one stage when, on rounding one of the corners of the zigzag descent, we almost ran into an old monk walking slowly upwards. John and I who were in the lead went straightway to the ground, but Alexis and the red-haired giant were moving less cautiously behind us and only got into the undergrowth in the very nick of time. We realised as he went past us, that one of the two guarding monks was now accounted for.

There was still a light in the house as we reached the rocky beach. I posted Nicki and the Greek officer at the end of the track up the hill, told Alexis and his friend to go beyond the house to watch from that direction, while John and I moved carefully closer.

We could hear someone talking inside. From the cover of some olive trees in a courtyard we listened, our hearts pounding with excitement. With relief we realised that the man inside was talking to a small dog, who yapped merrily in reply.

John favoured a quick sally into the house, to overpower the monk and tie him up, but I restrained him. I felt we were not dealing with soldiers or enemies, and if possible should avoid any violence. I decided that we should allow an hour for the monk to leave.

We did not have to wait that long. The monk appeared at the now darkened doorway, slammed the heavy door to, locked it, and made off slowly towards the track up the mountain. From inside a small plaintive wailing began which, no doubt, swamped our furtive movements as we moved out of the road to let the monk pass.

To allow a safe margin while he climbed up out of earshot, John and I passed the next twenty minutes or so in a careful reconnaissance of all the windows and doors of the house. All the windows were heavily criss-crossed with iron bars sunk deep into stone, and without days of filing were, we thought, impenetrable. On the side facing the sea were two heavy doors into the boat-shed, from which a well-constructed ramp ran down to the sea in between a natural break in the rocks. This was so stoutly barricaded and barred from the outside that we quickly despaired of ever opening it from without.

The only other door was the one by which we had seen the monk leave. It was on the first floor of the building and opened on to a rocky landing with hewn steps down to ground level. It was also very stout and firm, and I began to regret that we had not taken John's advice and captured the monk while the house was open.

However, I determined that we would get in somehow, even if we had to take the whole place to bits. The bay was some hundreds of feet below the village and we would have quite a margin of safety as far as noise was concerned. The only worry was that, if discovered, we knew of no exit from the bay other than that we had come down. By the cliffs all around I conjectured that we might easily be trapped there.

We called in Nicki and Alexis, leaving the other two to watch the approaches. From our first efforts, which drove the dog within to a shrill barking, we found that the door was held by a massive lock in the middle as well as some sort of bar about a foot from the top. What this last was we could not imagine until Nicki, quite by chance, found a latch hidden by one of the barred windows. This worked some string or wire to lift a bar inside. It was evidently some sort of additional lock the two monks used when they did not bother about the key. But the main lock in the middle was very stout; indeed, all our hammering with an axe brought by Alexis was to no avail, indeed hardly marked the door at all. Meanwhile, the dog inside unnerved us with its panic-stricken barking.

After an hour of endeavour by one and then the other, John suggested using a battering ram. A quick search found a pole some twenty feet long and almost a foot thick. It was too much for four of us, so we withdrew the sentries and staggered up the rock steps with six of us spaced along its length. With John at its head giving directions, we drew back, and then smashed the pole forward with terrific force on to the lock.

The first effort, and indeed the next ten or twelve, made practically no difference at all. The whole building seemed to jar and the pole bounced back in our hands. Soon, however, the tremendous weight of the weapon began to have an effect on the bolts and screws holding the lock. John announced triumphantly that there was a gap of half an inch, then an inch, and finally the door burst open, precipitating all of us on to the ground, some inside and some on the steps.

We picked ourselves up quickly and stumbled around in the dark of the room. The dog, too frightened now to do anything more than whimper, appeared at our feet as a small spaniel. In a few minutes we had lit a candle and had discovered the trapdoor which led down to the boat-shed. Here I divided our forces. Nicki was to remain at the door as sentry to avoid surprise as we got the boat ready, Demetrius was to forage with Simonides for food and water for the voyage, while John, Alexis and I went below to choose a boat and open the shed doors.

In less than ten minutes we had chosen a fifteen-foot open fishing boat with a stout mast and good sails, and had opened the doors to slide her out on the ramp. Meanwhile Demetrius had found bread, olives and salted fish, as well as a large water cask. The redhead, Simonides, appeared with several flasks of red wine which, in spite of my disapproving remarks, he loaded aboard. I did, however, put my foot down when both Alexis and Simonides made a second trip back and collected clothes, boots and small valuables. I insisted that they leave them on the ground; we would take only that which was absolutely necessary for the voyage and not turn ourselves into common thieves.

With all hands we launched our vessel down the runway of cross-beams to the edge of the water. The waves were surging up the runway with quite a frightening force, but with three of us aboard we managed to launch it easily. We drew in against the rocks carefully for the remainder. Just as they were in the act of clambering in, the small dog, now considering us as his owners off on a fishing jaunt, leapt from a rock above and landed in the centre of the boat. In the confusion and excitement of those minutes no one thought to throw him ashore again. I myself had a momentary pang of remorse as I thought how fond those lonely men would be of their pet, but a large wave struck us amidships at that moment and I turned my attention to helping Alexis to swing the boat into the running sea.

It was after midnight when we set out, and with a rising sea from an unfavourable wind, we decided to make along the coast to the end of the peninsula. We would hide up for the first part of the next day, and then sail for Turkey in the afternoon. Thus we considered that if we were pursued we would use our start to keep us ahead until darkness fell and then hope to make Imbros, a Turkish island, the next day. Just before dawn we pulled into a sheltered and lonely bay not very far from where I had lived with Costos. We covered the boat with branches and concealed ourselves in the trees.

During the morning differences arose about the control and command. I had made Alexis the skipper of the boat, and Simonides, who had been his friend, objected. Simonides had not shown himself much of a help during the night, so with the agreement of Nicki I decided that we should leave him behind. This course, which was also prompted by the fact that the boat was too small for six, was made easy by the man himself. Before midday he declared that there was going to be a storm and that he was not coming with us; furthermore, he was not going to be caught in the bay with the boat. With that he left us.

Soon after noon we drew out of the bay and headed east. There was a heavy swell, but we pulled on the four long oars with a will and were all highly optimistic and happy.

We were only a mile from the shore when we had our first fright. A fast German patrol boat rounded the point behind and sped towards us, leaving a wake of churning water behind it. But the steel-helmeted occupants scarcely looked at us as they passed less than a furlong away. In a few minutes the patrol boat was out of sight round the next headland.

As the afternoon went on the wind grew, and we hoisted the sail with a marked advantage. While the majestic peak of the Holy Mountain began to slip down into the sea behind us, ahead of us the features and buildings of the island of Lemnos became ever clearer. Navigation was most important. We were bound to go between Lemnos, which was a German strongpoint, and the Bulgarian-occupied island of Samothrace which was kept fully manned as a pressure threat against Turkey. To the east of the channel between these two lay the Turkish island of Imbros.

We were jubilant at our progress; by dusk we could see the houses on Imbros and had covered all of forty miles. We sang all the songs we could think of and were very content with our chances. But behind us from beyond the now tiny peak of Mount Athos a large black mass of cloud reached out towards us. With it came a strong wind and soon it became apparent that a storm was brewing. When the cloud mass began to cover us the sea was already whipped up into white horses and the heavy swell turned into tremendous and dangerous waves.

Alexis was at first confident and resourceful. He sailed into the darkness at a speed which must have exceeded twelve knots, shouting instructions to John and me to tighten this rope or loosen that, and controlling Demetrius who, with one oar, assisted him in turning. But soon it became apparent that we were very nearly out of control, the wind was too strong for the amount of canvas we were exposing. When I saw that the lad was losing his grip and was almost beside himself with terror, I suggested that we should drop the sail. His head jerked agreement frantically in the gloom, and John and I did our utmost to drop the mainsail. This was a type unlike any I have ever seen before or since. It was a long spar or boom which was hoisted into a deep angle formed by a short arm jutting forward off the mast near the top. The canvas swept down from this to the boom not unlike that of a small yacht. It had been relatively easy to rig, but to get it down was a different matter. Several times we were caught in the boom when Alexis turned and nearly swept overboard, and finally we decided that it was beyond us. The boat raced on into the night.

By this time the sea had risen to foam-crested waves as big as small steep hills which rushed down on to us from the rear, one following the other. One moment we were high in the air, looking over miles of foaming white in the darkness, and then we were down in an inky trough with black walls of water hissing on all sides. Both the wind and the waves came from behind us so that, in spite of our speed, we were often held on the very crest of a wave while it hurled us forward even faster. When this happened Alexis would fight to keep us with our pointed stern cleanly into the pursuing wave, and if he succeeded we got off lightly with only the foam licking over the sides of the boat. But if he failed in even the slightest degree the churning crest of the wave surged over the side of the boat, and times without number almost swamped us. We all bailed furiously, John and I with buckets and the others with hats, or mugs, or anything they could find. By the time the next wave arrived we would have the water down to about a foot in the bottom of the boat; we never seemed able to get it lower. Each of us realised as we worked frantically that it would need only two such waves taken consecutively side-on to swamp us completely.

It came on to rain heavily. Large drops mingled with the flying foam to drive against our faces and blind us in our frantic endeavours to keep the level of the water down. The dog, wretched and whimpering with fear, balanced uncomfortably on one of the cross-seats, from where he was washed into the centre of the boat by each wave we took broadside on.

Things were heading swiftly to a climax. Our chances of riding the storm slowly diminished. Nicki, worn out and racked with sea-sickness collapsed first—throwing himself on a small built-up decking near the bow and clinging there prostrate. Alexis, who had borne all the main stress of responsibility, passed his cracking point when a sudden and inexplicable cross-current of wind swept the boom from one side to the very opposite, tearing the ropes out of his hands. He thought the mast must have gone with the sudden strain and screamed in panic. When the boat lurched drunkenly before righting herself he let the tiller go free and splashed through the water to where we were bailing.

'It's no use ... it's no use!' he screamed. 'We are lost, we cannot live through this! Better to jump overboard and finish it quickly than carry on!' He collapsed on the seat by the dog, sobbing, moaning and praying.

It was touch and go at that moment: the boat lurched drunkenly from the side of a wave and in a moment was broadside on in the trough below. With every ounce of energy I could muster I floundered back to the tiller and forced it over. Heavy with water, indeed almost swamped, the boat responded sluggishly in spite of our speed, but as the next wave thundered behind us she straightened to a less dangerous angle. Even so, a great wall of seething water crashed down on to us, washing every loose thing overboard and forcing us to hang on for our very lives.

Before, with an experienced sailor at the helm, we had kept five men fully employed bailing. Now, with a complete novice struggling clumsily with the tiller and one oar, there was only John and the Greek officer to bail. It seemed hopeless. John continued to bail with all his might, pausing every few minutes only to try and curse the others into some action. The Greek officer began to pray aloud as he bailed and his prayers mingled with John's curses, Nicki's retching, and the sobs of the boy, Alexis.

In between the tremendous waves there was a brief respite which gave half a moment for reflection as I worked the tiller. I weighed up our chances each time. At first, I thought very selfishly what I could do to save myself alone when the boat finally went under; there were the water casks half empty for example, which would support one person if he could be lashed to them. And then I thought perhaps it would be only for a brief hour; would it not be better to dive and dive even deeper into the sea, straining and striving with the very last of my will-power until I collapsed. Somewhere I had read that this was a painless death.

After a while, however, these brief moments of reflection became more peaceful. I was strangely resigned. It was all going to be so very simple, but oh! how rotten for my mother and father at home! They would never know, no one would ever know, how it all happened. They would worry for years and pray against all probability that I would reappear. How much better to have been cleanly killed on Crete. So went my thoughts.

We took in another deluge from a partial broadside and John, exhausted, straightened from his bailing. He waded down to me and peered into my face. I called to him, but a gust of wind drove the words back into my mouth. He understood that and grinned a reply as he sat down opposite me on the end seat. The Greek officer had given up bailing and taken to prayer alone a few minutes earlier and was kneeling on the bottom of the boat, with his elbows on the centre seat, while the water swirled around his chest, rocking him from side to side. My own knees and lower thighs, as I sat, were under water.

The dog swam down from the bow where he had been sheltering with Nicki and clambered up on to my lap, whimpering with cold and fright. John reached over and fondled it and had his hands licked in return.

Raising my face into the driving rain I prayed quietly. My initial panic and dread had passed and I felt resigned, indeed peaceful and expectant. It was not for some miraculous deliverance that I prayed, but rather to prepare myself for what seemed quite inevitable. More as a gesture than with any idea of assistance John took over the single oar I was using to aid the tiller. He called something which I couldn't catch above the wind, and then we remained quiet and waited....

With the level of the water only about three or four inches below that of the ocean, the boat lumbered sluggishly along in spite of the unabated fury of the wind. Something had to give way soon, either the tall mast or the sail itself, for the strain was terrific.

Every so often, every seventh wave to be exact, a tremendous sea would overtake us and hurl us along for some hundreds of yards. To be caught broadside on by one of these would be the end; we could never hope to right the sodden boat.

Suddenly the climax came. A violent cross-wind tilted the boat almost on to its side and swung the boom right across. There was a terrific crack and in front of our eyes the sail split in two, flapped twice, and then disappeared in countless ragged threads.

This was the moment we had been waiting for. We braced ourselves mentally and waited for the boat to settle as she lost way. One of the tremendous seventh-wave seas rushed down on us from behind, and I felt the dog go rigid in my lap. Someone screamed. For another split second John and I waited for the end.

The giant wave poised above us, and in spite of its fury and speed it seemed to curl its seething crest slowly and deliberately before crashing down upon us. A great deluge of foaming water struck me on my head and shoulders and I felt the boat shudder beneath me. I closed my eyes. There was a roaring in my ears and the swirling of water all around me, but I was not at first swept from my seat.

Then I felt myself crushed to the bottom of the boat, smashed into the seat and thrown against John and the dog. While I was fighting to get my head above water again time seemed to stand still and I waited almost impatiently for the end. There was no great feeling of fear, no clutching panic such as I had always imagined would come at the moment of death; while my body twisted and fought I myself felt tranquil and mildly curious. A red glaze appeared before my eyes and I wondered if this was the start of my transition to the other world. From a long way off someone was calling my name, and I felt a flow of satisfaction that I was known in the new world. Then everything went black, although I could still faintly hear my name being called. It was all over.

'Mr Thomas, Mr Thomas, sir! You must make an effort! Speak to me!' floated into my consciousness. 'Good heavens,' I thought, 'that is John! Fancy still treating me as an officer after I am dead!'

Suddenly my mind cleared. I opened my eyes to find myself in the crook of John's right arm; his left arm was working the tiller furiously. The storm was in no way abated, but something was different. Of course, there was no sail, but also there seemed to be less water in the boat. While I wondered at this we were lifted over a large wave with scarcely a splash coming aboard. I roused myself into action.

'I thought you'd had it, sir,' called John, grinning up at me as I pulled away from him. 'I think we're better without the sail. She lifts over the crest of each wave now instead of pulling through them. As long as we can keep the old bitch stern on to these mountains I think we might live through the night!'

I took over the tiller from him, and with one oar kept the pointed stern straight into the pursuing rollers, using the old mariner's practice of keeping direction in the dark by the feel of the wind on the cheek.

Meanwhile, John busied himself with the bucket and, when they saw his marked progress, the others picked up fresh heart and went to his assistance. Presently, with satisfaction, I observed that the water was down below the level of the seats, and after a while there remained only six or seven inches.

I screwed up my eyes against the teeming rain and stared up into the darkness. Although I could not express myself adequately, I sought the same awareness of something divine which I had felt before the climax of the storm. For it was a true miracle I wished to acknowledge. However, only the rain came tumbling out of the murky blackness and I realised that the comforting Presence had passed on with the crisis, and that I was now able to proceed without it. However, as I wrestled with my oar and tiller throughout the night, I enjoyed a warm glow of wonder and devotion in recalling the certainty of Holy comfort and intervention.

The night was terribly long; dawn seemed to have forgotten us. But after what seemed an interminable period, measured only by the waves which passed us, a slight lightening of the sky appeared, and presently we were able to see some distance whenever we topped the crest of wave. The first reaction was of new fear for, strangely enough, the waves we had experienced all the night appeared more fearful when seen approaching from afar, toppling and frothing as their curled crests collapsed.

Towards midday the rain eased off and the wind began to drop, although for some time there was no perceptible change in the waves. The Greek officer, who was staring blankly into the distance, suddenly started into life.

'Land!' he cried excitedly. 'Look there, right down on the horizon, a small black peak!'

And sure enough we all picked it up. We estimated that it must be some thirty miles to the north of us and fell to wondering what it could be. I think we all had different ideas and that they ranged over islands spaced over several hundreds of miles of the Aegean, but no one could be sure. Alexis and Demetrius slipped an oar in opposite rowlocks and began to assist John and me. I swung the boat as near as I dared towards the new target. Be it Italian, German, Greek or Bulgarian, we were going to try our luck there.

Later in the afternoon we were still over ten miles from this land, but by then it had risen out of the sea so that its shape was unmistakable. With heavy hearts we recognised the features of the Holy Mountain itself. The storm must have beaten us over fifty miles to the west off our course, and now we had little alternative but to land where we might on the peninsula we had left. With the constant rowing our hands, unused to such work, blistered and finally peeled raw. In particular, John, who would stop for nothing, had two ugly bleeding hands and thus it was out of the question to start east to Turkey again, even if the weather abated at all. The only passenger who was at all happy to see the great Mountain again was the dog who had miraculously lived through the night. He stood up in the bow yapping excitedly as the land grew nearer.

It was well after dark when we came under the lee of the great cliffs of the easternmost tip of the peninsula, and we were more than a little concerned about our chances of effecting a harbour in such a sea. It appeared almost impossible to find a place where these tremendous waves would not be smashing against the rocky cliffs. We dared not go in too close lest we be caught into their fury.

I gave orders that everyone should loosen all buttons and remove shoes, for I was afraid that we might have to swim for it. John arranged to help Nicki, and I to help Alexis who professed not to swim at all.

The boat was swept along the face of the cliffs by a strong current running directly across the direction of the waves and wind. We rowed steadily to give control to the tiller and, after a series of attempts to get into small breaks in the cliff-face, we suddenly found ourselves thrust into a sheltered bay to the leeward of the storm. With every ounce of energy we had left we struggled across the current as it attempted to draw us out again, and presently we were in still water under a massive overhanging cliff. We moved carefully along its face and found a rough stone landing-stage built out from a large building which stood in darkness thirty feet from the jetty.

We were terribly weak from the long ordeal, and it was as much as we could do to tie the boat up securely, drag ourselves ashore and approach the house. Indeed, when we found that the place was deserted and the door locked we were forced to lie down on the stone courtyard outside and rest before we could do anything about it. When we had recovered sufficiently John declared the lock was too heavy to pick and we resorted to the same battering-ram tactics we had employed before. The door gave way quite easily to this treatment, and before long we had a roaring fire going inside and some food from the house larder cooking. Before many minutes we were all asleep on a rug by the fire with our clothes drying all round the main room.

Chapter Eighteen

The Three Musketeers

The period following the big theft was one of comradeship and adventure. Forced to flee before dawn the next morning, after a warning from the police, we had struck high into the mountain to get clear of the area. Here I divided the force into two bands, Demetrius and Alexis heading towards St Lawrence, and we three English north along the peninsula. Below us the sea continued to thrash and storm.

We made our way through the mountain monastery villages, calling on any friends we might know and spending the money I had collected on good food. We seldom stayed more than one night in any one place, and we made a point of giving false information about out destination, for the news of the theft had travelled swiftly through the monasteries.

After moving steadily north for a week we came into an area which both John and Nicki knew well. One morning soon after dawn we stealthily approached a small house standing on its own on the edge of a clearing. John had declared that this would make an ideal headquarters from which we could sally forth in search of boats. We were determined to repeat our theft when the opportunity presented itself, but not until the weather had settled down a little.

A careful reconnaissance showed that there was no one in the house, and we closed in. The door was heavily barred, and had a thick chain drawn through it and its stone framework. It looked as if it would be a ticklish business breaking in.

'I never intended getting in by the door, sir,' John explained. 'I was just looking to see if anyone had been here since I last made a visit. If such is the case there's probably some fresh food inside. I'll now show you how the Commandos get into a house of this kind.' Grinning broadly, he began to worm his way between the large stone foundations under the house.

Following him closely, we watched while he tapped the boards over his head until one responded to his liking. He forced it upwards. In a few moments we had all clambered into the room above. John fumbled about in the dark and lit a candle. We saw that we were in a small square room with a large open fireplace, in which wood was already laid for a fire, so we put a match to it and sat on the floor to warm ourselves.

'I stayed here last summer with a monk,' said John, 'and one day, while he was working in the field below, I loosened these boards. I knew he was going back to the monastery to live in the winter and I thought it would make a good hide-out. I wonder if he's anything in his larder?' He ferreted round the adjoining room, returning with some potatoes and salted fish. It was not until the meal was well under way that he told us the olive oil he was using to cook with came from the oil-lamps in the attached chapel.

We dished up the meal and were preparing to enjoy it when we heard a heavy step on the porch outside. We looked at one another in dismay and then quickly gulped a few mouthfuls of food in case we had to make a dash for it.

Meanwhile there was a rattling of heavy chains outside and the scraping of a massive key in the equally massive lock.

The door swung slowly inwards.

We kept absolutely still, our food in our laps, our heads turned towards the intruder.

The slight figure of a very old and stooping monk was silhouetted against the doorway. He came slowly into the room humming a chant in low monotone.

The fire had sunk low and was partially screened by our figures, so that at first he didn't spot us, but went into the chapel, where we could hear him moving about.

Presently his humming stopped and we heard an exclamation of surprise.

'He's found there's no oil in the lamps,' whispered John apprehensively and, I hoped, with some sense of guilt. The old man appeared at the dividing door again muttering into his beard.

Then he spotted us. His mouth dropped open in astonishment, and for a few moments he was speechless.

'It's all right, Papa,' John said in Greek. 'We are friends; we're only taking refuge. We want nothing but food and shelter, so don't worry.'

The old man certainly was not worried. He was thrilled to have found us, and genuinely amused at our ingenious entry into the house. He produced some dried herbs and made us a pleasant drink on the embers of the fire before he locked the door again and went back to the monastery.

We made good use of that hut. The old monk visited it regularly, and whether we were there or not left baskets of fresh food for us. Often while we were inside passers-by, no doubt attracted by the smoke, would come on to the porch and try the door. But the heavy lock and chains fastened from the outside always confounded them, and they never stayed long.

Another of our hide-outs was the lodge of the Monastery of St Paul, whose gatekeeper, a monk called Pavlas, was a friend of Nicki. It was Pavlas who brought us news of a boat. He found that a civilian fisherman from the small island of Amuliana was negotiating for a contract with the monks of a nearby village. He had arrived in a very suitable boat which he left each night in the middle of a beach below the village and, provided a really dark night was offered, there seemed no reason why we could not help ourselves.

Accordingly, the very night we were given this intelligence we left the lodge and marched the two hours to the bay Pavlas had mentioned. With no difficulty we made our way down the steep track which ran around the outskirts of the village and with stealth reached the beach.

Sure enough, hidden in the rocks, was a large whaling boat which would be quite adequate for the voyage. There was no mast, but we had decided that even if it took us a month we were prepared to row the full distance.

We had a strenuous time getting the boat down into the water, for it was very heavy. Finally, however, she was afloat, and we turned her head to the south-east and began rowing. There was no sign of any alarm from the village above; we could hear the sounds of merry laughter and revelry as we pulled away.

The weather for the preceding several days had been perfect, with a sea as smooth as glass. Thus, we had high hopes of a steady trip to Imbros; we had brought provisions for two or three days. Fate, however, was definitely against our maritime attempts for, as we rounded the headland of the peninsula, we ran into a swift current and a steadily rising sea. Reluctantly and with heavy hearts we pulled into a rocky cove and concealed the boat, praying that the next day might show some improvement.

But all next morning the waves mounted with the wind until there was a full-scale gale sweeping into the bay. To our consternation, the waves began to endanger our boat by dashing her against the rocks to which we had anchored her. After some deliberation we decided to beach her. As this meant exposing ourselves and the boat to observation from a cluster of houses several hundred feet above the bay, we realised that we would probably not get away with it.

We were not, therefore, greatly surprised when, soon after we had got her up to safety, we spotted a file of armed policeman making their way down the steep hillside towards us. We had the choice of putting to sea immediately, which was not very inviting, or escaping on foot up a steep track on the far side of the bay. Sad as we were to leave the boat, the last course seemed the wiser, and we made off with all possible speed.

The track, which was obviously little used, took us along some breath-taking ledges and cliffs, and then across a giant landslide of house-sized rocks. We spent the night in a large cave entrance.

We were not the only occupants of the cave which evidently ran deep into the mountainside. Soon after we had arrived we were almost trampled down by a herd of large goats which rushed into the cave entrance and disappeared into the darkness. They were followed by an old shepherd monk who clambered slowly in and approached us.

He was not surprised to find us. He said that the cave had been used for centuries by wayfarers and that, before the great landslide, the main route had passed its entrance. He pointed to a well dug in the rock floor and to cast-iron fittings for faggot torches on the wall. The old monk insisted on sharing his meal with us and, as he had had a good day fishing, we had a good spread. We lit a fire on the floor of the cave and cooked the fish on the embers.

The next morning we said goodbye to the old man and continued on our way. We had travelled only about an hour when we came over a ridge and looked down on to a large, cliff-lined bay. We recognised it at once as the bay where we had stolen our first boat.

'I don't suppose we could get that boat again?' I wondered aloud. 'We could almost manage it with the three of us now that we've had a little experience.'

'I'm on,' said John. 'Let's go down and see what the form is.'

We could see two monks working in the courtyard of the house. One of them turned and saw us.

'It's all right. He doesn't know who we are,' said John. 'You can see that he isn't at all suspicious.'

'We'll go right down to the house then and have a look round,' I said, 'and if things look at all favourable we'll climb up into the trees on the other side and wait until dark.'

We went a little closer.

'Look!' said Nicki, pointing excitedly. 'Look, there's the little dog which came with us.'

'The police must have returned the little beggar when they brought back the boat,' said John. 'I hope the poor little blighter was no worse for the trip.'

The two monks were both facing us now. They still looked unworried.

Then something unforeseen happened. Something which changed the situation and exposed us as effectively as though we had shouted who we were to the two monks.

The little dog which had been lying at the feet of the elder monk suddenly looked up in our direction. In one bound it was out of the courtyard and running, yapping, towards us. At first, we thought it was merely going to greet our approach with some barking. But the little brat was thrilled to see us again. It leapt into our arms in turn, licking our faces in a frenzy of recognition and welcome. There could not have been a worse give-away.

The two monks stood gaping for a few seconds, and then called the dog. But, suddenly, one of them saw the reason for the dog's welcome and shouted to the other. They both made a hurried departure from the courtyard into the house and we could hear doors banging and bolts being driven home. They were in a great panic.

'That fixes that,' said John, grinning in spite of the set-back. 'This little beggar has served them better than they thought.'

'Let's get out of here,' said Nicki, looking apprehensively around the bay. 'I've got a feeling we're not wanted, and those old fellows might have a gun!'

'What about the dog?' asked John, fondling it in his arms. 'Should we take it?'

'No, certainly not,' I admonished him. 'That dog probably means a tremendous lot to these people. Put him down and let him run back to the house.'

After this we were very closely watched whenever we went near the sea. Our friends warned us there was a sizeable price on our heads and that the Germans were searching us out. Obviously we must leave the peninsula. Travelling north, after two days we crossed the isthmus near the village of Pyrgos and entered the world once more.

Chapter Nineteen

His Majesty's subjects

'Blimey!' said John, turning to me in agreement. 'It's a fair risk, I reckon! There don't seem to be any Germans round here, and if we couldn't pull it off we could easily fix these people. Besides, it'll be dark in three hours.'

We looked down on to the busy scene below from the cover of the brushwood. All along a wide, clean beach there were small groups of men and women doing the chores of a fishing village; some were mending nets hung over high wooden railings, others were scrubbing boats and cleaning fish. Everyone was fully occupied. Ten yards from the water's edge, and a safe distance from the nearest group, was the most perfect small sailing craft we had ever seen.

The point we were considering that afternoon was whether it would be possible to walk boldly down the beach and take her. It was extraordinarily tempting.

It was several days since we had left the Holy Mountain and we had moved slowly through a series of small fishing villages, always on the lookout for a boat. We had made our way almost to the extremity of the second great peninsula of Longos without finding anything suitable, but here was a discovery which appeared more promising. There was something so foolhardy and reckless about the thought of stealing a boat from under the very eyes of so many people that it was decidedly attractive. We looked at one another in silence for a few minutes, grinning like schoolboys about to raid an orchard, in spite of a dread that the consequences might be disastrous, particularly if there were any Germans within rifle fire. The sense of adventure prevailed. With one accord we moved down on to the beach.

Some of the girls working on the nets looked up idly as we passed, and I saw John wink openly at one dark lass, but on the whole our presence seemed to raise no particular comment. From a safe distance we would appear as three rough seamen, foreign perhaps, but then the fishing villages were used to foreigners.

As we approached the boat we could see that she had four large oars lying on the sand alongside, and that all the sails were furled against the single mast.

We picked up the oars as we arrived and threw them carelessly aboard. Without further ado we commenced to shove her down the sand to the water. It was not easy by any means, for she was a heavy craft, but in a few minutes we had her afloat and were safely aboard. As we slipped a pair of oars into the rowlocks I glanced apprehensively along the beach, but no one seemed at all interested. We rowed only a few hundred yards and unfurled the sail. A gentle breeze from the land filled the canvas and we began to make way.

'Seems to be a lot of water about,' said Nicki, who was already looking a little green around the gills, for he was a hopeless sailor. He had told us once that he was often seasick while rowing on the Thames.

'Well, set to and bail,' said John from the tiller. 'She has probably been lying in the sun all day and the cracks have warped open a little. They'll soon close up.'

This view was, however, not born out by events. The level of the water rose slowly but steadily in spite of Nicki's efforts with the small bailing can. When it was over our ankles we looked at one another in consternation. Something was wrong.

'Hullo, what's that?' said Nicki, straightening up from his bailing, and pointing to a three-inch stick of wood which was floating out from the seat across the bow. There was a dark ring up the first inch or so of its length, as though it had been used as a cork.

'Blimey!' cried John, splashing up the boat and seizing it. 'It's the bung. No wonder we're shipping water.'

We all fell to a frenzied search for the hole where the bung belonged. We splashed about from stem to stern, poking our fingers in every possible place, but to no avail. The level of water crept higher now that Nicki had left off bailing to assist. We tore up all the millboards on the bottom of the boat and felt every inch of the planks in spite of the swirling water. Determined to leave no stone unturned in our endeavours John even stripped and dived over the side in the remote hope that the hole might show better from there.

The water continued to make progress and at last, when it was almost up to our knees, we realised that there was no choice but to make back. By some strange twist of humour I found myself more amused than disappointed at that moment, for the picture of the three of us with our hands thrust deep in water frantically poking with our fingers seemed excruciatingly funny.

Meanwhile, the scene back on the beach had changed. People were rushing this way and that, and their excited shouts could be plainly heard across the water. A party of youths were heaving a large sailing boat down the beach from a boat-shed, and we guessed that whatever had happened they would have given us chase. It was a matter of conjecture whether we would have been able to hold our lead until darkness gave us the chance of giving them the slip.

When everyone saw that we were making back to the beach there was a general lessening of tension, and we noticed that the sailing boat which had been launched was not putting to sea. A small crowd began to gather at the point from where we had made the theft, and in the centre of this one man stood out as the most concerned. He was a short dark fellow and he was striding up and down the beach in front of the interested and admiring crowd, waving his fists in the air, tearing his hair, stamping on the sand, and generally demonstrating a Greek version of the Highland Fling. We presumed this man to be the outraged owner.

'What are we going to do, sir?' asked John, eyeing the reception as we drew nearer. 'Punch that little man on the nose or apologise?'

Two or three young men of the village waded out to meet us and guided the boat towards the shore. Heavy with water, she was drawing at least eighteen inches more than normal, and the shallow keel ran aground some twenty yards from the high-water mark. We clambered off and waded through two feet of water for the rest of the way.

The little man darted in front of us, reaching his fist up to within inches of our noses and waving his hands to the heavens in fury as he drew down every known curse on to our heads. He was obviously a past master at invective and even the crowd of fisher-people, who have a remarkable standard in that direction, were visibly impressed with this effort. We were amazed at his vitality. He went on for over twenty minutes. We did not have the opportunity to say a word.

However, at last he finished. He paused to regain his breath and glared at us balefully as though surprised and indignant that we should still be standing. Making use of one of the favourite Greek gestures, I shrugged my shoulders and opened my hands in front of me.

'What can we do?' I demanded, smiling at him. 'We are English and are bound to get back somehow to our army to fight your enemy and ours.'

The little man started off on another round, but perceived to his astonishment that the crowd had shifted its sympathy; indeed, one man had come forward and taken John by the hand in welcome. He paused, perplexed for a moment, and then pushed aside those who were moving over to us and, facing the crowd, began to harangue them instead. He spoke too fast and with such a difficult dialect that I could not follow all he said, but the gist appeared to be that, after all, it was his boat that had been stolen by the English, and therefore it was for him only to offer us welcome to the village. It was typical of Greek reasoning and we three grinned at one another as we realised that things had changed for the better.

There was a small amount of opposition to this change of front, but I was certain no Greek present thought it in any way incongruous. They just wanted the chance to welcome us, too. The little man, however, was not going to waive his claim. Finally, he broke off from cursing the crowd and came beaming towards us. He seized and pumped our hands in turn and then, with his arm round Nicki's shoulder as the smallest of us, he led us up the beach. He talked volubly all the while.

Some three hours later we were seated around the hearth of this strange little man, the very same man whose boat we had stolen, drinking his wine, and discussing, of all things, the possibilities of *stealing another boat belonging to a friend of his*! The Greek is quite delightfully enigmatic.

Greatly interested in the topic and obviously excited with the adventure of having English fugitives in their house, the two elder daughters of our host kept our glasses filled and captivated us with their laughing charm. Both of them were attractive, not beautiful, but radiating good health and vitality. Trudi, the elder of the two, sat by my side, and whenever I looked I seemed to find her brown eyes staring boldly into mine; it was both pleasantly stirring and disconcerting after so many months of life in the monasteries. The second lass was called Eta, and she made no secret of her admiration for John.

'About half an hour from here,' said our host, speaking a little thickly from the effects of the wine, 'there is a small bay surrounded by thick trees. It is very lonely nowadays, as the owners have moved to Salonika.

'The only building on the foreshore is a boat-shed. It is a very big boat-shed and very, very strongly built. It would be very hard to get into.' He paused and looked at each of us in turn with a tipsily knowing expression, enjoying our full attention. 'But inside that shed is a boat, one of the most wonderful boats on this coast. She is, in fact, a launch, but there is, of course, no fuel to run her these days. That is why she is laid up.'

'Has she oars, could we row it?' demanded Nicki, all agog.

'She has oars, that I know, for I have often been out in her, but you couldn't row her far, she is too big.' He laughed at our consternation. 'What's wrong with using the sails, though? Are they not better than oars? That is, if you do take her, for I am suggesting nothing. Why should I, anyway? It belongs to my brother-in-law by my first marriage. Not that it wouldn't serve him right to lose it; he is always so stuck up and proud.'

'I am sure that dear Uncle Hadsi would not mind if John and Thomas and Nicki took his boat for a while,' pouted Eta, showing a generous if hardly practical mind. 'It is not doing any good there; anyway, it will probably be rotting.'

It seemed too good to be true. How anyone could leave a shed unguarded for even a day in this land of happy thieves was beyond us, and we felt confident at that stage that a building would have to be very strong indeed to resist our force, provided we had a few uninterrupted hours. The evening took on a new atmosphere of expectation and excitement, in which the girls joined to the full. We had found some sound allies.

Before dawn the next morning we were round in the bay and examining the lonely and deserted-looking boat-shed from the cover of the trees. It certainly had every appearance of sound construction, but we had no doubt that we could break in somehow. A more pressing problem was the thought of our small numbers. It would be tragic, we decided, to steal such a boat, which by all accounts could weather any storm, and find that we could not handle her. However impatient we were to be gone, this plan was better approached carefully and methodically. Someone would have to go back to the Holy Mountain, brave the German patrols there, and make contact through Philippas, the Police Sergeant at St Lawrence, with Demetrius and whoever else was with him.

My leg was in no state for such a long march, and I would have liked to see Nicki tackle it, as he was the fittest by far, but it was John who said firmly that he would undertake the task. We all turned back towards the village together to collect some food for the journey.

Just as we began to climb, however, we heard someone running lightly through the trees ahead and, to our astonishment, suddenly observed Trudi stumbling and falling over herself as she rushed to join us. She was panting and sobbing, and when she reached us she could not at first speak, but threw her arms around my neck and lay breathless, while her lithe body heaved and shuddered in agitation.

'Hide ... Germans ... eleven of them this morning,' she gasped presently, tightening her hold around my neck. 'They are looking for you now; someone must have sent them news.' She buried her head in my neck and commenced to cry.

'They took Father away. He did not tell them anything, though,' she sobbed. 'He said that after stealing his boat you forced him to give you food and shelter for the night and that you left for Salonika. I came as soon as I could while Eta stayed to watch the house. You must fly, you must fly as far from here as you can!'

I looked at John and Nicki over her black wavy hair, wondering for a moment what we should do. It soon became clear that whatever transpired we should not willingly leave the wonderful chance which the boat-shed represented, not even for a hundred Germans. The news of our host's capture was alarming and I felt a deep concern for him and for the worry his absence would bring the girls. Somehow, however, I guessed that he would talk his way out of this predicament and even enjoy himself in the process. If he was to get away with it he would be the hero of the village.

'What's the form, boss?' said John, unruffled as usual. 'Do we chance our luck now, lie low for a few weeks, or stick to our original plan?'

'Nothing will divorce me from this boat, John,' I replied. 'We'll continue much as before, but it looks as if Nicki and I will have some uncomfortable nights until you return. We will stay in the woods above this bay whatever the weather. I suggest that you set off right away and get back as soon as possible. How many days do you think it will take?'

'Four. Two there and two back, allowing me a safe margin for rest. I should be back here next Friday evening. Where will I find you two ... inside the boat-shed perhaps?'

'No, John, it would be foolish to approach that building until we are all prepared for the actual theft. We will collect food and water and wait for you. Do you see that tall fir jutting out from that clump of elms? The track runs near there. When you get back place three stones in a small triangle at the foot of that tree and then wait nearby by. When it is safe Nicki and I will search you out.'

There was nothing indolent about John. If there was something to be done he liked to get straight into it, and with his training as a regular soldier was never happy until he had brought it off satisfactorily. He turned on his heels and, with a half-smile for a farewell, strode off into the trees.

Nicki and I comforted Trudi as best we could before she left to return to Eta. We showed her the little hollow we had chosen for a headquarters, and she promised to smuggle out blankets and food and water for us. We also asked her to look into the possibility of getting some tools suitable for housebreaking; we had only vague ideas what was required for this purpose, but asked her to concentrate on a crowbar, an axe and a saw.

We were deeply indebted to Trudi in the few days that followed John's departure. Risking the punishment of the German patrol in the village, which could quite conceivably have been death, she slipped out of the village each evening past the roving sentries. She would skirt round to avoid any betrayal of her direction and would make her way to our hiding-place in the trees. Each time she would bring something for us to eat and something for the voyage. One evening, against our protests, she made a second trip, to stagger back with an iron crowbar as long as herself. That night she stayed with us under the trees and slept like a child in my arms.

Friday evening came, but there was no sign of John and his party. I tried to convince myself that he was delayed by Demetrius being farther afield than we had anticipated, but my knowledge of John and his emphatic declaration that he would be back on Friday started me on alarming thoughts of the active patrols reported on the Holy Mountain. Trudi arrived as usual, bringing her sister Eta who, no doubt, was anxious to see John. They were full of news. First, their father had been released, although they thought he was still under observation. He had to report to the Mayor's house, where the patrol was living, every evening and was not allowed to leave the village. Then, as if it did not concern us at all, they went on to tell us that the Germans were going to organise a wide sweep of the area the next morning in which all men of the village were to take part. The Germans were confident that they would find the English, but the girls laughed merrily at the thought that we were so far away.

I was not so sure. The Germans could be very thorough when they liked, and this lonely bay might seem an ideal place for investigation. I walked up to the fir tree again, feeling far from happy.

There were no stones at the base, but as I turned to go back to the girls I heard a movement in the trees nearby. A dry twig snapped and a branch swished as though it had been bent back and then released. I dropped to the ground, my heart in my mouth, but for a few minutes all was eerie and quiet. Then, suddenly, something came whistling through the air at me. I ducked in fear of a grenade, but to my embarrassment a single pine cone plopped on to the ground by my head and out of the darkness came the sound of John laughing quietly.

I rushed up to him and hugged him, so pleased I was to have him safely back. With him was Demetrius and two others, both soldiers from the British Colony of Cyprus. John introduced them quickly: Carlos, a short, olive-complexioned lad whose teeth shone brightly even in the dark, and a lanky, older man, Petra. Without any further ado, I explained the urgency of the situation to them all and we hurried down to Nicki and the girls. In a few minutes we had made a brief but very memorable farewell to these stout-hearted heroines and were on the way down to the beach. As they were new to the problem I placed Demetrius and the two Cypriots on guard, each at some distance from the shed in different directions, and we set to work.

When we had had a closer look we were not so surprised as we had been that it had been left unguarded. It was a real fort. The walls were of well-fitted and closely mortared stone, and the windows were heavily barred with iron. There was no way of finding a weak link underneath as the whole building was embedded into natural rock. There were but two alternatives, the main double doors or the small entrance door.

We looked to this latter, confident that our old ally, the battering ram, would fill the bill. We found a large pole, twenty feet in length, and withdrew the sentries so that we could lift it do to its task. The door, however, took the full weight stolidly, and after two solid hours of straining and smashing all there was to show for our labours was a large crack from top to bottom and a few splinters. We realised that this door differed from the others we had tried, because it normally opened outwards. Thus, any force from the outside only embedded it further into its frame. We decided to leave it for a while.

The two main doors stood about twenty feet high, no doubt to allow mast clearance for the boats. They were constructed of timber about three-quarters of an inch thick and felt very solid. By exerting our weight against them we were able to find out that there was something which held the doors as firm as a wall about four feet up from the ground. We decided that this was a long bar running the full width of the doorway and probably deeply embedded into sockets in the stone. The doors would be held to it by two large iron clasps.

Where the two doors joined there was an overlap of a piece of timber which we managed to remove with the crowbar, but this did not get us very far. We were able, however, to slip the blade of John's sheath knife through the crack between the doors and to gain some idea of the size of the bar. We thought it was at least five inches wide and three inches thick. By that time it was nearly midnight and things looked a little hopeless.

It was at that stage Nicki had his brilliant inspiration. He suggested that we widen the crack between the doors with the axe and then slip the saw through to hack the bar in two.

This sounded very simple. We set to with enthusiasm but found it far from easy. The doors were of well-seasoned and tough timber and the little axe bounced back in the hand rather than into them. However, bit by bit we splintered off shavings until there was an eighth of an inch gap above the bar. We inserted the saw.

It was not a good saw, was probably more suitable for pruning small branches than cutting through a thick slab of seasoned wood. In contrast to the English type of handsaw, the teeth were so arranged that the bite was on the pull and not the push. We worked steadily on, hour by hour. In turn, each of us would saw furiously for as long as he could and then pass it on to the next. There was no perceptible progress made by each individual effort on the hard wood, but we reckoned on making an inch every hour.

The night dragged on and still we were unmolested, while no doubt in the village over the hill the Germans were resting content with their chances of ferreting us out on the morrow. A pale half-moon sank below the bank of clouds on the seaward horizon, leaving us with only the light from the stars.

We made better progress than we had anticipated. Little by little, each of us found how best to make the worn teeth of the saw bite out a maximum of the hard, dry wood, and about four in the morning John finished it off. We all gathered around expectantly, but even then there was still some obstacle. It appeared that the bottom of one of the doors was fastened somehow to the stone flooring and that the other door was unable to open first. We set to work with the axe again and in a few minutes had hewn the corner off the bottom of the obstructed door sufficiently to insert the large crowbar. Then, with all of us on the end, we exerted all our weight. There was a tearing and a splintering and suddenly both the doors swung open.

Inside, taking up nearly all the space of the large shed, was the most wonderful boat we had so far seen. It was forty feet long and was completely decked, even to the provision of a smart cabin. There was a relatively small main mast and a second small one at the very stern, both of which had sails neatly furled to their respective boom. Twin propellers denoted that she was normally power driven and that the sails were merely a standby.

We had been a little worried about getting her out of the shed and were delighted to find that she was on a roughly constructed but thoroughly adequate wheeled cradle. Indeed, when we untied the restraining ropes it was all we could do to prevent her from rushing there and then into the sea. Profiting always by experience, we first made a thorough search of her hull and satisfied ourselves that the bung was in position, and then eased her gently down the concrete runway into the water.

There were four great oars, each of them twice as long and three times as heavy as any I had ever seen, and we used these, with the uprights of the railing as a rowlock, to manoeuvre her out into the open sea. It was still very dark, but we took our direction from the coastline and moved ponderously away from the bay.

The first glimmerings of dawn were just showing in a clear sky as we rounded the headland of the peninsula and entered the Aegean proper. As there was a slight but steady wind from the north we unfurled both sails and ran with it, shipping our oars. By sunrise we were several miles from the nearest land and were heading south at a comfortable three or four knots.

There was every reason for jubilation, but I was worried about the search just commencing in the village we had left. I was sure that the girls would be all right, for they were accomplished young ladies and could take care of themselves as well as anyone, but there was the very real danger of the Germans discovering the empty shed. I cursed myself for the lack of foresight which had made us leave the doors wide open to be seen by any passing boat. I called the others together at the tiller and we had one of our frequent councils of war.

We all agreed that it would be too much to expect that the theft would not be noticed that day and decided that it would be sound to assume that by nightfall the Germans in the village would have signalled their headquarters, and that there would be some attempt to head us off. I thereupon proposed that we should not make east to Imbros as we had planned, but continue south, making full use of the present wind which was, in fact, coming more from the east than the north at that stage; thus we would avoid the most obvious heading-off area between Lemnos and Samothrace and would seem to disappear. Then we would swing east, when we were well south of Lemnos and land somewhere on the more southern coast of Turkey.

There was general agreement to the plan.

But the decision to ride the present wind south for at least two days meant a careful stock-taking of our rations and water, for we had counted on less than three days for the whole voyage. I was particularly impressed, however, at the cheerful manner everyone accepted for the inevitable portioning out of our resources organised by John and Demetrius. A happy find was several inches of not too stale water in an old cask in the cabin so that we were able to manage about a litre per person per day.

For three days of perfect weather we made south with only a slight easterly gain. By day and by night the sails billowed gently to give us an average of something less than four knots, although I considered that any sailor could have made a good five or six with the steady wind. We organised ourselves into three watches of one English and one Greek or Cypriot in each watch, and in this way kept alert for any eventuality, whether it was a sudden squall or the appearance of an enemy craft or plane. On the evening of the third day we thought we must be some eighty or ninety miles south of the dangerous island of Lemnos, and as we had seen no sign of German aircraft or patrol boats we decided that it would be safe to turn east. In actual fact, we had seen one enemy ship, a large liner, which had shown for some hours on the horizon, but as she was cutting across ahead of us in much the same direction we were not at any time greatly concerned about her.

We all felt a new thrill of anticipation and excitement as our boat, which had been christened the *Blighty* by John, swung her bow to the east. The weather, which on every previous occasion had thwarted our endeavours, now seemed to be seeking our forgiveness and favour, for within the same hour that we turned to the east it swung too, and sent a gentle but ample breeze from almost due west. We may not have gone any faster than a good walking pace, but the steady, definite progress was a joy to all of us after so many long months of inactive waiting. In spite of a nagging hunger we sang and laughed together and discussed the meals we would have and the comforts we would seek when we arrived.

All the day following our change of direction, we watched the hills of Turkey rise out of the sea, change from a deep blue into a hazy grey, and then slowly become green and real. After midday it was possible at first to pick out hedgelines and then even to see the tiny shapes which denoted houses and farms. The scene on the good ship *Blighty* that afternoon was more like a happy Mediterranean yacht tour than the escape of a band of fugitives from Hitler's Europe. We all lay on the deck in the sun drinking in the beauty of the green rolling hills which meant, in different ways, so much to each of us.

To the south, now on our right, land was much nearer in the form of the large occupied island of Mytelene, and we steered to avoid it by a safe margin. Towards dusk, when we considered ourselves to be in view of the German garrison there, we made a great show of industry with the one large fishing net which was aboard, hauling it up the side of the mast and going through the motions of mending it.

We had a few nasty moments at this stage when an ugly, wide-winged flying boat rose from a bay and flew low out towards us. It approached us slowly and deliberately, so that we could clearly see the two pilots at their controls and the dreaded black crosses on the wings and fuselage but, although it passed less than a hundred feet over our heads, I doubted whether any of the passengers we could see even bothered to crane their necks to get a better view of us. As they faded into a speck on the darkening horizon to the north they little dreamed our humble *Blighty* was capable of carrying hated English to safety under the very eyes of one of their strongholds.

No one was greatly interested in sleep that night. We were all keyed up with the approach of our freedom, for we had few doubts that, by hook or by crook, we would be able to get through Turkey. It was Nicki who roused us to the peak of our excitement with a loud cry of joy.

'There it is, land ahead,' he cried, pointing into the darkness. 'Wake up and turn about, we are almost on a beach.'

We rushed up to the bow to join him and straight away realised that we were under the lee of a hill. Not more than half a mile ahead we could hear the waves breaking on a beach. What sweet music it was, the sound of those waves surging and receding on Turkish shores; we went wild with glee, hugged one another and danced madly around the deck. There was no doubt now. We had made it.

There was a tremendous temptation to beach the launch there and then and take our chance. But, in conference with John and Nicki, I decided that if it was at all possible we should go farther south along the coast towards Smyrna or Izmir. I had a secret desire to skirt even farther if we could pick up provisions and perhaps make the British port of Famagusta at Cyprus but, in any case, as I pointed out to the remainder, it was well known that Turkey divided herself neatly in her neutrality. The northern provinces gained by assisting the Germans in every way while the south was more disposed to aid the English. It was an unpopular suggestion, but in a few minutes all hands turned reluctantly to assist in resetting the two booms to allow us to proceed slowly down the coast.

All the next morning we hugged the land, keeping well within the internationally recognised three-mile limit of territorial water, and watching the idle life of the farming communities on the hills that passed slowly by. We were hungry and thirsty, but there was a contented sense of achievement mingled with anticipation which easily overshadowed all discomforts. Even those who wanted to land immediately now joked and laughed like carefree schoolchildren.

All was tranquil and happy until the middle of the afternoon, and up to that time no one was anything but certain in their minds that we had, in fact, achieved our escape. But Demetrius, who had remained quietly watchful all the time, suddenly jerked to his feet and with an oath pointed to a splash of white to the west.

'Look! Look!' he cried, his eyes protruding from his head. 'What's that ... it's a German patrol boat!'

His announcement burst upon us like a bomb, swamping our happiness like a douche of ice-cold water. We all strained our eyes at the fast-growing speck, sick with apprehension. It was as yet a good five miles from us, but there was no doubt of its direction.

'They can't touch us here!' exclaimed Nicki, though without much conviction. 'This is within the Turkish three-mile limit!'

'They're likely to grab us first and argue about that later,' growled Petra, scowling darkly in my direction. 'If we had not listened to some foolery last night we would have been safely ashore by now!'

I could not understand how we could have been spotted unless the Germans kept a long-range telescope on Mytelene, but we were indeed in great danger. I was at the tiller at the time, so I forced it hard over and the *Blighty* swung slowly in answer to face a muddy-looking beach a little over five hundred yards away. John, Nicki and Demetrius jumped to alter the booms and we began to creep shorewards, for the first time horribly impatient of *Blighty*'s snail-like speed. Behind us the white wash of the pursuers enlarged rapidly to show the unmistakable lines of the German 'E' boat still bearing at top speed in our direction.

We quickly made preparation to quit the boat in two parties as soon as we grounded, the English to strike to the south and Demetrius and the Cypriots to the north. Meanwhile, quite unruffled by all the fuss, *Blighty* sailed on serenely, not deigning to alter her speed as we began to plough through the hundred-odd yards of bulrushes laced with old seaweed which screened the foreshore. With an almost imperceptible shudder she sliced through the deep mud beyond them and came quietly to a halt, her sails flapping a farewell as we scrambled over her side. She had finished her task like the lady she was, for there was hardly a yard from the point of her bow to the firm turfy bank of the shore. Thus, we arrived in Turkey with dry feet, and ready for anything.

We immediately divided into our two parties, calling quick farewells, and struck inland in our different directions as fast as we could go. A tremendous sense of urgency spurred us forward; I half expected at any moment to hear the rattle of a machine-gun. We could now plainly hear the roar of marine engines.

It was not until we had gone perhaps half a mile that John, who was bringing up the rear of our party, gave a terrific shout and then commenced to laugh aloud as though he was never going to stop. Turning in bewilderment, we followed the direction of his pointed hand to see that the 'E' boat had swung north and, even as we watched, was diminishing as she skirted out to the three-mile limit again. We realised that in all probability she had been on a normal patrol duty and had thought to give us a bit of a scare as she passed on her way. No doubt her commander had been very amused to see the reaction of what appeared to be a Turkish fishing smack.

We pressed forward with the idea of making a small village which we could plainly see on the side of a rolling range some five miles inland. We were soon overtaken by Demetrius and his party who, as we had expected, preferred to stay with us now that the danger was passed.

The sun set as a great red ball over the distant hills of Mytelene Island as we entered the office of the local Turkish Chief of Police. With some difficulty we explained how we had come into his area. He was a fat and pompous little man, obviously over-inflated by his position, and he looked down his nose at our ragged clothes, our unshaven and unkempt heads. He said a few things about all Englishmen and spat when the Greeks were mentioned. We did not feel we were very welcome, particularly when we were shown to the village jail for our overnight accommodation. Here we were further insulted by a stream of curious and slightly hostile villagers who came in procession to view the strange people given up by the sea. However, the fat Chief of Police, after great persuasion and, incidentally, the offer of all rights to the good ship *Blighty*, agreed to despatch a telegram in French to the British representative in Izmir. I wrote out about a hundred words telling of our predicament and the Post Office official accepted it without a murmur.

In spite of the hostility of the villagers all round us and the initial disappointment at the coolness of our reception, we passed a happy night of comradeship in that Turkish cell, cheerfully eating the frugal meal that they brought us and singing well into the night. At least, we were out of Nazi Europe, and if the worst came to the worst anyone could get away from these rather sordid people. Though the cell was filthy and there were obvious signs of vermin, we felt content with our success and our chances for the immediate future.

Our high feelings were justified next morning. Soon after ten there was a great stir in the village, shouting and even cheers. We rushed to the iron-barred windows of our common cell to investigate. We saw two splendid Rolls-Royce cars sweep up the narrow mud tracks between the rough houses and come to a halt in a cloud of dust outside the Police Headquarters.

In a matter of moments we were being shepherded out of the jail by a now effusive Chief of Police and presented to a smiling gentleman who looked clean and fresh in grey flannels and a Royal Yacht Club blazer. His Majesty's Consul for Smyrna welcomed us with enthusiasm, clasping each of our hands in turn and somehow appearing just as happy and overwhelmed as we were. I found a hard lump in my throat and could not think of anything to say. Meanwhile, the crowd of gaping villagers increased and pushed closer with children pressing their faces against the shining windows of the cars in wonderment.

His Majesty's Consul impatiently signed some documents for the obsequious Chief of Police and then bustled us into the two cars. We drew out of the village, joined a better class of road, and headed south at speed. John and I and Nicki looked at one another as we relaxed in the leading car and grinned from ear to ear. This was the perfect ending. This was the complete reward for nights of anxiety and privation; this was the end of our adventure in Greece. In front of us, sitting next to the white uniformed chauffeur was His Imperial Majesty's representative who had come over eighty miles to personally take charge of us. We snuggled back into the soft cushions and, as the green, rolling country slid swiftly by, we allowed our thoughts to drift tenderly homewards. We were in good hands.

Postscript

Walking on air

Hell's bells!' exploded Colonel Blunt throwing up his hands in horror.

'You can't possibly have spent it *all!* That was supposed to last you for at *least* ten days. You chaps will be the ruin of me yet.' Colonel Blunt had proved to be a real friend. A veteran from the first war, Australian born, he was serving as Military Attaché at the British Consulate. But I must admit we had been testing him quite a bit.

On arrival in Izmir (Smyrna), he had taken us to a medical building where we were showered, embarrassingly de-loused, issued with a sort of bathrobe and then examined, in turn, by a charming old Turkish doctor. Dr Kavacik tut-tutted as he swabbed the remaining festering patch of my wound then, as he expertly bound it all up said, 'There is now in London a brilliant plastic surgeon from your country. McIndoe will be able to pull in the rough sides of that gash ... but, my boy, you will not be able to serve in the army again.' I did not say so, but I knew I would be able to prove him wrong.

Our examinations over, Colonel Blunt took us to a high-class shop and bought us all civilian clothes. From there he introduced us to the motherly old proprietor of a small *pension* on the sea front, over-looking the ancient port. Oh ... the almost forgotten *luxury* of a long, hot bath, clean clothes and a real bed with linen sheets!

He had given me some money for meals, and it was the squandering of that which so irritated him now. We had spent it all on a tour of bars and restaurants, having much wine and impossibly rich meals and then, unaware that we were under surveillance, we ambled along the neat waterfront footpaths. We came to a row of imposing two and a half storey buildings, one of which had a great black-on-red swastika hanging from the upper balcony rails right down to the street.

It seemed too good a chance to miss, and Nicki, having noticed a street photographer further back, persuaded him to come and take our picture in front of the German Consulate. We thought we had a wonderful souvenir but had gone only a few hundred yards when a car pulled up and a *very* angry Colonel Blunt jumped out.

'Give me those damn photographs!' he demanded, thrusting out his hand. 'Don't you realise how important it is to keep a low profile while you are here! The Turks are almost *paranoid* about their neutrality and the last thing they want is to let it be known that there are English soldiers wandering around their streets.' He broke off, quietened, and continued, 'Look chaps, things are not gong too well for us down in the Western Desert. If Tobruk falls the Germans could sweep on to Cairo. The Turks are terrified that Hitler might be tempted to strike through Turkey to join up with those troops at Suez.' He paused, perhaps thinking he was being too matey, and finished briskly, 'So you chaps had better watch your step or I'll confine you to your rooms!'

After some days of resting, medical treatment and enjoying our freedom, we were finally put on a train to go initially north towards Istanbul and then to swing south to the Turkish border with Syria. Colonel Blunt came to the station to see us off. In his generous way he slipped us some extra cash, which I sensed may have come from his own pocket rather than the public purse. But he seemed unusually pensive and less able to share our excitement. Just before the whistle blew to herald our departure he blurted out, 'Look chaps, I've got to tell you something. I *think* everything will be OK, but our Intelligence guys have just told me that the German Ambassador put pressure on the Turkish President yesterday. The Huns are furious that so many English, and particularly Greek, soldiers are being allowed to pass through Turkey, so play it careful at the border crossing and ... well, I'll keep my fingers crossed for you.'

I don't think, then, we really took in his sudden pessimism, we just clambered into a rather decrepit carriage, leant out of the windows and waved happily to him as the train pulled out of the station.

On that journey, over three days and long nights, we seemed to stop

Rail route through Turkey

at a thousand small stations. As we slowed to approach each one a quite friendly, but always silent, armed railway guard appeared and stood by us until the train left the station. But his presence could in no way diminish a steadily rising elation. Even the train wheels on the rails seemed to clang, 'We're gonna make it! We're gonna make it! We're gonna make it!' Only my half-Scot caution stopped me changing it to, 'We've done it! We've done it! We've done it!' Then Colonel Blunt's warning began to seek some unwanted presence in my mind. There was still one possible hurdle; the border crossing into Allied-controlled Syria.

The countryside changed from hour to hour; scrubby barren hillsides, to neat farmhouse-dotted fields, stations with ill-clad peasants loading fat-tailed sheep, then prosperous towns and well-dressed men and women. We changed trains at Ankara, escorted by our silent guard, and at last the train swung south, south towards Syria and freedom.

We had a particularly long, dark night, in which exaggerated fears of possible new dangers denied me sleep. How did one 'play it careful' at a

241

border crossing? Just *why* did the Military Attaché need to keep his fingers crossed for us? What were the perils and risks ahead?

Dawn slowly revealed the passing countryside, and also the signposts flashing by:

Maydan lkbis 50 kilometres, Aleppo 280 kilometres ...

Maydan lkbis 30 kilometres ...

Maydan lkbis 20 kilometres ... Customs ... Douane ... Zoll ...

Maydan lkbis 10 kilometres....

Then, alarm! The train slowed and ground to a halt. No station, just open fields.

Through the carriage door appeared our mute guard and with him a soldier, smart in an almost German-type uniform. He wore the badges of a corporal in Turkish Intelligence. Stopping before us, he clicked his heels and saluted. I half rose in my seat, apprehensive.

'Lieutenant,' he said in English, 'you must leave the train here.'

'But, but,' I stammered, 'where will we go ...?'

'Relax, relax Lieutenant,' interjected the corporal. 'Just pick up your gear and follow me.' And he set off down the carriageway. As we hurried to follow, the face of the ever-silent train guard suddenly brightened into a wide grin. He grabbed our hands in turn and, astonishingly breaking into perfect English, cried, 'Good luck! Good Luck! I pray to Allah that today will bring you freedom.'

As we clambered down on to the railway track and hastened after the corporal, curious faces emerged from nearly every carriage, some passengers waving as the train moved slowly away. The corporal led us across some open fields until we found a track which took us by a few rather poor homes and up the side of a gently sloping hill.

How wonderful that morning was! The air was pure and free. Above us was a blue sky with the most beautiful cumulous clouds. The countryside was welcoming; there seemed nothing to prevent an enormous, welling feeling of exhilaration and expectation.

We came over the crest of the small hill and looked down across a valley onto a different scene. The hillside was covered with small pockets of soldiers all digging and preparing defences. There also seemed to be an awful lot of barbed wire across the bottom of the gully. The Turkish Corporal stopped in his tracks and pointed to the figures on the other side. 'Those are British soldiers,' he said. 'Those are your friends. They are building trenches there in case the Germans try to come through our country. If you walk down the side of this hill to the stream there and call out, I think you will find that you are at the end of your journey.' With that, he saluted, turned smartly about, and marched back the way he had come.

The three of us set off down the side of the hill. Initially the workers on the hillside over the stream took no notice. Then they put down their tools, picked up their rifles, and watched us rather more closely. When we got within calling distance, I shouted out, 'Hullo there. Don't shoot! We are English escaped prisoners. The Turks have let us come here to make contact with you.'

'Put your bloody hands up!' a voice shouted from the group gathering near the wire closest to us. 'Don't do anything fast ... just move slowly towards us, we'll see who you are.' There was an accent in that voice that sounded familiar.

The next seconds, the next minutes, the next hours were quite indescribably wonderful. In no time we had made ourselves known, the wire so meticulously put up was cut and a pass made for us to cross the stream and into a huddle of excited, kindly and exuberant faces. Everyone crowded in to hug us, to clap us on the back, and to somehow be just as thrilled as we were.

My recognition of the accent was right ... they all were New Zealanders, and what seemed *absolutely impossible*, they were members of my old, my beloved, 23rd Battalion. They had been sent to Syria with the whole of the Division, partly to rest after their fierce battles in the Western Desert and partly to prepare for the threatened German attack through Turkey.

In a matter of minutes they were carrying the three of us shoulder high up the side of the hill, shouting to everybody else to come and see us.

'It's old Sandy! Sandy Thomas from 15 Platoon!' shouted a voice.

'Don't be daft,' cried another; 'the bastards got Sandy on Crete!'

'It's him I tell you ... if it's not Sandy it's his bloody ghost!'

Then, from a more authoritative voice, 'Yes that's him! That's Sandy! But how the hell.... Here, get out of my way! Let me grab his hand. Mr Thomas, Mr Thomas, it's me, Sergeant Irvine, sir, remember? 14 Platoon. We thought you were a goner, sir! Welcome back, sir, welcome back!'

Then, to crown it all as they pressed in around me, someone shouted, 'Sandy, Sandy! Your brother Godfrey is here! He's just over the hill—he's with your old Platoon!' Godfrey? Could it be? Surely he was still in New Zealand fretting over regulations forbidding farmers to volunteer for active service.

Sergeant Irvine seized command, 'Let's take him over to see Godfrey! Come on, lads, hoist him up again and the other two as well—let's go!'

We came over the top of the hill, John and Nicki, grinning from ear to ear, and the exuberant shouting welled even higher. I could see more and more soldiers dropping their tools and hurrying towards us.

'Get Godfrey. Get Godfrey, tell him we've got Sandy here!'

(Strangely, in the ever-mounting thrill of the moment, I became aware of a voice at the back of my mind saying, 'They really *shouldn't* be calling me "Sandy", I'm an officer!')

My brother Godfrey.
2nd Lt G. J. Thomas MC

The surging mass around us parted. The stalwarts who had me on their shoulders lowered me carefully to the ground. The shouting, the clapping, the excited exclamations died away to an expectant hush.

Godfrey, stripped to the waist, bronzed, hatless, was pushed in towards me. For perhaps half a second, we looked at one another. Then, we did something we had never done before. We rushed into each other's arms and hugged and hugged.

Hardly aware of the cheering, the shouting, the excited faces all around, I looked up through those lovely white clouds and beyond into that perfect blue sky: and I thanked God.

17/5/42

Dearest of Mothers, and Dad,

I'm free and having leave with Godfrey. My welcome here I'll never forget: the old Battalion hadn't forgot us. But it's your welcome I'm waiting for, and please God it won't be long before we can clean everything up and come home.

I know you will be longing for my story—but honestly I can't write more than a line just now—being a bit restless, and in any case security reasons require a month of silence. Just briefly—after 3 attempts, a court martial and other trifles, I finally escaped from Salonica on Nov 16/41 and have been all over North Greece and Salonica, in monasteries, homes and cowsheds, and after many unsuccessful boating expeditions stole a boat and made Turkey. Give my love to Adele and tell her to tear up a letter I wrote in Germany.

All my love to you both and to Frances and Joan.

Your loving son
Sandy

Note: The date of the letter was actually 17/5/42 not 17/5/41 as shown on the original.